Introductory Economics

STUDY GUIDE

SJ Grant and GF Stanlake

LONGMAN

Addison Wesley Longman Limited
Edinburgh Gate, Harlow
Essex CM20 2JE, England
and Associated Companies throughout the World

ISBN 0 582 30256 0

First published 1997
Produced by Longman Singapore Pte Ltd
Printed in Singapore

The Publisher's policy is to use paper manufactured from sustainable forests.

Acknowledgements

We are grateful for permission to reproduce copyright material:

Extracts from the article 'Economics of the Media' by Robert Paisley from *British Economy Survey* Vol.24 No.1 Autumn 1994; The Economist for extracts from the articles 'Monopolies and Merger Omission' © *The Economist*, London 20.4.96 and 'Shooting at Inflation' © *The Economist,* London 18.7.96; The Guardian for extracts from the articles 'Traffic growth "will be severe"' by Keith Harper in *The Guardian* © 26.4.96, 'Hitting the jackpot first time' in *The Guardian* © 5.6.96; the Controller of HMSO for an extract from *Labour Market and Skills Trend* 1996/1997. Crown Copyright.

We are also grateful to the following for permission to use copyright material:

The Controller of HMSO and of the Office for National Statistics for an extract from the *DTI Statistical Bulletin June 1945*, quoted in *Labour Market Trends 1996/7*, Crown © 1997 (page 14); The Controller of HMSO and of the Office for National Statistics for an extract from *National Income Blue Books, 1986 & 1996*, Crown © 1997 (page 22); National Institute of Economic & Social Research (pages 48, 62, 69, 75, 76, 85, 90); *The Guardian* 28.3.96 (page 54); The Controller of HMSO and of the Office for National Statistics for an extract from the *Monthly Digest of Statistics, April 1996*, Crown © 1997 (page 84); the Controller of HMSO and of the Office for National Statistics for extracts from *Social Trends 26*, 1996, Crown © 1997 (pages 90, 91).

Contents

Introduction

Section 1 – Questions

Section 2 – Answers

This workbook is designed to be both a complementary text to *Introductory Economics* and an independent aid to students pursuing A Level Economics, AS Level Economics, Scottish Higher Economics, GNVQ Advanced Business, HND Business and Finance, and first-year Economics degree courses.

Each part covers a major subject area and starts with an introduction which gives a reference to the relevant chapters in *Introductory Economics* and identifies the key topics and skills. The introduction is followed by ten short questions, ten multiple choice questions, two data response questions and two essay questions. These questions are intended to probe the understanding of economic theory and the ability to apply that theory in different contexts.

Detailed answers are provided for each question. These are not intended to be model answers. What they do seek to do is to clarify topics, provide suggested solutions to short questions, data response questions and essay questions, explain why a particular option to a multiple choice question is the correct one and in some cases why other options are not correct.

Suggestions on how to use the book

This book can be used to help to develop your understanding and skills as you work through your course or as a revision guide towards the end of your course.

It is useful first to consult the syllabus and examination papers of the course you are following. You can then assess which topics are of particular relevance to you and the question format of the examination papers you will be sitting.

You may wish to check which of the topics and skills you possess, both before and after you work through the questions, by ticking the objectives in the introduction to each part.

In answering the short questions, data response questions and essay questions, try to include up-to-date, relevant examples wherever possible. For example, it would be useful to describe briefly current government measures to increase investment in your answer to short question 7 in Part 12. As another example, it would be a good idea to include current arguments advanced by the British government, other countries' governments and international organisations as part of the discussion in your answer to essay question 1b for Part 11.

When you have worked through a section of questions, check the answers. If you are finding that you are unable to answer some of the short questions, data response questions or essay questions, or that you are getting a significant number of the multiple choice questions wrong, it would be advisable to refer back to your notes, to *Introductory Economics* or another textbook and/or to consult your teacher/lecturer.

Advice on answering short questions

Remember that a 'short' question does not mean that the question itself is necessarily short. It means that the *answer* is intended to be short. First, check the wording carefully, paying particular attention to the instructions. If, for example, the question asks you to discuss two causes of market failure, discuss only two and pick two that you can explain clearly and for which you can give examples drawn from real life. Do not discuss more than two as you will not get extra marks and you could be using the time more productively. If the question instructs you to outline an argument or theory, concentrate on the key points and do not go into unnecessary detail.

Write clearly but succinctly and make sure that everything you include is relevant. When you have finished, read over your answer to see if you have made any mistakes or left anything out.

Advice on answering multiple choice questions

The questions in this book and on the majority of examination papers are simple completion questions. This means that there is a question or an incomplete statement (known as the *stem*) followed by a number of options. There are usually four options, labelled A to D. The correct option is known as the *key*.

Multiple choice questions test knowledge, understanding, data handling, interpretation, analysis, application, and evaluation. They vary in degree of difficulty, with those testing knowledge and understanding tending to be the easiest. In recent times there has been an increase in the proportion of questions based on real world data.

It is very important to avoid answering multiple choice questions too quickly. Read the stem of the question very carefully. In some cases it is useful to think through the answer before looking at the options. When you have considered the stem, then consider each option in turn, referring back to the stem each time. With some questions it is a good idea to draw diagrams to work out the answer. Other questions require you to undertake calculations, often involving percentages.

Advice on answering data response questions

Data response questions test your ability to interpret, handle and analyse data and to apply your knowledge and understanding of economics. There are three main types of question. One is based on a prose (text) extract from a newspaper article or articles, a periodical or a textbook. Another is based on factual data often presented in a table of numerical data but sometimes in a graphical or diagrammatic form. The third type is one which combines both a prose extract and factual data.

General advice

First, check the data very carefully. Then read through all the questions, checking for a general theme running through the questions, their individual meaning, seeking to avoid overlap in your answers and noting the number of marks per question part.

In answering data response questions you must make use of both the data and your knowledge and understanding of economics. Spend longer on question parts which carry more marks. If appropriate, draw diagrams to help your explanations. You do not have to answer the questions in order – it is often relatively easy to pick up points on the last question part.

Prose extracts

First, check if there is a heading as this will give you an idea of what the extract is about. Also check the source and the date of publication. Then read through the extract, getting an overall impression of what it is about. You may find it useful to note this down at the side of the extract. Then read through all the question parts, following the general advice above. Check the extract again, considering the meaning of each paragraph and bearing in mind the question parts. Then answer each question part. Write in your own words but if you wish to quote from the extract, put the words in quotations.

Numerical form

First, check what the data are showing. If there is a table of statistical data, pay particular attention to the headings of the columns. For example, are the figures in current or constant prices (nominal or real values) and are they in index numbers, or in for example £ millions? If the data are in the form of a graph or diagram, check the axes carefully. For example, a graph may be a time series graph or a cumulative frequency graph (*ogive*). The scale on the axes may differ.

Look at any footnotes as these may provide extra information. Read through the question parts carefully. Then consider what relationships or trends you would expect to find, what relationship or trend appears to exist and whether it is consistent with what you expected. Note any unusual figures.

In analysing a relationship, consider whether there is a direct, inverse or time lagged relationship. It may be useful to calculate actual or percentage changes which you can present in a table. Keep statistical analysis relatively simple, concentrating on percentages and averages, as appropriate. Alternatively, you may wish to plot the data on a graph to establish the nature of the relationship.

Support your answers with evidence drawn from the data and from any calculations you have made based on the data.

Advice on answering essay questions

The essays in this book are structured essays. This means that they are in two or three related parts. This format helps you to organise your thoughts in a logical manner. Structured essays are becoming increasingly popular, although single part essay questions are still asked. You may find it useful, in a few cases, to select a question part which carries a high number of marks and answer it as a complete essay in its own right.

When you are answering an essay question you must first decide what the question is asking. You must note carefully the instruction given in the question and the key words. For example, more detail is needed in an answer to a question which asks you to *explain* than in one which asks you to *outline*.

When you have interpreted the question, you should then research it using existing notes you may have and, if necessary, taking new notes from books, articles, lectures and TV programmes. Alternatively, you can practise answering the question under exam conditions.

You should plan your answer before you write it. There is no one right way to construct a plan. It is for your use and so should be in a format that is suited to your thought processes.

When you write your answer you should start answering the question set, right from the start of the question: everything you write should be relevant. Do not wander off the subject of the question and do not pad out your answer. Quality is much more important than quantity.

Your answers should show thorough knowledge and understanding, the abilities to analyse and evaluate and an awareness of current issues and problems.

Write clearly in short sentences, taking care with grammar, punctuation and spelling. Explain all your points clearly and fully. Devote a paragraph to each major point you make. Use only acceptable abbreviations and first write out the word or words in full, followed by the abbreviation; for example, price elasticity of demand (PED). Include real world examples which illustrate your points wherever possible, as discussed before. It is also often beneficial to include diagrams to help your explanations. These should be drawn large enough (approximately one third of a side) and the axes should be labelled.

When you have completed your answer read it through to check for errors and for anything you have missed out.

Advice on preparing for examinations

Early on in your course, check details of the examination papers you will be sitting – in particular the dates of the papers you will be sitting, the coverage of the papers and the format of the papers.

Throughout your course you will be preparing for your final assessment. You will be gaining knowledge, developing the skills of interpretation, application, analysis and evaluation and in some cases writing reports or dissertations or researching the topic of a special study.

Revision should also be a continuous process. After you have studied a topic or a part of a topic, review it and if you are unclear about any part, research it further and/or ask your teacher/lecturer. Many students find it useful to draw up a glossary of key words and terms as they come across them.

As the date of your examination papers approaches, you will need to engage in further, more intensive revision. Give yourself time for this and draw up a realistic revision timetable. Engage in active revision. Examples of active revision include summarising notes, updating examples, producing lists, spider diagrams, tables, diagrams and graphs and practising answering, or producing plans for, questions from workbooks and past examination papers.

The least productive method of revision is merely to read through your notes.

Advice on answering questions under examination conditions

Take the relevant, permitted equipment to the examination, e.g. two black or blue pens, a ruler, a pencil, a pencil sharpener, an eraser and a calculator. Arrive in plenty of time.

When you are permitted to look at the examination paper, first read carefully the instructions on the front of the question paper. It is important that you answer the correct number of questions and that you select these from the relevant sections.

Then take note of the time allocated. This gives an indication of the time you should spend on each question and each question part. On short questions, data response questions and essay questions this time is intended to be used to interpret the question, structure the answer and write it. If you have a choice, select those questions which are on topics you know well, which you are confident about answering and on which you can answer each part.

Follow the general guidelines on answering questions given earlier in this introduction. Remember that quality and relevance are very important. Glance at your watch frequently to make sure you are keeping within the time limit. Most papers have reasonable time limits. If, however, you find that you are running out of time on an essay paper, do a complete essay plan for the last question.

On a multiple choice paper remember that each question carries an equal number of marks, although they are of different degrees of difficulty. If you find a few questions particularly difficult, leave them and then go back to them. Take particular care with any questions which have a negative stem. In working out which is the key, you can write, carry out calculations and draw diagrams on the question paper. Answer all the multiple choice questions. If you are completely uncertain about the correct answer to a few questions, guess – you do not lose marks for incorrect answers. If you change your mind about an answer, rub out your first answer and mark in your new answer firmly.

When you have finished an examination paper, forget it and turn your concentration to the next paper. When you have completed all your papers, relax and enjoy yourself!

Section 1
Questions

PART ONE

The economic problem

Introduction

In answering the questions in this part you may find it useful to consult Chapters 1–5 in *Introductory Economics* or appropriate chapters in other books.

The questions in this part seek to test and improve your understanding of the nature of economics, production possibility curves, economic systems, changes in economic systems, and economic resources.

The specific objectives are to develop your ability to:

- define key economic concepts, i.e. scarcity, choice and opportunity cost

- apply opportunity cost to a wide range of choices which consumers, workers, firms and governments make

- appreciate the difference between positive and normative statements

- understand the meaning of a production possibility curve (boundary or frontier) and to draw it accurately

- recognise the significance of points inside, on and outside a production possibility curve

- understand what can cause a shift and a change in the slope of a production possibility curve

- use production possibility curves to illustrate a range of economic decisions and events

- compare and contrast the workings of different economic systems and how they solve the issue of resource allocation

- understand the relative advantages and disadvantages of economic systems

- analyse the causes and consequences of the move to market economies

- describe the main features of the factors of production.

Short questions

1 Explain the relevance of the concept of opportunity cost in a student's decision as to whether to go on to university.

2 What are the basic economic concepts illustrated by a production possibility curve?

3 Use a production possibility curve to illustrate the effect of a famine in a developing country.

4 What are the three fundamental questions that all economies face?

5 What type of economic system did the UK operate between 1940 and 1945? Explain your answer.

6 How may planners assess consumer demand in a command economy?

7 Why is a country that is changing its economic system from a planned to a market economy likely to experience inflation?

8 Explain how the price mechanism functions to allocate resources in the case of the demand for tea falling and the demand for coffee increasing.

9 Define land, labour and capital.

10 Giving examples, explain the types of risks entrepreneurs bear.

Multiple choice questions

1 Which of the following is a normative statement?

   A Government expenditure on higher education provides both private and external benefits.

   B Student grants should be increased and student loans should be phased out.

   C Additional funding for university education could be provided by switching expenditure from other government programmes.

   D More students from higher income groups undertake degree courses than those from lower income groups.

2 What is an economic good? One which:

   A is sold at a profit

   B has an opportunity cost

   C is supplied by the private sector

   D is produced under conditions of decreasing average cost.

3 What does the existence of scarcity imply?

   A All goods are economic goods.

   B Economic agents have to make choices.

   C It is not possible to increase resources.

   D Production occurs within the production possibility frontier.

4   XY is a production possibility curve. Which points are attainable?

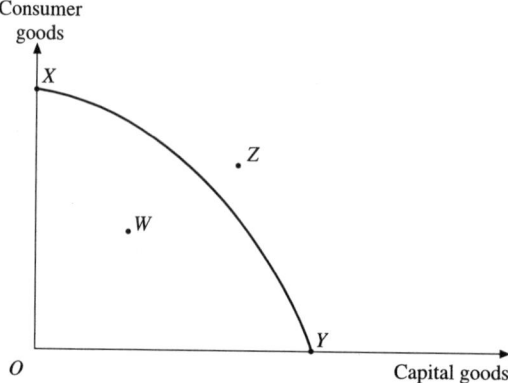

Fig. 1.1

A W   **B** X and Y   **C** W, X and Y   **D** W, X, Y and Z

5   What is implied by the shape of the production possibility frontier shown?

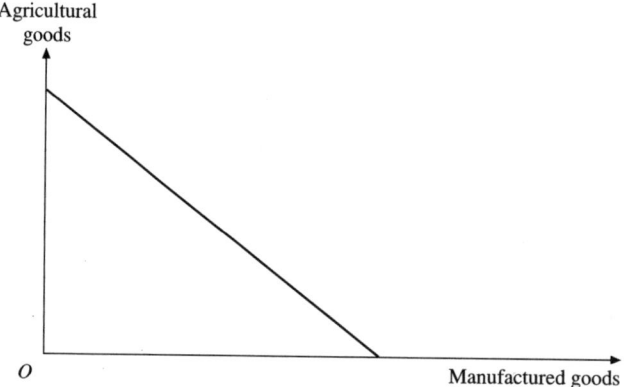

Fig. 1.2

A   The economy will operate at full employment.

B   The output of manufactured goods will be greater than the output of agricultural goods.

C   There is a constant rate of opportunity cost involved in transferring resources from the production of agricultural goods to manufactured goods.

D   Resources are not equally good at producing both manufactured and agricultural goods.

6   WX and YZ are two production possibility curves. Which of the following could explain the movement from point R to point S?

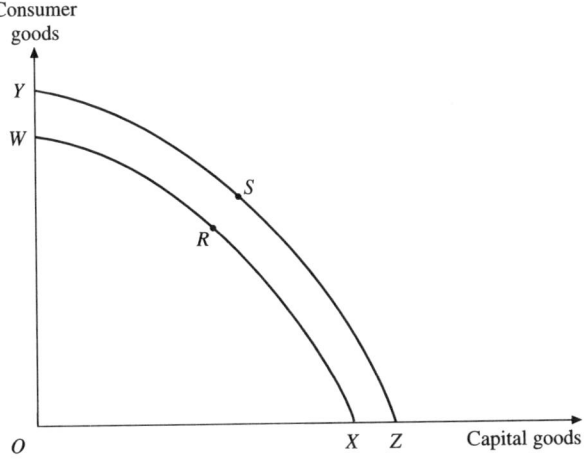

Fig. 1.3

A   a reduction in unemployment

B   an increase in the price of both consumer and capital goods

C   improvements in technology affecting both consumer and capital goods

D   a more efficient allocation of resources between consumer and capital goods.

7   The diagram shows a production possibility frontier, XZ.

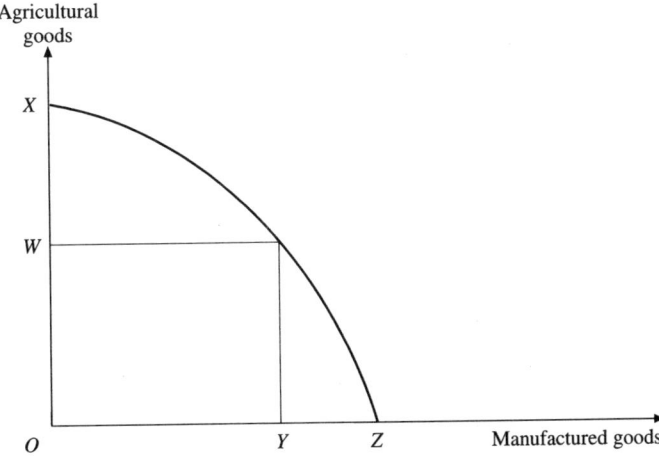

Fig. 1.4

What is the opportunity cost of producing OY quantity of manufactured goods?

A   OW quantity of agricultural goods

B   WX quantity of agricultural goods

C   OX quantity of agricultural goods

D   YZ quantity of manufactured goods.

8   What is the main difference between a planned and a market economy? In a market economy:

A   most of the economy is state owned and controlled

B   government officials are the ultimate decision takers

C   the private sector provides both public and merit goods

D   the price mechanism is the main mechanism for allocating resources.

9   What is meant by consumer sovereignty?

A   Products are sold at low prices.

B   Consumers are able to satisfy all their wants.

C   The preferences of consumers influence the pattern of production.

D   Output decisions are taken on the basis of social costs and benefits.

10   Which is the most likely reason why some industries in a planned economy may fail to reach their output targets?

A   a lack of aggregate demand

B   a change in consumer preferences

C   an increase in the general price level

D   problems of coordination between industries.

Data response questions

1   In all societies people want more than they are capable of producing. At any given moment in time the supply of economic resources is limited so that more of one thing can usually only be produced if less of something else is produced. Likewise, incomes are limited and in spending our incomes we have to choose between alternatives. Economists use the term opportunity cost to describe the idea of measuring cost in terms of the alternatives forgone. This is a very important concept. We have to make choices all the time. We have to decide how we spend our time, how we spend our incomes and what employment we undertake. For example, in choosing to visit the cinema I may be forgoing the opportunity to play badminton. In buying one model of car I am forgoing the opportunity to buy another model, and in working as a teacher I am unable to work as a civil servant.

Producers and governments also have to make choices. A producer must decide what goods to produce and which factors of production to employ. For example, a farmer selecting to use an area of land for growing corn has chosen not to use it for another purpose, such as keeping sheep. In growing the corn he has the choice of using labour- or capital-intensive methods. Governments also have to consider the opportunity cost of any decision they make. The real cost of building an NHS hospital is not the cost in terms of money but the cost in terms of the alternative uses of the resources, i.e. the opportunity cost.

a   What is meant by economic resources?   (2)

b   Explain the link between scarcity, choice and opportunity cost.   (5)

c   Which economic agents have to make choices and why?   (4)

d   In what circumstances might it be possible to increase output
    without incurring an opportunity cost?   (5)

e   What factors influence which products firms choose to produce?   (5)

f   Give two examples of the possible opportunity cost of a
    government building a new hospital.   (4)

2

According to the central deduction of economic theory, under certain conditions markets allocate resources efficiently. 'Efficiency' has a special meaning in this context. The theory says that markets will produce an outcome such that, given the economy's scarce resources, it is impossible to make anybody better-off without making somebody else worse-off.

Economic theory, in other words, offers a proof of Adam Smith's big idea. In a market economy, if certain conditions are met, an invisible hand guides countless apparently uncoordinated individuals to a result that is, in one plausible sense, the best that can be done.

In rich countries, markets are too familiar to attract attention. Yet a certain awe is appropriate. When Soviet planners visited a vegetable market in London during the early days of *perestroika*, they were impressed to find no queues, shortages, or mountains of spoiled and unwanted vegetables. They took their hosts aside and said: 'We understand, you have to say it's all done by supply and demand. But can't you tell us what's really going on? Where are your planners, and what are their methods?'

Source: *The Economist*, 'State and Market', 'Schools Brief', 17 February 1996

a   Explain what is meant by:

   i   efficiency   (3)

   ii a market economy.   (3)

b   Comment on two conditions which have to be met for a market
    economy to work efficiently.   (4)

   c What evidence of market clearing did the Soviet planners find on their visit to London? (4)

   d In the context of the extract, explain what is meant by 'it's all done by supply and demand'. (6)

   e What was the role of Soviet planners in the former Soviet Union? (5)

Essay questions

1 **a** Explain what is meant by a production possibility frontier. (5)

   b What effect will the following have:

      i a movement from inside to on the frontier (5)

      ii a movement along the frontier (5)

      iii a movement from one frontier to another one further to the right? (5)

   c Discuss the main factors which can cause a production possibility frontier to shift to the right. (5)

2 **a** What are the main criteria for distinguishing between different types of economic system? (6)

   b Explain how the price mechanism acts as a rationing and signalling device in a market economy. (9)

   c Discuss the economic problems which planned economies may experience in moving towards a market system. (10)

PART TWO

The organisation and scale of production

Introduction

In answering the questions in this part you may find it useful to consult Chapters 6–13 in *Introductory Economics* or appropriate chapters in other books.

The questions in this part seek to test and improve your understanding of specialisation, mobility, diminishing returns and increasing returns, costs of production, economies and diseconomies of scale, growth of firms, mergers, small firms, size and structure of UK industry, finance of industry and influences on the location of industry.

The specific objectives are to develop your ability to:

- define division of labour and recognise its advantages and disadvantages

- appreciate the difference between occupational and geographical mobility

- define, calculate and illustrate the law of diminishing returns

- recognise the link between returns to scale and economies of scale

- define, analyse and illustrate short- and long-run costs of production

- understand the meaning of economies and diseconomies of scale and give examples of different types

- discuss the motives for growth

- recognise the different forms of growth and their implications

- distinguish between horizontal, vertical and conglomerate mergers

- appreciate the reasons for the survival of small firms

- understand the meaning and significance of industrial concentration

- distinguish between the main sources of the finance of industry

- recognise the main influences on the location of industry.

Short questions

1 Explain how specialisation is limited by the size of the market.

2 Distinguish between the geographical mobility and the occupational mobility of labour.

3 How would the rate of return on capital be expected to change if the supply of labour is fixed and the quantity of capital increases?

4 Distinguish, with examples, between a firm's fixed and variable costs.

5   Why are most short-run average cost curves usually expected to be U-shaped?

6   Describe two economies of scale which could be gained by a car manufacturer as it grows in size.

7   What are the main motives behind horizontal mergers?

8   Give, and briefly explain, three reasons for the survival of small firms.

9   What are the three main sources of finance for firms?

10 Distinguish between a bulk increasing and a bulk reducing industry and explain where they are likely to locate.

Multiple choice questions

1   What is happening to the total variable cost curve when the law of diminishing returns begins to operate?

   A It falls at an increasing rate.

   B It falls at a decreasing rate.

   C It rises at a decreasing rate.

   D It rises at an increasing rate.

2   The table shows the total cost of different levels of a firm's output.

Output (units)	Total cost (£)
0	15 000
10	20 000
20	23 000
30	24 000
40	27 000
50	35 000

The firm's average variable cost curve is U-shaped. Within which one of the following ranges of output will average variable costs be minimised?

A 10–20 units   **B** 20–30 units   **C** 30–40 units   **D** 40–50 units

3   A firm initially produces 200 conservatories at an average total cost of £4000 each. It then increases production to 201 conservatories. The production of the additional conservatory reduces average fixed costs by £15 but raises average variable costs by £12. What is the marginal cost of this additional conservatory?

A £3   **B** £12   **C** £3397   **D** £3997

4 When marginal product is equal to average product:

A average product is rising

B marginal product is rising

C average product is at a maximum

D marginal product is at a maximum.

5 The diagram shows a firm's short-run total cost curve.

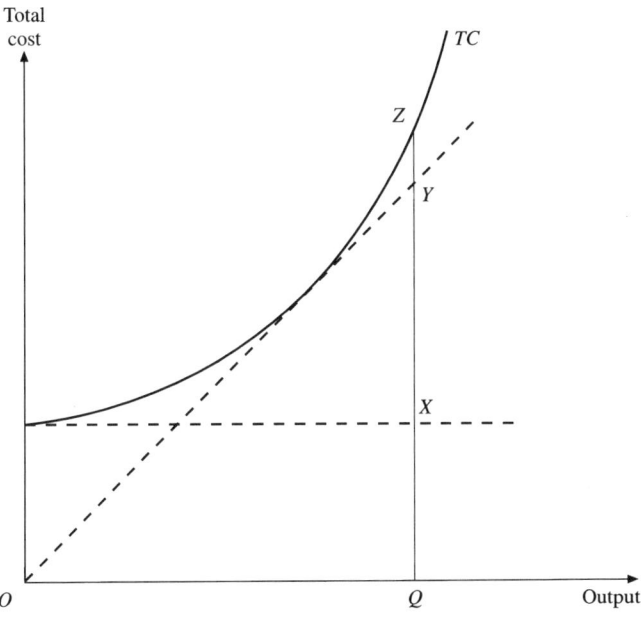

Fig. 2.1

At output OQ average variable costs are:

A XQ   **B** YZ   **C** $\dfrac{\text{XZ}}{\text{OQ}}$ **D** $\dfrac{\text{XQ}}{\text{OQ}}$

6 The table below shows a firm's short-run and long-run costs.

Output	1	2	3	4	5
Short run Total cost (£)	10	18	24	28	30
Long run Total cost (£)	10	22	36	52	70

From this information, what conclusions can be drawn about the characteristics of production in the short and long run?

	Short run	**Long run**
A	increasing average costs	economies of scale
B	increasing average costs	diseconomies of scale
C	decreasing average costs	diseconomies of scale
D	decreasing average costs	economies of scale

7   What is meant by financial economies of scale?

   A   the ability of a firm to raise finance more easily and more cheaply as it grows in size

   B   the ability of a firm to buy raw materials at a discount as it grows in size

   C   the fall in unit costs experienced by firms working in the financial sector as they grow in size

   D   the fall in unit costs experienced by larger firms arising from the more efficient handling of revenue.

8   A tobacco company purchases an insurance company. This is an example of:

   A   a horizontal merger

   B   a conglomerate merger

   C   a vertical backwards merger

   D   a vertical forwards merger.

9   Which of the following is most likely to result in a firm being able to benefit from external economies of scale?

   A   an increase in its output

   B   a diversification into a wider range of products

   C   location in the same area as other firms in the industry

   D   introduction of new, more capital-intensive methods of production.

10 **Number of enterprises by size (number of employees), 1993**

	UK (thousands)	Percentage
All	3581	100.0
0	2589	72.3
1–9	791	22.1
10–19	107	3.0
20–49	59	1.6
50–99	19	0.5
100–199	9	0.2
200–249	2	0.05
250–499	3	0.1
500	3	0.1

Note: 0 = 1 or more self-employed people with no employees.
Source: DTI *Statistical Bulletin*, June 1995

It can be deduced from the figures that in the UK:

A   small firms produce a higher percentage of output than large firms

B   most people in the UK are self-employed

C   small firms employ more workers than large firms

D   most firms employ a small number of workers.

Data response questions

1   The diagram shows the average fixed cost, average variable cost, average total cost and marginal cost curves of a firm.

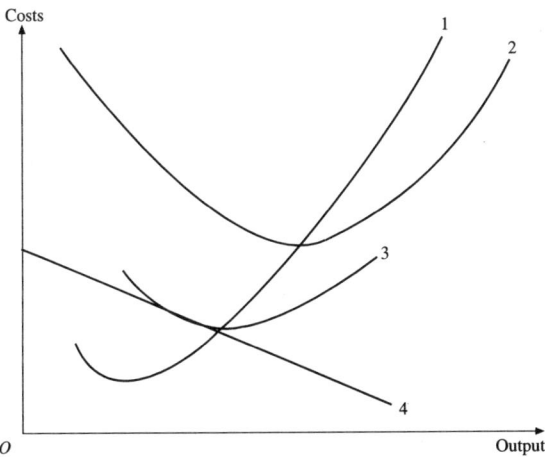

Fig. 2.2

a Identify each curve. (4)

b Explain the shape of the average fixed cost curve. (4)

c Illustrate and explain the shape of the total cost curve this firm would have. (6)

d Discuss the relationship between the marginal cost curve and the average total cost curve. (5)

e Explain the difference between diminishing returns and diseconomies of scale. (6)

2

Horizontal integration occurs when firms combine at the same stage of production, involving similar products or services. During the 1960s over 80% of the total number of UK mergers were of the horizontal type, and despite a subsequent fall in this percentage, some 80% of mergers in the early 1990s were still of this type. The British Airways takeover of British Caledonian in 1988, and the Ford takeover of Jaguar in 1989, and the Hong Kong and Shanghai Banking Corporation's acquisition of Midland Bank in 1992, were examples of horizontal mergers. Horizontal integration may provide a number of economies at the level both of the plant (productive unit) and the firm (business unit). Plant economies may follow from the rationalisation made possible by horizontal integration. For instance, production may be concentrated at a smaller number of enlarged plants, permitting the familiar technical economies of greater specialisation, the dovetailing of separate processes at higher output, and the application of the engineers' rule whereby material costs increase as the square but capacity as the cube. All these lead to a reduction in cost per unit as the size of plant output increases. Firm economies result from the growth in size of the whole enterprise, permitting economies via bulk purchase, the spread of similar administrative costs over greater output, and the cheaper cost of finance, etc.

Source: *Applied Economics*, sixth edition, edited by Alan Griffiths and Stuart Wall, Longman, 1995

a Explain why the three mergers mentioned are examples of horizontal mergers. (2)

b How do the other two main types of integration, vertical and conglomerate, differ from horizontal integration? (4)

c In your own words, distinguish between plant and firm economies. (4)

d Explain the sentence 'Plant economies may follow from the rationalisation made possible by horizontal integration.' (6)

e Identify two firm economies of scale not mentioned in the extract. (2)

f Discuss whether horizontal mergers always result in a 'reduction in cost per unit'? (7)

Essay questions

1 **a** Explain what is meant by division of labour.   (4)

   b To what extent can car manufacturers take advantage of division of labour?   (7)

   c Discuss the advantages and disadvantages of division of labour from:

   i the firm's point of view   (9)

   ii the worker's point of view.   (5)

2 **a** Distinguish, with examples, between internal economies and diseconomies of scale.   (10)

   b Explain which types of industries may experience a downward sloping long-run average cost curve.   (6)

   c Discuss the external economies and diseconomies of scale which computer firms may experience.   (9)

PART THREE

Price determination

Introduction

In answering the questions in this part you may find it useful to consult Chapters 14–18 in *Introductory Economics* or appropriate chapters in other books.

The questions in this part seek to test and improve your understanding of demand, supply, the concept of elasticity, price determination and relationships between markets. The specific objectives are to develop your ability to:

- understand the meaning of effective demand

- recognise the difference and link between individual and market demand curves

- distinguish between movements along and shifts in demand curves

- explain the effects of a price change

- understand the concept of diminishing marginal utility and its relationship to the demand curve

- explain how a consumer can maximise total utility

- define consumer surplus and illustrate it on a diagram

- identify the main causes of shifts in the demand curve

- define, explain, calculate and illustrate price, cross and income elasticities of demand

- appreciate the implications of price elasticity of demand for changes in total expenditure for firms and for government policy

- apply the forms of elasticity in analysing real-world examples

- define supply

- distinguish between movements along and shifts in the supply curve

- identify the main causes of shifts in the supply curve

- define, explain, calculate and illustrate price elasticity of supply

- appreciate the influence of time on price elasticity of supply

- define, explain and illustrate equilibrium price

- understand the effects of changes in demand and supply on equilibrium price and output

- appreciate the significance of price elasticity of demand and supply in determining the extent of changes in price and output

- identify the main demand and supply relationships
- explain the relationship between product and factor markets.

Short questions

1 Define effective demand and explain what may cause an extension in demand for a product.

2 Give three reasons for an increase in demand for apples.

3 Explain the impact of a rise in the price of pork on demand for pork.

4 Why is water, which is essential, cheap, whereas diamonds, which are non-essential, are expensive?

5 What type of goods have:

   i negative price elasticity of demand

   ii negative cross elasticity of demand

   iii negative income elasticity of demand.

6 Giving reasons, explain what size of price elasticity of demand cigarettes have.

7 Give three reasons for a decrease in the supply of cabbages.

8 Discuss three determinants of the elasticity of supply of televisions.

9 Giving examples, explain which type of goods are:

   i in joint demand

   ii in joint supply.

10 What effect is a rise in demand for duvets likely to have on the market for blanket workers?

Multiple choice questions

1 Which of the following would cause the demand curve for a good to shift to the left?

   A a rise in the price of the good

   B an increase in the supply of the good

   C a decrease in the price of a substitute good

   D a decrease in the tax imposed by the government on the good.

2 The following table shows the total utility gained by an individual from the consumption of three goods.

Units consumed	Total utility (utils)		
	Cabbages	Carrots	Peas
1	10	7	9
2	18	14	16
3	25	21	21
4	30	28	23
5	32	35	22

Which of the goods are subject to diminishing marginal utility?

A   peas only

B   cabbages and peas

C   cabbages and carrots

D   cabbages, carrots and peas.

3   The diagram shows the marginal utility a person gains from the consumption of successive units of good Z.

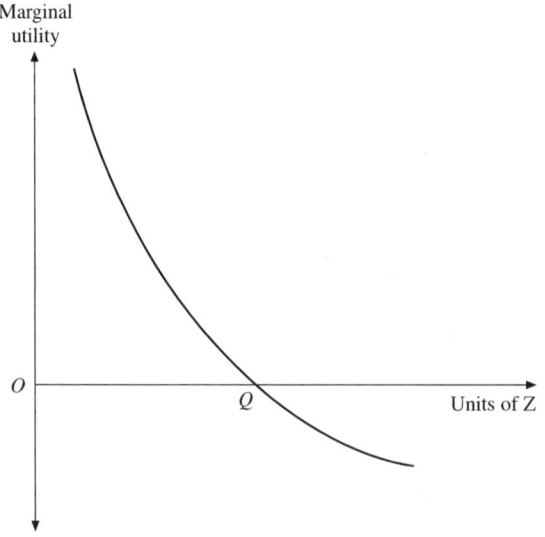

Fig. 3.1

If the person is consuming OQ units, what can be concluded?

A   Total utility is at a maximum.

B   The person is gaining no satisfaction from consumption of the good.

C The person is in equilibrium with their purchases of Z.

D Disutility is experienced.

4 The diagram shows the effect of an increase in the supply of a good.

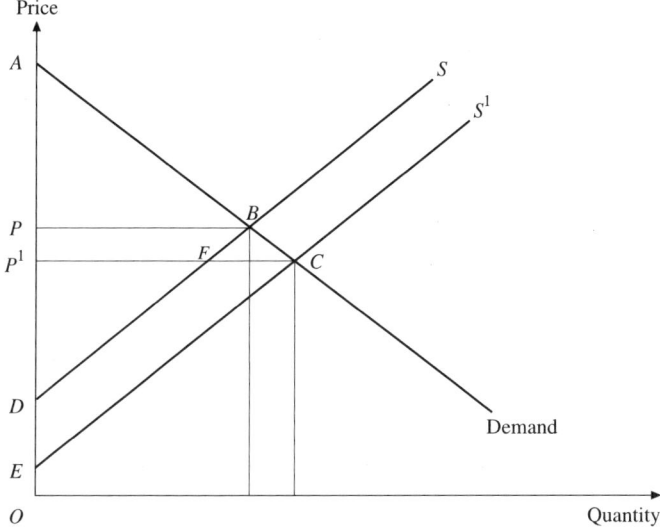

Fig. 3.2

Which area represents the resulting increase in consumer surplus?

A PAB

B P1PBC

C P1FD

D DBCE

5 A good has unit price elasticity of demand. What will decrease as a result of an increase in the price of the good?

A quantity demanded

B quantity supplied

C expenditure on substitutes

D expenditure on the good.

6 Which of the following diagrams illustrates negative cross elasticity of demand?

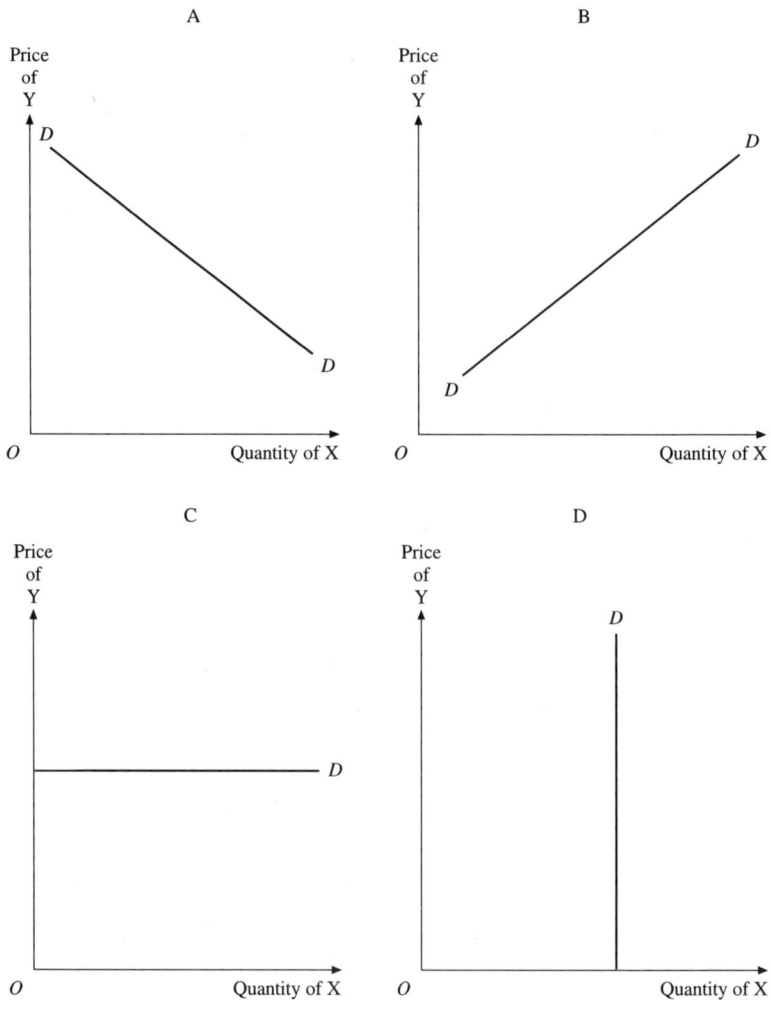

Fig. 3.3

7   A person's real income rises from £600 per week to £630 per week. As a
     result they increase their spending on wine from £20 per week to £22 per
     week. What is their income elasticity of demand for wine?

     A 0.5   **B** 0.67   **C** 1.0   **D** 2.0

8   The price elasticity of supply for a firm's good is 0.8. At a price of £40 the
     quantity supplied by the firm is 600 units. Then the price rises to £50.
     What is the firm's revenue after this rise in price?

     A £24 000   **B** £30 000   **C** £32 400   **D** £36 000

9 The diagram shows the demand and supply curves for a consumer good. The initial equilibrium price is P. Which of the following would explain a fall in price to P1?

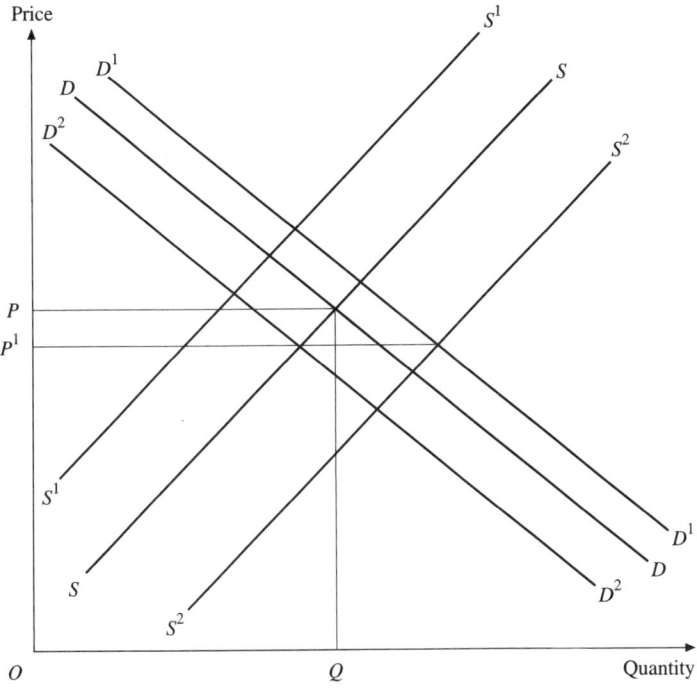

Price

Fig. 3.4

A an increase in real incomes and a fall in raw material costs

B a subsidy granted to producers and an increase in the price of a complement

C an increase in income tax and the introduction of improved technology

D an increase in population and an increase in value added tax.

10 **Consumers' expenditure £m 1990 market prices**

	1983	*1993*
Food	38 582	42 957
Clothing & footwear	15 441	22 463
Housing	41 161	49 584
Transport & communication	43 968	60 544
Tobacco	9 566	7 866
Total consumers' expenditure	261 200	341 922

It can be deduced from the data that:

A   Expenditure on transport and communication rose by a greater percentage than expenditure on clothing and footwear.

B   Expenditure on food formed a smaller percentage of total expenditure in 1993 than in 1983.

C   The price of cigarettes and other tobacco products fell over the period 1983 to 1993.

D   The supply of housing increased by a greater percentage than the demand for housing between 1983 and 1993.

Data response questions

1

The combination of accelerating power, falling costs, and a competitive market has resulted in a rapid growth in sales of PCs (personal computers) in the UK market. The upward growth in sales continued through the latest recession, and at a time when consumer confidence continues to be relatively low, the market for PCs for home use continues to be buoyant. According to Dataquest, the UK PC market as a whole grew from 1.7 million units in 1991 to 2.3 million units in 1994, and the 'professional' sector (including business and education) grew from 1.2 million units in 1991 to 1.8 million units in 1994.

In the business sector, as the performance of PCs increases, main-frame and minicomputers have been losing markets. In 1994, 80 per cent of worldwide spending on information technology (computers and associated hardware and software) went on PCs. Most businesses use standard software such as word processors, spreadsheets, databases and desktop publishing. The main area of development in the business market is likely to be the use of on-line networks such as the Internet and electronic conferencing. The corporate market for PCs is expected to grow at about 8 per cent over the next five years.

However, more rapid growth (about 17 per cent per year) is expected in the market for home computers. This difference is partly explained by the importance of CD-ROMs (compact disc, read-only memory) to the home computer market, and, over the longer term, by the potential for multimedia interaction between computers, television and telecommunications networks.

Falling production costs and increased competition in the UK market for PCs is reflected in the continuing fall in the selling price.

Source: 'The Personal Computer Industry', Robert Paisley, *British Economy Survey*, Vol. 24, No. 2, Spring 1995

a   What are the two main sections of the PC market in the UK?   (2)

b   Discuss the causes of the rise in demand for PCs.   (6)

c   What does the passage suggest is the relationship between
    computers and televisions?   (2)

d   Explain, and draw a diagram to illustrate, the cause of the fall
    in price of PCs.   (5)

e   What effect is the increase in demand for PCs likely to have on
    the market for computing magazines?   (4)

f   Discuss three influences on demand for PCs not mentioned in the
    extract.   (6)

2

Changing technology has had a major impact on the supply of newspapers. In the 1980s, computerised production methods replaced the 'hot
metal' process traditionally used in Fleet Street, and newspaper publish-
ers moved out of the Fleet Street area of the City of London. The acquisition of *The Sun, News of the World, The Times* and *The Sunday Times* by
Rupert Murdoch's News International resulted in a move to Wapping in
the East End.

The boom in the economy in the late 1980s was reflected in the newspaper industry, not only as a result of increased revenue from sales, but
also as a result of the boom in advertising revenue. The profitability of
the industry combined with the concern about the concentration of market power in a few hands contributed to the entry of *The Independent*
into the broadsheet market in 1986.

The Guardian and *The Daily Telegraph* managed to limit the loss of
sales during the recession by developing features which may have
helped to reinforce brand loyalty. *The Daily Telegraph* updated its image
by increasing its appeal to younger readers (for example, through the
Young Telegraph on Saturday and more emphasis on lifestyle features)
without offending most of its traditional readers. *The Guardian* developed its tabloid section covering social and political issues, the media
and the arts, in a digestible format.

In an attempt to recover market share, News International followed a
cut in the cover price of *The Sun* from 25p to 20p with a cut in the cover
price of *The Times* from 45p to 30p in September 1993.

The effect of the price cuts on News International titles was
significant. All five showed an increase in sales in the six months to
March 1994, compared to the significant decline in the corresponding
period a year earlier. Although this was partly due to an upturn in
incomes as a result of the recovery, only two out of the six other national
dailies showed a significant increase in sales over this period. However,
with *The Daily Telegraph* resorting to a price cut from 48p to 30p in June
1994, the cover price of *The Times* was cut further to 20p, the same price
as *The Sun*. In August, *The Independent* finally relented and cut its price
for the Monday to Friday editions to 30p.

Source: 'Economics of the Media', Robert Paisley, *British Economy Survey*,
Vol. 24, No. 1, Autumn 1994

   a Explain what happened to the supply of newspapers in the 1980s. (3)

   b Discuss two causes of a change in the supply of newspapers not
       mentioned in the extract. (4)

   c What does the extract suggest about the income elasticity of
       demand for newspapers? (4)

   d How did the newspapers mentioned in the extract seek to attract
       buyers? (4)

   e Newspaper owners were seeking to raise revenue by cutting the
       price of their papers. What must they have believed about the
       price elasticity of demand for their products? (4)

   f What factors influence the price elasticity of a particular
       newspaper? (6)

Essay questions

1 **a** What factors influence the demand for lamb? (6)

     b What effect will an increase in the price of lamb have on the
        markets for:

        i   lamb (4)

        ii mint sauce (5)

        iii beef (5)

        iv shepherds? (5)

2 **a** Define and explain price elasticity of demand, cross elasticity
       of demand and income elasticity of demand. (12)

     b How may knowledge of these concepts be used by a coach
        firm seeking to increase its revenue? (13)

PART FOUR

Market structure

Introduction

In answering the questions in this part you may find it useful to consult Chapters 19–23 in *Introductory Economics* or appropriate chapters in other books.

The questions in this part seek to test and improve your understanding of perfect competition, monopolistic competition, oligopoly, monopoly and how these market structures compare.

The specific objectives are to develop your ability to:

- understand the meaning and the interrelationship between marginal, average and total revenue

- identify the key characteristics of perfect competition, monopolistic competition, oligopoly and monopoly

- explain the factors which determine the structure of markets

- describe the characteristics and assumptions of the different market structures

- distinguish between normal profits, supernormal profits and losses

- draw accurate diagrams showing different output positions of firms

- distinguish between the short-run and long-run output positions in both perfect competition monopolistic competition

- recognise the relationship between marginal cost and the short- and long-run supply curves under perfect competition

- distinguish between collusive and non-collusive behaviour under oligopoly

- explain the main types of barriers to entry

- understand the meaning, conditions needed and consequences of price discrimination

- analyse the effect of changes in costs and demand on a firm's output under different market structures

- compare the characteristics of different market structures including the existence or non-existence of barriers to entry

- assess the behaviour of firms operating in different market structures, including types of competition and ability to influence price

- understand when a firm would leave the industry

- evaluate the performance of firms in different market structures, including profit levels, efficiency, consumer surplus and innovation

- appreciate that firms may have a variety of objectives, e.g. profit maximising, growth
- consider alternative pricing policies
- explain the meaning and significance of contestable markets.

Short questions

1   What factors determine the structure of markets?

2   What is so perfect about perfect competition?

3   Explain three similarities and three differences between perfect competition and monopolistic competition.

4   Explain the significance of game theory in analysing the behaviour of oligopolistic firms.

5   Explain under which market structures the following UK industries operate:
    commercial banks
    civil airlines
    public houses.

6   A discriminating monopolist may separate markets on the basis of, for example, age. Explain two other bases for separating markets.

7   Who gains and who loses from price discrimination?

8   Explain, giving examples, four forms of non-price competition which firms may engage in.

9   How, and why, do the total revenue curves of firms producing under monopoly and perfect competition differ?

10 Under what conditions will firms produce at minimum average cost?

Multiple choice questions

1   A firm is producing under conditions of perfect competition. Under which of the following conditions would it close down in the short run?

    A   Marginal cost exceeds average revenue.

    B   Average cost exceeds average revenue.

    C   Average fixed cost exceeds average revenue.

    D   Average variable cost exceeds average revenue.

2   The following table shows the revenue and cost schedules of a firm.

Output	Total revenue (£)	Total cost (£)
11	70	54
12	80	56
13	90	60
14	100	66
15	110	76

Within which of the following ranges of output will profits be maximised?

A 11–12 units   **B** 12–13 units   **C** 13–14 units   **D** 14–15 units

3 The diagram shows the output of a firm producing under conditions of imperfect competition.

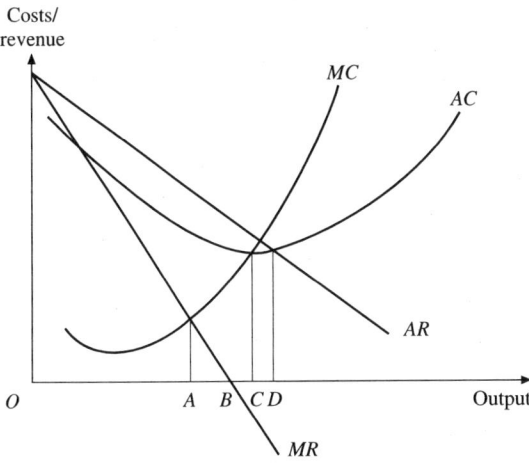

Fig. 4.1

At which level of output will the firm maximise sales revenue?

4 The table below shows the marginal cost schedules of three profit maximising firms which produce under conditions of perfect competition.

Units of output	Marginal costs (£)		
	Firm R	Firm S	Firm T
5	2	2	1
6	4	3	3
7	6	4	4
8	9	5	6
9	12	6	10

What is their combined elasticity of supply for an increase in price from £4 to £6?

A 0.4   **B** 0.5   **C** 1.33   **D** 2.5

5 The diagram shows the total revenue and total costs of a firm.

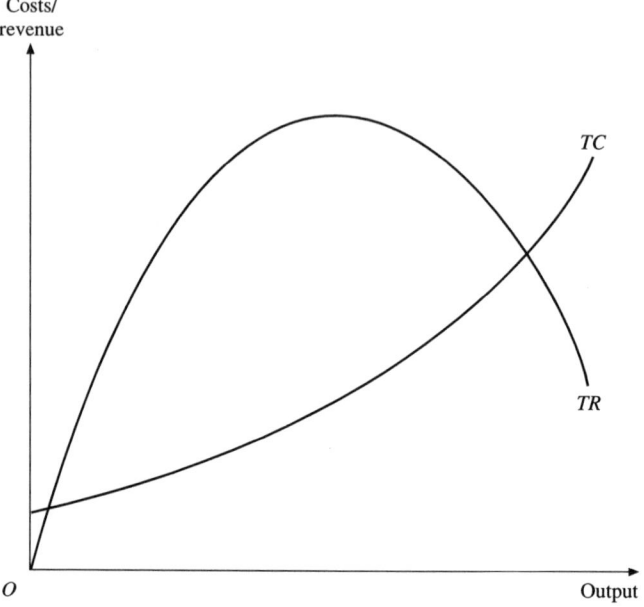

Fig. 4.2

Which situation does the diagram represent?

A monopoly in the short run

B monopoly in the long run

C perfect competition in the short run

D perfect competition in the long run.

6 Monopolistic competition is best described as a market situation where:

A the firms are price takers

B there are barriers to entry and exit

C the firms produce differentiated products

D most of the firms make supernormal profits in the long run.

7 The kinked demand curve suggests that firms operating in oligopolistic markets will:

A sell their products in more than one market

B   follow price cuts initiated by rival firms but not price rises

C   have a downward-sloping average revenue curve but a horizontal marginal revenue curve

D   face inelastic demand above and elastic demand below the current market price.

8   A monopolist decides to maximise profits by engaging in price discrimination. They sell their output in two separate markets, Y and Z. The diagram shows the average revenue and marginal revenue curves for the good in the two separate markets.

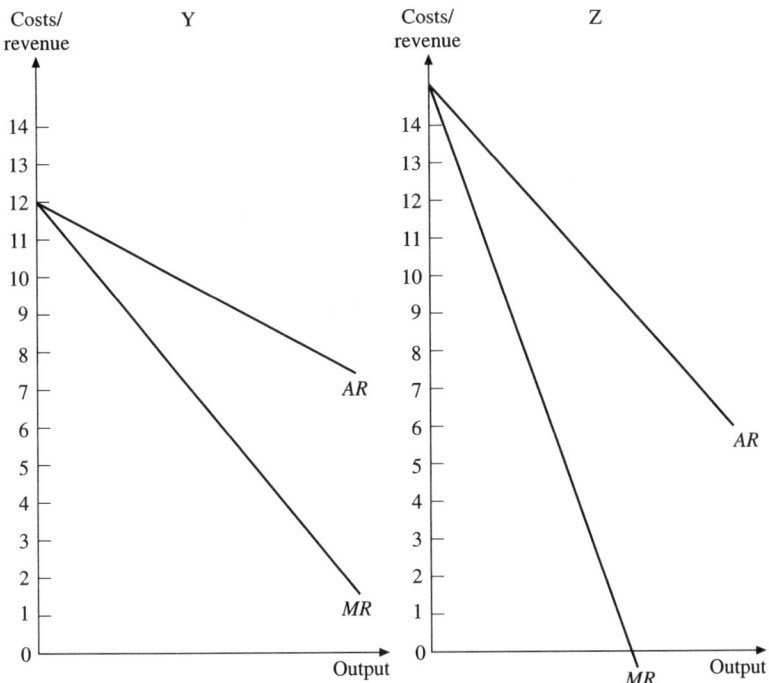

Fig. 4.3

The marginal cost of production is £5. Which set of prices would maximise the monopolist's profits?

	Price in market Y (£)	Price in market Z (£)
A	5	6
B	9	8
C	11	5
D	12	7

9 The diagram shows the cost and revenue curves of a monopolist.

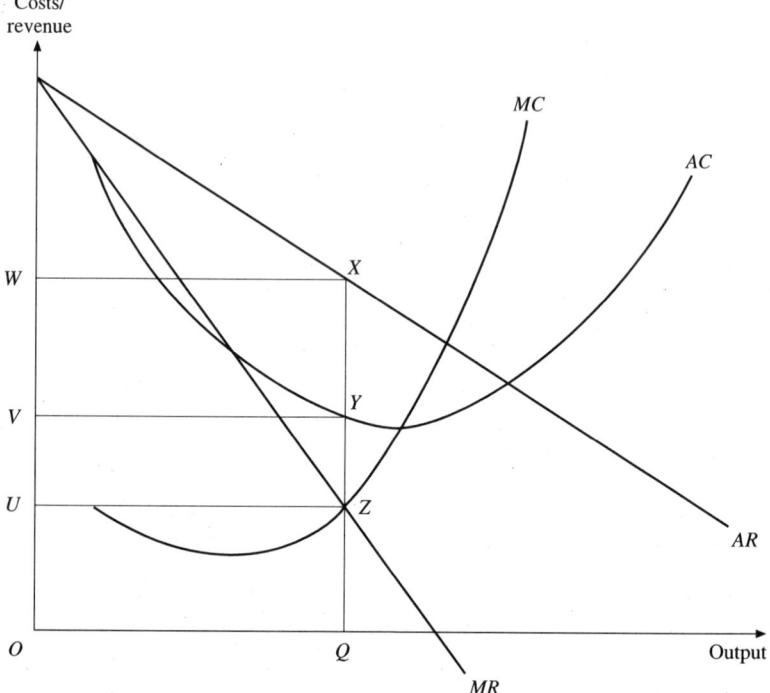

Fig. 4.4

To maximise profits the firm produces an output of OQ. Which area includes the normal profit earned by the firm.

A OUZQ

B UVYZ

C VWXY

D OVYQ

10

> Car output is dominated by seven groups, accounting for 99 per cent of the total: Rover (which became a subsidiary of BMW in 1994), Ford (including Jaguar), Vauxhall, Peugeot-Talbot, Honda, Nissan and Toyota. The remainder is in the hands of smaller, specialist producers such as Rolls-Royce, whose cars are renowned for their quality and durability.
>
> Source: *Britain 1996, An Official Handbook* (page 243), HMSO

The data provide a description of the UK car industry. Under which market structure is it operating?

A   perfect competition

B   monopolistic competition

C   oligopoly

D   monopoly.

Data response questions

8

The theory of contestable markets is relatively new and is based on the assumption that there is freedom of entry into an industry and that exit is costless. Free entry means that potential entrants to a market are at no disadvantage in terms of higher costs than firms already in the market or from consumers preferring the products of existing firms. Costless exit means that firms are able to leave the market without financial penalty. The result of a contestable market is that potential entrants are not deterred from entering an industry by the possibility of existing firms reducing their prices since they can always leave the market given the absence of unrecoverable or *sunk* costs.

Unlike the traditional theory of price and output determination, most notably perfect competition and monopoly, the theory of contestable markets states that the structure of a market, and how firms behave within that market, cannot be determined simply by the number of firms which operate in the industry. Thus, in contestable markets, the number of firms operating is not important, what is important is the *threat* of entry. The threat of entry is sufficient to make existing firms, whether large or small, behave competitively. Contestable markets experience *hit and run entry* since the existence of super-normal profit encourages new firms to enter the market obtaining a share of the profits and leaving the industry when profits are creamed off. If there are unrecoverable or sunk costs involved then these are a cost of entry and as such therefore a barrier to entry. In a contestable market there are no such sunk costs to inhibit entry.

Although first impressions would appear to support the idea of the local bus service market being a contestable market, in that entry costs are low, given the active second-hand bus market, and sunk costs are small, given that the vehicles can be resold, there are in fact certain barriers to entry. For example, new entrants may find it difficult to obtain access to certain bus stations and there may be passenger loyalty to existing operators.

Source: 'The Structure of the British Bus Industry, Stephen Ison, *British Economy Survey*, Vol. 25, No. 1, Autumn 1995

a   Explain what is meant by:

  i   sunk costs   (2)

  ii   hit and run entry.   (2)

b How does the theory of contestable markets differ from the traditional theory of price and output? (3)

c Discuss whether a monopoly market can also be a contestable market. (3)

d Discuss two barriers to entry not mentioned in the text. (4)

e What effect does the existence of supernormal profits have in a perfectly contestable market? (4)

f Discuss whether the UK telecommunications industry is a contestable market. (7)

2

Privatisation has created a number of large corporations which are dominant suppliers in their respective markets and possess considerable market power. Monopoly is usually regarded, by economists, as a 'bad thing' because a monopolist may charge higher prices, and hence earn excess profits, compared to a competitive market; a monopolist is also said to lack the incentive to minimise costs of production. On the other hand, monopoly may result from greater efficiency and innovation. Taking the last point, economists are often less concerned, in practice, with the size of the firm as such, and rather more so with the actions of dominant firms trying to preserve their market share by anti-competitive behaviour, such as predatory pricing (pricing below production cost), the purpose of which is to deter rival firms.

A special case, but one of considerable importance to the privatised firms, is that of 'natural monopoly'. Natural monopoly is where a single supplier can operate at a lower unit cost than can two or more suppliers. One source of natural monopoly can arise in other ways. In the privatised markets it is most commonly associated with the evidence of distribution networks which would not be economic to duplicate, given the capital costs involved. Examples include the national grid and local distribution networks for electricity, gas and water pipelines, telephone lines, and in the most recent case under discussion, railway track. In each case there is a mixture of technical and economic (cost) factors which indicate that a single supplier is the most efficient way of providing a network.

Source: 'Regulating Natural Monopolies', Stuart Swift, *British Economy Survey*, Vol. 22, No. 2, Spring 1993

a In the context of the extract, define 'excess profits'. (3)

b Why might a monopolist not seek to minimise 'costs of production'? (4)

c Distinguish between predatory and limit pricing. (4)

d Identify and comment on two examples of anti-competitive behaviour not mentioned in the extract. (4)

e Explain, in your own words, the meaning of a natural monopoly. (5)

   f Discuss whether a monopolist will necessarily charge higher
prices than a perfectly competitive firm.   (5)

Essay questions

1 **a** Distinguish between normal and supernormal profit.   (5)

   b Explain why firms producing under conditions of perfect
competition may enjoy supernormal profits in the short run
but not in the long run.   (15)

   c Under what conditions is a perfectly competitive industry in
long-run equilibrium?   (5)

2 **a** Explain what is meant by oligopoly.   (5)

   b Discuss the strategies an oligopolistic firm might take:

      i to maintain its market share   (10)

      ii to increase its market share.   (10)

PART FIVE

Market failure and government response

Introduction

In answering the questions in this part you may find it useful to consult Chapters 24–28 in *Introductory Economics* or appropriate chapters in other text-books.

The questions in this part seek to test and improve your understanding of social costs and benefits, causes of market failure, government response to market failure, nationalisation and privatisation.

The specific objectives are to develop your ability to:

- distinguish between private, external and social costs and benefits
- define market failure
- identify reasons for government failure
- define private, public, merit and demerit goods
- recognise the impact of imperfect competition on welfare
- discuss the causes of an imperfect distribution of income and wealth
- analyse policies to deal with market failure, including legislation, giving property rights, taxation and subsidies
- distinguish between specific and ad valorem indirect taxes and subsidies
- analyse the effects of indirect taxes and subsidies on welfare
- explain the effect of setting a maximum and minimum price
- analyse the workings of a buffer stock
- discuss government competition policy
- recognise the role of the MMC, Restrictive Practices Court and the EU in promoting competitive practices
- discuss the arguments for and against nationalisation and privatisation.

Short questions

1   Distinguish between a public and a private good.

2   Explain why education is a merit and not a public good.

3   What are the social costs associated with people smoking?

4   Explain what is meant by the optimum level of pollution.

5   Discuss the effect on the market for tobacco of an increase in taxation on the product.

6   Discuss one example of a positive external benefit of consumption and one example of a positive benefit of production.

7   Explain how a buffer stock operates.

8   Discuss whether mergers between banks and building societies are in the public interest.

9   How may the extension of property rights reduce market failure?

10   Discuss three arguments for and against privatisation.

Multiple choice questions

1   What is a demerit good? A good:

A   that is both non-rival and non-excludable

B   where the average revenue obtained is exceeded by the average costs of production

C   where the private costs of consuming the good exceed its social costs

D   that the government believes consumers will buy too much of if it is provided by the private sector at market prices.

2   The table shows the demand and supply schedules for a good.

Price (£)	Quantity demanded	Quantity supplied
10	20	1280
9	60	1000
8	150	850
7	260	600
6	400	400
5	600	150
4	900	50

If a tax of £3 is imposed on the good, by how much will its price rise?

A £2   **B** £3   **C** £6   **D** £8

3   In the following diagram demand is shown by the curve DD. The introduction of an expenditure tax shifts the supply curve from SS to S1S1.

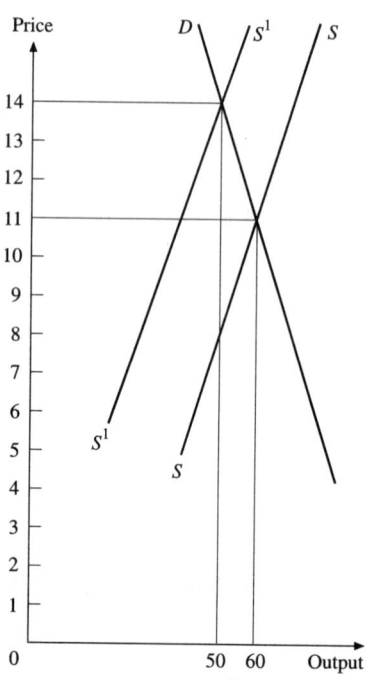

Fig. 5.1

What is the revenue received by the government as a result of the tax?

A £100   B £150
C £250   D £660

4 In the diagram the initial supply curve is SS.

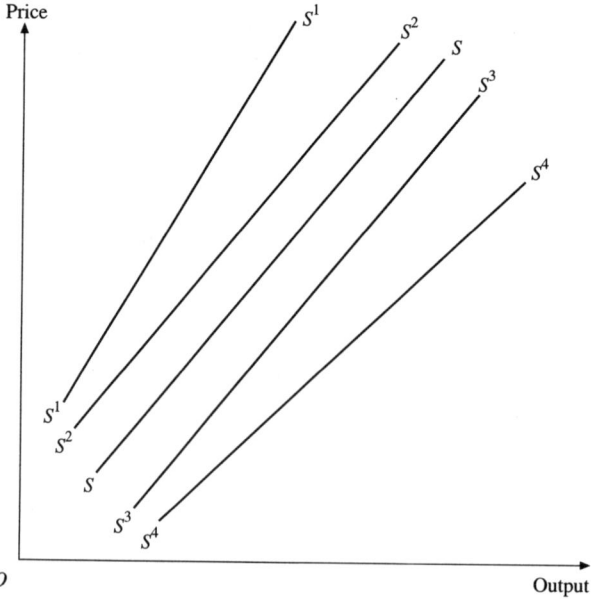

Fig. 5.2

Which curve shows the effect of the introduction of a specific subsidy?

A S1S1   **B** S2S2   **C** S3S3   **D** S4S4

5   Which of the following would give rise to market failure? A firm producing an output where:

A   price exceeds marginal cost

B   average revenue exceeds average variable cost

C   average revenue equals average total cost

D   marginal social cost equals marginal social benefit.

6   Which one of the following is a private, as opposed to external, cost of building a new car manufacturing factory?

A   visual pollution

B   increased traffic congestion in the vicinity of the factory

C   purchase of the land on which the factory is built

D   damage to the natural environment of the land on which the factory is built.

7   What would a socially efficient tax on alcohol achieve? It would:

A   maximise government revenue

B   eliminate alcohol consumption

C   reduce alcohol consumption to an optimal level

D   raise revenue for the government but have a neutral effect on the consumption and production of alcohol.

8   Which of the following is a public good?

A   health care

B   public libraries

C   seat belts

D   street lighting.

9   The diagram shows the output of a monopolist.

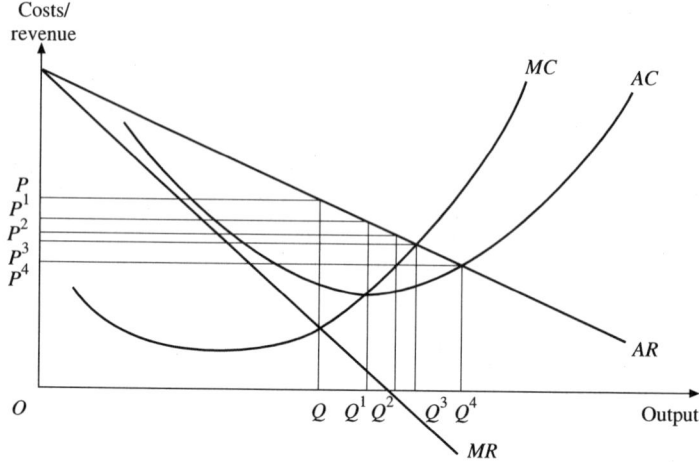

Fig. 5.3

The firm seeks to maximise profits. By how much do output and price differ from the allocatively efficient levels?

	Price	Output
A	PP3	QQ3
B	P1P4	Q1Q4
C	P3P2	Q3Q2
D	P2P	Q2Q

10   'Cost-benefit analysis (CBA) is an attempt to provide a monetary valuation of the perceived costs and benefits of any particular investment project.'

(Source: *Applied Economics* edited by A. Griffiths & S. Wall, 6th edition, page 214, Longman)

Which type of costs and benefits is being referred to here?

A   financial

B   private

C   external

D   social.

Data response questions

1

A series of recent MMC reports have dismissed complaints about restraints to competition in markets ranging from instant coffee and ice-cream to perfume and cars. Even where the MMC has decided to act, its proposed remedies have sometimes been so weak, notably on newspaper distribution and gas supplies, that they have had to be toughened up by the Office of Fair Trading, the MMC's sister body, which in theory is supposed to carry out initial investigations while the MMC does the in-depth work. The weakness of government competition policy may spring partly from concerns about whether or not tough anti-monopoly legislation is good for an economy; but it has manifested itself as dithering. In 1989, Mrs Thatcher's government published a white paper (which normally precedes legislation) setting out proposals to reform the 1976 Restrictive Practices Act. Instead of legislation, the government followed this up with a green paper (which normally precedes a white one) in 1992. Then last month Ian Lang, president of the board of trade, published 'a consultation document' (which normally precedes a green paper) on plans to tighten up laws against illegal cartels.

Since Michael Heseltine, then president of the board of trade, appointed Mr Odgers as the MMC's chairman three years ago, the line has at least been clearer. Mr Odgers, a former managing director of Tarmac, argued on taking office that overzealous enforcement of competition rules 'risked damaging our great enterprises'. It was vital, he added, that the interests of industry were properly looked after: 'Competition can be enormously beneficial in many cases, but where it involves the destruction of strong interests in a wider context, it could be weakening from UK PLC's point of view.'

Source: 'Monopolies and Mergers Omission', *The Economist*, 20 April 1996, pages 22 and 23

a Explain the difference between the role of the MMC and the OFT. (4)

b Why might anti-monopoly legislation be bad for the economy?   (6)

c Explain the meaning of:

  i restraints to competition   (3)

  ii cartels.   (3)

d Discuss the benefits of competition.   (5)

e Discuss two methods a government can use to promote
   competition.   (4)

2

'Carrot and Stick' Could Cut Car Addiction

The Government is to consider ways of reducing traffic congestion by charging car drivers to enter cities or limiting access to certain areas. But the measures, set out in a green paper released yesterday, are unlikely to be enacted before the election because ministers need more time to consult. Stung by resentment at road projects such as the Newbury bypass, Sir George Young, the Transport Secretary, has also called for a new planning system for trunk roads, and closer consultation with local authorities.

Sir George made it clear that he wanted to reduce car dependency. Some 60 per cent of car journeys were shorter than five miles, and concern about pollution and other effects had focused the need to promote alternatives, with the possibility of doubling cycle use by 2000.

He said the Government had narrowed things down to about 20 specific measures. To get people off the roads, he said, 'we have to use a carrot and stick approach'. The stick already existed in making it difficult for people to park; the carrot was to make bus travel more attractive.

The document, *Transport – The Way Forward*, is the Government's response to views put forward by various bodies, who were invited to comment when Sir George's predecessor, Brian Mawhinney, initiated the 'great transport debate'. The paper says that 'without additional measures aimed at reducing their impact, currently forecast levels of traffic will lead to increasingly severe pressures of congestion'. It says local authorities may need to examine traffic restraint measures, while sustaining the local economy.

Source: '"Carrot and Stick" Could Cut Car Addiction"', Keith Harper, *The Guardian*, 26 April 1996

a Explain briefly how the government could:

    i charge drivers 'to enter cities' (4)

    ii 'limit access to certain areas'. (4)

b Discuss the negative externalities caused by the high numbers of people using their cars for short journeys. (4)

c Distinguish between carrot and stick measures to reduce traffic congestion. (4)

d Discuss two economic measures to reduce traffic congestion that were not discussed in the extract. (4)

e Explain the meaning of the last sentence. ('It says local authorities may need to examine traffic restraint measures, while sustaining the local economy.') (5)

Essay questions

1 **a** Explain and give examples of:

     i private and external costs   (5)

     ii private and external benefits.   (5)

  b Evaluate, using diagrams where appropriate, the economic
     policies which a government may use to:

     i reduce external costs   (7)

     ii increase external benefits.   (8)

2 A government wishes to encourage an increase in the consumption
  and production of domestic smoke detectors.

  a Explain why the market mechanism may result in the
    underconsumption of smoke detectors.   (6)

  b Assess the effectiveness of setting a maximum price, providing
    a subsidy to producers and cutting income tax in achieving the
    government's objective.   (15)

  c Discuss two other government policy measures which could
    be used.   (4)

PART SIX

The markets for factors of production

Introduction

In answering the questions in this part you may find it useful to consult Chapters 29–31 in *Introductory Economics* or appropriate chapters in other textbooks.

The questions in this part seek to test and improve your understanding of marginal revenue product, profit and economic rent.

The specific objectives are to develop your ability to:

- appreciate that demand for a factor of production is derived from the demand for the product

- understand the meaning of marginal revenue productivity (MRP)

- appreciate the relationship between TRP, ARP and MRP

- recognise the link between MRP and the demand for a factor of production

- identify the causes and effects of changes in MRP

- define profit

- distinguish between supernormal profit, normal profit and loss

- recognise the role of profit in a market economy

- define and distinguish between economic rent and transfer earnings

- understand the factors which influence the proportion of economic rent and transfer earnings earned by a factor

- analyse the arguments for taxing economic rent

- explain the meaning of quasi-economic rent.

Short questions

1 Identify the four factors of production and the reward which each one receives.

2 Define the marginal revenue productivity of any factor of production and explain how MRP can change.

3 How does the economist's definition of profit differ from the accountant's definition?

4 Explain the functions of profit in a market economy.

5 Discuss two benefits a firm may gain from introducing a profit-sharing scheme for its workers.

6   How does profit differ from the other three rewards to factors of production.

7   Discuss whether supernormal profit is a form of economic rent.

8   Explain whether it is possible for economic rent to be negative.

9   When will a factor of production's earnings consist entirely of transfer earnings?

10   Both premier league football players and barristers receive high salaries. Explain which group's pay is likely to consist of the higher proportion of economic rent.

Multiple choice questions

1   'It is the addition to output resulting from employing one more unit of a factor of production, when the quantities of all other factors of production are held constant.' Of which of the following is this a definition?

A   marginal revenue

B   marginal factor cost

C   marginal physical product

D   marginal revenue product.

2   A firm uses two factors of production: X and Y. The marginal physical product of X is MPx and the marginal physical product of Y is MPy. The price per unit of factor X is Px and the price of factor Y is Py. To minimise the cost of production the firm should substitute the factors until:

A $MPx = MPy$

B $MPxPx = MPyPy$

C $\dfrac{MPx}{MPy} = \dfrac{Py}{Px}$

D $\dfrac{MPx}{Px} = \dfrac{MPy}{Py}$

3   A firm employs labour, land and capital as inputs. The table shows the marginal products of these inputs at the current level of output and their costs.

	Labour	Land	Capital
Marginal product (units)	15	10	18
Cost per unit of factor (£)	3	2	6

Which of the changes in the employment of the inputs would move the firm nearer to the least cost combination of inputs for its current output level?

	Labour	Land	Capital
A	less	less	more
B	more	more	less
C	more	no change	less
D	less	less	no change

4 Normal profit is earned by a firm when:

A marginal cost is equal to marginal revenue

B marginal cost is equal to average cost

C marginal cost is equal to average revenue

D average cost is equal to average revenue.

5 Under which market conditions may firms earn supernormal profits in the long run?

A perfect competition and monopolistic competition

B monopolistic competition and monopoly

C monopoly and oligopoly

D oligopoly and monopolistic competition.

6 What is the share of profits which shareholders receive called?

A dividends

B interest

C capital gain

D retained profit.

7 The supply of a factor of production is completely inelastic. Its earnings will consist:

A entirely of economic rent

B mostly of transfer earnings

C equally of economic rent and transfer earnings

D entirely of transfer earnings.

8 Which of the following is a definition of transfer earnings?

A payments made to workers during periods of training

B payments made to students, pensions and holders of the national debt

C that part of the earnings of a factor of production which consists of economic rent

D the minimum payment necessary to keep a factor of production in its current employment.

9 The diagram shows the market for a factor of production.

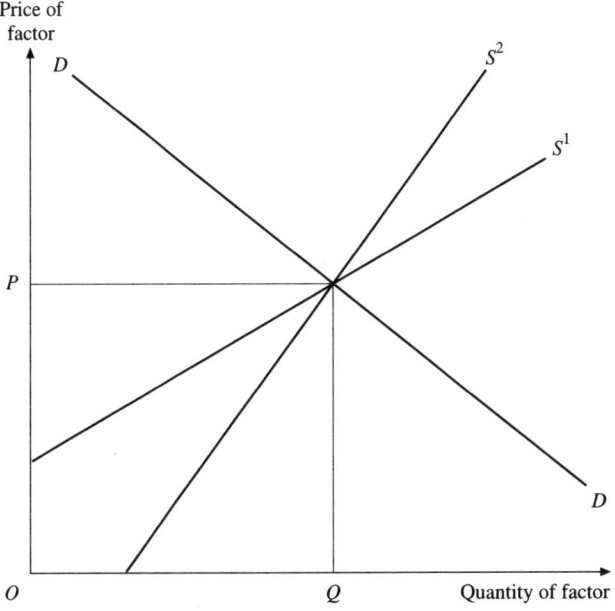

Fig. 6.1

What is the effect on economic rent and transfer earnings of a change in the supply curve from S1 to S2?

	Economic rent	Transfer earnings
A	rises	rise
B	rises	fall
C	falls	rise
D	falls	fall

10 What is meant by 'quasi-economic rent'?

A rent on property held below the equilibrium level by means of government controls

B the payment which a factor of production can earn in its next best paid occupation

C   the 'rent of ability' earned by any factor of production in the long run

D   a surplus in the short run which becomes a transfer earning in the long run.

Data response questions

1

'Hitting the Jackpot First Time'

By any business criterion, the National Lottery is an astonishing success. It sprang from nowhere to achieve sales of £5.2 billion in its first full year – over 25 per cent better than the highest forecasts made by the eight lottery applicants in 1994. Has any other company in British business history ever done so well? Over £1.41 billion was raised for good causes and £677 million paid in taxes. This will finance countless capital projects – from the Tate's Bankside gallery to village halls across the country – forming all in all the most lasting monument of John Major's tenure as prime minister (Mrs Thatcher eschewed such 'state gambling').

Instead of applause, Camelot has run into criticism because of high profits of £77 million (less than one per cent of sales) in its first full year with bonuses of up to £120 000 for its directors. Quite rightly too. Camelot has no legal obligations to give away its profits and it claims anyway that the £500 000 allocated for its first year already puts it into the top 30 UK corporate donors to charity. But that is not the point. It has a strong moral obligation to do so. First, as a new company in a new era of corporate responsibility it should set standards. Second, although it won the contract against fierce competition, it is a monopoly and ought to be sensitive to accusations of monopoly profits. Third, a company so totally dependent on good causes for its very existence ought to be setting its own agenda for corporate donations. If it rejects these arguments, then for public relations reasons alone a huge increase in charitable donations would have been priceless in defusing an inevitable public outcry. For a start, Camelot should atone by adopting one of its own techniques – by rolling over a large slice of last year's profits to be given away this year. With bonuses.

Source: leader article, *The Guardian*, 5 June 1996

a   In what sense were Camelot's profits high?   (3)

b   Explain what is meant by monopoly profits.   (4)

c   Briefly discuss two possible reasons why Camelot's first-year profits were higher than predicted.   (6)

d   Explain in your own words the arguments for Camelot giving more money to charity.   (6)

e   Assess whether it is justifiable for the company running the National Lottery to earn high profits.   (6)

2 **Index numbers 1990 = 100 at 1990 prices**

Year	Gross trading profits	GDP at factor cost	Total fixed investment
1986	93.4	88.6	77.7
1987	110.9	92.7	81.3
1988	113.5	97.3	87.0
1989	110.1	99.4	94.6
1990	100.0	100.0	100.0
1991	85.6	97.9	100.3
1992	84.8	97.4	97.6
1993	100.6	99.6	98.0
1994	115.4	103.6	100.2
1995	120.0	106.1	105.3

Sources: Table 1.1 *NSO Monthly Digest of Statistics*, May 1996, and Tables 1 and 6 (adapted) *National Institute Economic Review*, No. 156, May 1996, National Institute of Economic and Social Research

a Explain what is meant by 'gross trading profits at 1990 prices'. (3)

b With the aid of a graph, analyse the relative movements of gross trading profits and GDP over the time period shown. (6)

c Explain whether the relationship you found in **b** is the one you would have expected to find between profits and GDP. (5)

d Again with the aid of a graph, analyse the relationship between the relative movements of gross trading profits and investment. (6)

e Explain whether the relationship you found in **d** is the one you would have expected to find between profits and investment. (5)

Essay questions

1 **a** Explain what is meant by the marginal revenue product of a factor of production. (8)

b Analyse what could cause an increase in the marginal revenue productivity of an area of farmland. (8)

c What implications does the mobility of an area of land have for the proportion of economic rent it earns? (9)

2 **a** Distinguish between transfer earnings and economic rent. (10)

b Which factors of production can earn economic rent? (6)

c Evaluate the arguments for taxing economic rent. (9)

PART SEVEN

Labour markets

Introduction

In answering the questions in this part you may find it useful to consult Chapters 33–36 in *Introductory Economics* or appropriate chapters in other textbooks.

The questions in this part seek to test and improve your understanding of the demand for and supply of labour, wage determination, labour market failure and government action to correct labour market imperfections. The specific objectives are to develop your ability to:

- identify the key influences on the demand for labour

- analyse the main influences on the elasticity of demand and supply of labour

- apply income and substitution effects in analysing the supply of labour

- distinguish between the determinants of the supply of labour to a given occupation or industry and the aggregate supply of labour

- discuss changes in the nature of the labour force and trends in employment and pay determination

- analyse the factors determining the relative wages in different occupations and industries and between different categories of workers

- discuss the effects of trade unions on wages and employment

- understand the nature and effects of gender, ethnic, social and age discrimination

- understand the role of marginal revenue productivity in the determination of employment levels

- distinguish between wage and employment levels in competitive and monopsonistic labour markets

- discuss the other causes of labour market failure

- recognise the role and effects of education and training

- evaluate the arguments for and against a national minimum wage

- discuss recent trends in trade union membership and their impact on economy.

Short questions

1 What factors determine the aggregate supply of labour?

2 Explain why the participation of women, particularly married women, in the labour force has increased in recent years.

3 In what circumstances will an increase in wages not result in an increase in a firm's total wage bill or change in output?

4 Explain why firms pay overtime rates which are usually higher than standard wage rates.

5 Discuss three arguments a trade union could advance in support of a pay claim for its members.

6 What economic effects may trade unions have on the wages of non-unionised labour?

7 In November 1995 the Disability Act came into force. What major form of labour market discrimination is not covered by legislation and what impact do you think this omission has?

8 Apart from pay, what factors influence a person's choice of job?

9 Use demand and supply analysis to explain the effect of an increase in the resources devoted to training teachers on the market for teacher trainers.

10 Discuss the effects of the trend away from national to local pay determination.

Multiple choice questions

1 Which of the following would reduce the elasticity of demand for labour in a particular market?

A an increase in the proportion of labour costs in total costs

B an increase in the ease of substituting capital for labour

C a reduction in the elasticity of demand for the final product

D a reduction in the national level of employment.

2 In order to increase their labour force from 20 to 21 workers, an employer is obliged to raise the weekly wage rate from £510 to £530. What is the marginal cost of employing the twenty-first worker?

A £420   B £530   C £930   D £1590

3 Real wages are:

A money wages adjusted for inflation

B money wages expressed as a percentage of the national average wage rate

C nominal wages divided by the number of people in employment

D nominal wages adjusted for changes in gross domestic product.

4 The following diagram shows a supply curve for labour to a particular firm.

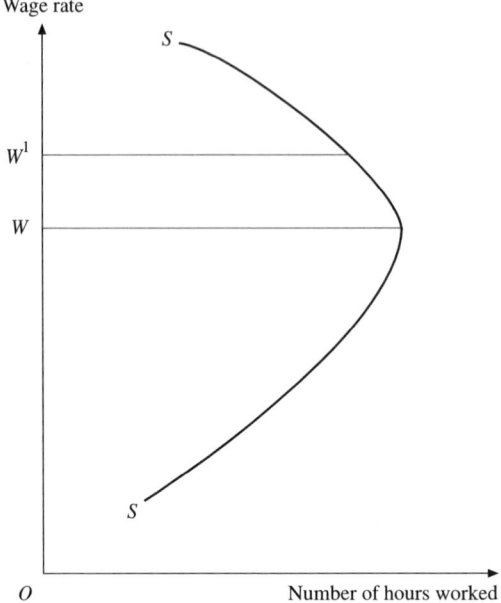

Fig. 7.1

What could explain the change in the supply curve from W to W1?

A the firm substituting capital for labour

B the workers substituting leisure for work

C consumers switching to another firm's products

D the government imposing an indirect tax on the good.

5 Which of the following will influence the elasticity of supply of a specific type of labour?

A the elasticity of supply for the final product

B the marginal revenue productivity of the workers

C the qualifications required to undertake the job

D the ease with which labour can be substituted for capital.

6 A firm operates in product and factor markets which are both perfectly competitive. Labour is its only variable factor input. In the following diagram the line YZ shows the relationship between the marginal physical product of labour and the labour hours hired.

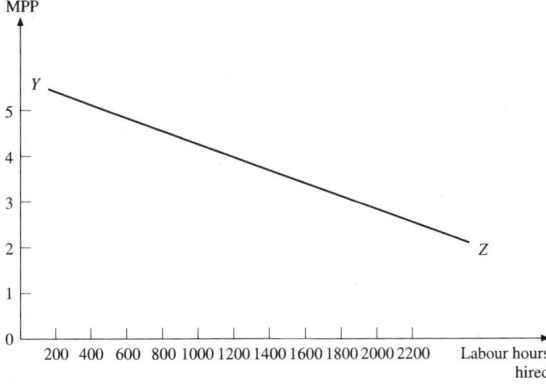

Fig. 7.2

When the price of the product is £5, the firm employs 2000 labour hours per day. What is the wage per labour hour?

A £3   **B** £5   **C** £10   **D** £15

7 Which of the following could cause a perfectly competitive firm's demand for labour curve to shift to the right?

A an increase in the wage rate

B a rise in the price of the final product

C a decrease in labour productivity

D a decrease in the supply of labour.

8 The diagram shows the relationship between the total output of a firm and the number of units of labour employed.

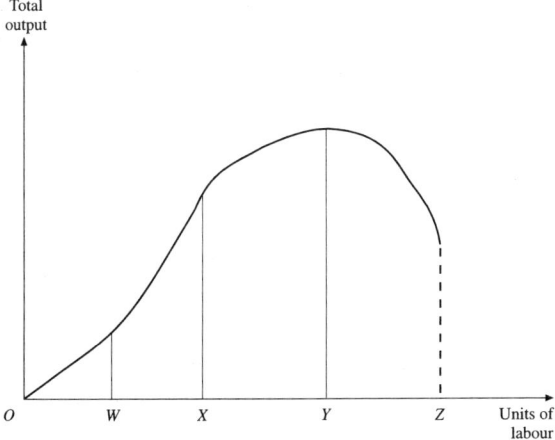

Fig. 7.3

At which point does diminishing marginal productivity set in?

A after OW units of labour are employed

B after OX units of labour are employed

C after OY units of labour are employed

D after OZ units of labour are employed.

9 The diagram shows the demand for and supply of labour in a monopsonistic market.

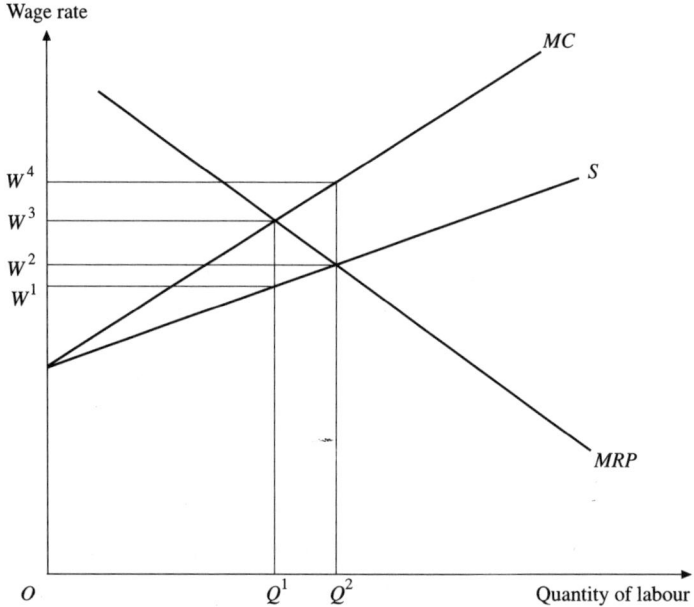

Wage rate

Quantity of labour

Fig. 7.4

What will be the quantity of labour employed and the wage rate paid?

	Quantity of labour	Wage rate
A	Q1	W1
B	Q1	W3
C	Q2	W2
D	Q2	W4

10 The data show the average gross weekly earnings in different occupations in the UK in 1995.

	Men £	Women £
Managers & administrators	537.0	367.8
Teaching professionals	482.9	400.6
Professional & technical occupations	442.9	333.3
Printing & related trades	343.6	235.3
Sales occupations	310.3	199.9
Receptionists, telephonists & related occupations	305.5	197.7
Plant & machine operatives	293.7	201.5
Catering occupations	209.5	158.8

Source: *New Earnings Survey*, 1995

What can be concluded from this data?

A   The average gross weekly earnings in the printing and related trades were £289.45.

B   Managers and administrators worked more overtime than those working in catering occupations.

C   The gender differential, in percentage terms, was greatest in sales occupations.

D   Women paid a higher percentage of their earnings in income tax than men.

Data response questions

1

'Flexibility of Employment'

Increased part-time working, and indeed self-employment, can be seen as part of a wider trend towards progressively greater flexibility of employment. The CBI estimates that nearly a quarter of UK employees are now employed on a part-time or temporary basis. Both businesses and individuals are increasingly looking at, and using, alternatives to full-time permanent employment.

For employers, flexibility aids competitiveness by adjusting the amount of labour used more quickly and closely to prevailing market conditions. They say the main benefits are cost effectiveness, efficiency and response to customer demands. Because companies increasingly operate in an uncertain environment, they need to be able to respond quickly to new circumstances and this means that labour flexibility and adaptability are vital.

Many employees find positive advantages in working on a part-time or temporary basis. For instance there can be increased employment opportunities and it allows work to be balanced with other commitments, such as a family. Over a quarter (27%) of employers using flexible working methods adopted them in response to employees' demands. The majority (81%) of women working part-time report that they do not want a full-time job.

Part-time working is one of the most common and, as has been discussed, increasing flexibilities in the UK labour market. Varying the hours or days worked by employees is often termed temporal flexibility. There has also been a growth in flexible working patterns that apply to full-time staff, such as annual hours contracts and flexitime (worked by 9% and 12% respectively in 1993), overtime or short-time working.

Source: *Labour Market & Skill Trends 1996/97*, Skills and Enterprise Network

a Briefly define flexibility of employment. (3)

b Explain how a more flexible labour force may increase 'effectiveness, efficiency and response to customer demands'. (5)

c Discuss why some people work part time. (4)

d Identify and explain three disadvantages employees may find in working on a part-time or temporary basis. (6)

e Temporal flexibility is one type of labour market flexibility. Explain two other forms of flexibility. (8)

2

Year	Trade union membership (millions)	Working days lost in all stoppages in progress (millions)	UK unemployment (%)
1989	8.96	4.13	6.3
1990	8.85	1.90	5.9
1991	8.63	0.76	8.1
1992	7.99	0.53	9.9
1993	7.81	0.65	10.4
1994	7.55	0.28	9.3
1995	7.28	0.42	8.3

Sources: *Labour Market Trends*, May 1996, and *The Annual Abstract of Statistics*, Office for National Statistics

a Identify and briefly comment on two other measures of labour disputes. (2)

b Comment on the changes in trade union membership over the period shown. (6)

c Analyse the relationship between UK unemployment and working days lost in stoppages. (5)

d Do your findings in **c** accord with what you would expect from economic theory? (6)

e Discuss three other influences on the number of working days lost in any one year. (6)

Essay questions

1 Analyse the effects that the following would be likely to have on the market for McDonald's counter staff:

a a reduction in the length of training required (7)

b an increase in vegetarianism (6)

c an increase in the wage rate offered by Wimpy's (6)

d a decrease in unemployment. (6)

2 **a** What are the main sources of household income? (3)

b Explain why stable grooms receive low pay. (9)

c Assess the arguments for and against the introduction of a national minimum wage. (14)

PART EIGHT

Economic activity

Introduction

In answering the questions in this part you may find it useful to consult Chapters 37–43 in *Introductory Economics* or appropriate chapters in other textbooks.

The questions in this part seek to test and improve your understanding of the distribution of wealth and income, measures of living standards, models of national income determination, aggregate demand and supply, changes in national income, growth and business cycles.

The specific objectives are to develop your ability to:

- differentiate between wealth and income

- identify the main sources of income and wealth

- describe the distribution of income and wealth in the UK

- discuss the main causes of the uneven distribution of income and wealth

- differentiate between relative and absolute poverty

- evaluate the various approaches to alleviating poverty

- understand the main measures of national income and appreciate that income equals output equals expenditure

- convert nominal (money) into real data

- recognise the uses of national income data

- discuss the value and limitations of national income data as a basis for measuring and comparing living standards

- identify alternative measures of living standards

- discuss the main components and determinants of aggregate expenditure

- show some familiarity with the marginal efficiency of capital

- understand the main influences on consumption, saving and investment

- explain the circular flow model of the economy

- distinguish between injections and withdrawals in closed and open economies

- use the injections-withdrawals, algebraic, aggregate demand and aggregate supply and Keynesian cross models to explain national income determination

- distinguish between movements along and shifts in the aggregate demand curve and discuss their causes

- distinguish between movements along and shifts in the short-run aggregate supply curve
- discuss the causes of shifts in the long-run aggregate supply curve
- appreciate the differences between the Keynesian and new classical approaches to the elasticity of the long-run aggregate supply curve
- analyse the effects of shifts in aggregate demand and supply curves using both Keynesian and new classical views on both output and the price level
- recognise that an initial change in expenditure can result in a large change in local or national income
- understand the differences and relationship between the multiplier and the accelerator
- discuss the causes, benefits and costs of growth
- define business cycles
- discuss explanations of business cycles.

Short questions

1　Why is the distribution of wealth more unequal than the distribution of income?

2　Compare cash benefits and the direct provision of services as means of alleviating poverty.

3　Why would it be misleading to calculate national income by adding up the values of the gross outputs of all the enterprises in the economy?

4　Will an increase in savings result in an increase in investment?

5　What factors influence the level of investment in an economy?

6　Explain how the level of national income is determined. Illustrate your answer with a diagram.

7　What can cause a movement along and a shift in the short-run aggregate supply curve?

8　If the long-run aggregate supply curve is vertical, what effect will an increase in demand for exports have on output and the general price level? Illustrate your answer.

9　Discuss two benefits and two costs of economic growth.

10　Identify two economic variables which provide useful information on which to base economic forecasts. Explain your choice.

Multiple choice questions

1   What is the difference between gross national product at factor cost and gross domestic product at factor cost?

   A   imports

   B   capital consumption

   C   indirect taxes and subsidies

   D   net property income from abroad.

2   In 1998 the gross domestic product of a country was £10 000 million and the price index was 100. By the year 2002 the GDP has increased to £12 075 million and the price index is 105. By what percentage has real GDP increased from 1998 to 2002?

   A 5   **B** 14.71   **C** 15   **D** 20.75

3   What is meant by the average propensity to consume?

   A   the proportion of total disposable income spent on consumption

   B   the proportion of additional disposable income spent on consumption

   C   the annual average consumption over the period of a year

   D   the annual average spent on domestically produced goods.

4   The table shows figures for government spending (G), investment (I), imports (M), savings (S), taxation (T), exports (X) and national income (Y) for an open economy.

	Y	G	I	*£ million* M	S	T	X
A	100	40	20	10	10	20	40
B	200	30	40	20	30	20	50
C	300	20	50	40	50	10	30
D	400	10	15	60	60	10	5

What is the equilibrium level of national income?

   A £100m   **B** £200m   **C** £300m   **D** £400m

5   Which of the following is a transfer payment?

   A   the pay of public sector workers

   B   the allowance paid to job seekers

   C   government expenditure on defence equipment

   D   the profits earned by foreign companies based in the UK.

6   The paradox of thrift refers to the fact that in a community:

   A   the rate of saving is inversely related to the rate of consumption

   B   the greater the propensity to save, the smaller the multiplier

   C   an increase in the propensity to save might reduce the level of total saving

   D   a fall in the propensity to save discourages investment and causes income to fall.

7   Which of the following concepts explains how changes in the level of aggregate demand may bring about changes in new capital formation?

   A   the accelerator

   B   the consumption function

   C   the multiplier

   D   the speculative demand for money.

8   Which of the following would cause an increase in the marginal efficiency of a new capital project?

   A   an increase in corporation tax

   B   an increase in the rate of interest

   C   a reduction in the purchase price of new machines

   D   a reduction in government subsidies on investment.

9   The diagram shows the aggregate demand in an economy increasing from AD to AD1.

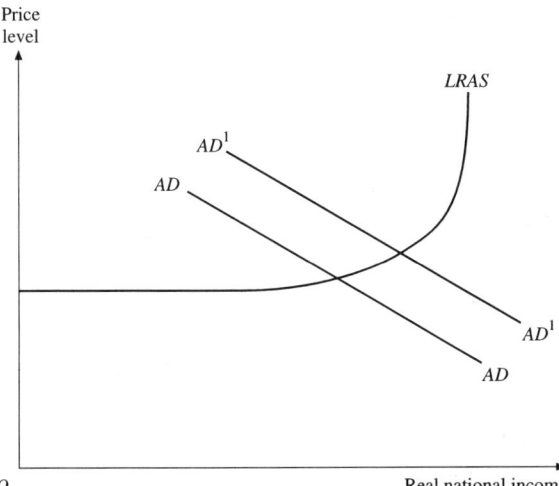

Fig. 8.1

What could have caused this increase?

A   an improvement in training

B   an increase in the rate of interest

C   a reduction in the exchange rate

D   a reduction in the general price level.

10   The graph shows a collection of Lorenz curves for different countries.

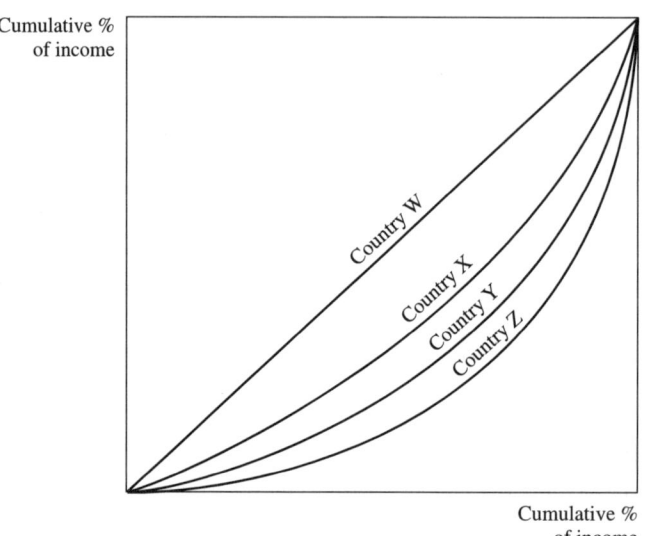

Fig. 8.2

What can be concluded from the graph?

A   Income levels are lowest in Country Z.

B   Country W has the most desirable distribution of income.

C   Country X has a higher rate of employment than Country Z.

D   Income is more unevenly distributed in Country Y than Country X.

Data response questions

1

Year	Real personal disposable income (£ million at 1990 prices)	Consumption ratio	Savings ratio (%)
1986	323 633	295 622	8.7
1987	334 706	311 234	7.0
1988	354 632	334 591	5.7
1989	371 603	345 406	7.1
1990	377 570	347 527	8.1
1991	377 115	339 915	10.1
1992	385 831	339 537	12.2
1993	392 285	348 447	11.4
1994	395 070	357 949	9.6
1995	406 715	366 236	10.1

Source: Table 8, *National Institute Economic Review* No. 156, May 1996, National Institute of Economic and Social Research

a Explain the meaning of 'real personal disposable income'. (3)

b Analyse the relationship between real personal disposable income and consumption in the period shown. (9)

c Do your findings in **b** accord with what you would expect from economic theory? (5)

d Explain the meaning of the savings ratio. (2)

e Identify and briefly comment on any three factors, other than income, which may influence the savings ratio. (6)

2

Investment has a dual role to play within any economy. In the short run, investment may be seen mainly as a component of aggregate demand which, if increased, will have the effect of stimulating the economy and, through the multiplier, substantially raising the level of National Income. Fixed and inventory investment together made up over 13% of TFE in 1993.

In the long run, investment will also affect the supply side of the economy, raising its productive potential and thereby pushing outwards the production frontier. Economic growth is sometimes strictly defined in this way, being that increase in GDP which results from raising productive potential. More usually it is loosely defined as any increase in GDP, even when that is within the existing production frontier.

> There have been a number of studies into the importance of invest-
> ment as a generator of growth, though the results have not been conclu-
> sive. For example, Kuznets (1961), using time-series data for a number
> of countries, found little relationship between the *share* of investment in
> GDP, and the growth in output over time. Similarly, a 1970 OECD sur-
> vey based on cross-sectional data found no clear well-defined relation-
> ship between investment shares and growth in output.... It could, of
> course, be argued that the growth in output is the *cause*, rather than the
> *effect*, of the growth in investment. To expand production may require
> additional capacity, giving rise to extra investment!
>
> Source: *Applied Economics*, edited by A. Griffiths & S. Wall, 6th edition,
> (page 325), Longman

a   Identify the other three components of aggregate demand.   (3)

b   Explain, with the use of a diagram, why an increase in
    investment will increase national income.   (6)

c   Distinguish between the two meanings of economic growth
    discussed in the extract.   (6)

d   Discuss two causes of an increase in a country's productive
    potential other than investment.   (4)

e   Discuss why, in practice, it is difficult to establish a relationship
    between growth in investment and growth in output.   (6)

Essay questions

1   a   Explain why economists compare living standards over time and
        between countries.   (5)

    b   Analyse the problems which may arise in using national income
        figures to make these comparisons.   (14)

    c   Discuss two possible alternative measures.   (6)

2   a   What factors determine the level of aggregate supply in an
        economy?   (5)

    b   Compare the Keynesian and new classical views on the shape
        of the long-run aggregate supply curve.   (7)

    c   Analyse the effects of an increase in government expenditure
        on output, employment and the general price level.   (13)

PART NINE

Money, financial institutions and the rate of interest

Introduction

In answering the questions in this part you may find it useful to consult Chapters 32, 45–48 and 61 in *Introductory Economics* or appropriate chapters in other textbooks.

The questions in this part seek to test and improve your understanding of interest rate determination, the effects of interest rate changes, money, financial institutions, credit creation, measures of changes in the value of money and the quantity theory.

The specific objectives are to develop your ability to:

- distinguish between the loanable funds and liquidity preference theories of interest rate determination

- discuss factors affecting influences on the marginal productivity of capital

- analyse the effects of changes in interest rates on consumption, investments, exchange rate, employment

- define money

- identify the main forms of money used in a modern society

- discuss the functions of money

- distinguish between narrow and broad measures of the money supply

- outline the key functions of the main financial institutions

- explain the concept of liquidity

- distinguish between a commercial bank's assets and liabilities

- explain how commercial banks are able to create credit

- calculate a weighted price index

- distinguish between RPI, TPI and the GDP deflator

- recognise the limitations of the RPI as a measure of inflation

- identify the quantity theory (Fisher) equation

- distinguish between the Monetarist and Keynesian views of the quantity theory.

Short questions

1 What is meant by the real rate of interest?

2 Distinguish between the transactions, precautionary and speculative motives.

3 Explain why a fall in the price of bonds is associated with a rise in the rate of interest.

4 What is money?

5 Outline the functions of money.

6 How are the functions of money affected by inflation?

7 Distinguish between the M0 and M4 measures of the money supply.

8 Why are profitability and liquidity conflicting objectives for a banker?

9 Discuss the main limitations of using changes in the Retail Price Index as a measure of changes in the cost of living.

10 Use the quantity theory to explain why an increase in the money supply may result in an increase in output or prices or both.

Multiple choice questions

1 In choosing a commodity to serve as money, which of the following is the most important characteristic? It must be:

A divisible

B issued by the state

C easily recognisable

D generally acceptable.

2 A banking system is obliged to maintain 10 per cent of its deposits in the form of cash and always lends out the remainder in the form of advances. If a new deposit of £10 million cash is made into the banking system and the public's demand for cash remains unchanged, what will be the value of the additional deposits created by bank lending?

A £9m   **B** £10m   **C** £90m   **D** £100m

3 The table shows data for the velocity of circulation (V), output (T), the price level (P) and the money supply (M).

Year	V	T	P	M
1	100	100	100	100
4	100	110		140

According to the quantity theory identity, what would be the approximate value of the index of prices in year 4?

A 79   **B** 127   **C** 130   **D** 154

4 Which of the following items, extracted from a bank's balance sheet, is the most profitable asset?

A advances

B money at call

C customers' deposits

D treasury bills discounted.

5 Other things being equal, what will result from the open market purchase of securities by the Bank of England?

   A The money supply will increase.

   B The rate of interest will rise.

   C The commercial banks will restrict advances to customers.

   D Commercial banks will call in loans from the discount houses.

6 The money supply in a country is £5000m and the national income is £30 000m. What is the income velocity of circulation?

   A 1/6   **B** 5   **C** 6   **D** 30

7 What do the weights in the Retail Price Index reflect?

   A changes in the price of each good

   B relative expenditures on different goods

   C changes in the rates of taxation on goods

   D the extent of seasonal fluctuations in prices.

8 The table shows consumers' spending patterns and the price indices of the categories of the goods they buy.

Commodity	Index of prices in year 1	Index of prices in year 2	Consumers' expenditure in year 1
Tobacco & alcoholic drink	100	100	100
Housing	100	90	300
Food	100	105	200
Other goods & services	100	120	400

By how much did the general level of prices increase between year 1 and year 2?

   A 2.5%   **B** 6.0%   **C** 15%   **D** 25%

9 Which of the following influences the speculative demand for money?

   A the value of current transactions

B   the marginal efficiency of capital

C   the expected level of interest rates

D   the frequency with which income payments are made.

10   What is meant by liquidity preference?

A   the desire to hold wealth in the form of money

B   the demand for loans by firms wishing to expand

C   the wish to earn a high rate of return on financial assets

D   the preference of financial institutions to hold treasury bills.

Data response questions

1

'The Determination of Interest Rates'

In most textbooks 'the' rate of interest is said to be determined by the demand for, and supply of, money. The demand curve is drawn downward sloping while the supply curve is drawn vertical and is said to shift when the central bank uses open market operations to increase or decrease banks' reserve assets (*the monetary base*). It is difficult to match this account with what one observes *in practice*, for three reasons. First, and most obviously, the news media frequently have us on the edge of our seats with speculation about what exactly the Bank of England (with or without the Chancellor of the Exchequer) is going to make the next change in rates. Changes in interest rates are therefore presented as an *administrative decision* rather than the outcome of the laws of supply and demand. Second, when the money supply does enter the picture, it is because the authorities are concerned with its *rate of growth*, not with its absolute size. Third, we know that in practice there are many different interest rates in an economy, and while they may move in the same direction most of the time, they do not do so always and they do not do so by the same amount.

In the UK, and in most other developed economies, the level of short-term interest rates is indeed set by administrative decision taken by some combination of the country's Treasury (or Ministry of Finance) and the central bank. The balance of power between the two is a topical issue at the moment, especially in the UK where some commentators would like to see more independence for the Bank of England. This follows a substantial literature suggesting that countries which give the central bank more independence in the conduct of monetary policy (including the setting of interest rates) tend to have lower inflation rates.

Saying that the authorities set rates does not mean that they are free to set them at whatever level they like.

Source: 'The Determination of the Level of Interest Rates', P. Howells, *British Economy Survey*, Vol. 24, No. 2, Spring 1995

a What theory of interest rate determination is being discussed in the first sentence of the extract? (4)

b Identify and briefly discuss an alternative theory of interest rate determination. (5)

c Explain what is meant by open market operations. (4)

d Discuss one advantage and one disadvantage of the Bank of England being given more independence. (6)

e Explain why the authorities are not free to set interest rates at 'whatever level they like'. (6)

2

Year	Base rate (%)	New car registrations (thousands)	Housing starts (private sector) (thousands)
1988	10.1	2210	222
1989	13.8	2305	170
1990	14.8	2005	137
1991	11.7	1596	137
1992	9.6	1603	120
1993	6.0	1778	141
1994	5.5	1900	157
1995	6.7	1938	136

Source: Tables 3 and 10, *National Institute Economic Review*, No. 156, May 1996, National Institute of Economic and Social Research

a Explain the meaning of 'base rate'. (2)

b What evidence is there in the data to suggest changes in the economic activity over the period shown? (4)

c **i** Changes in the rate of interest and new car registrations would be expected to have an inverse relationship. Do the data bear this out? (3)

    ii The data show the nominal base rate. Would the real base rate provide a better understanding of the relationship between changes in the rate of interest and new car registrations? (5)

d Explain how a change in the base rate may affect private sector housing starts. (6)

e Explain how two economic variables, other than new car registrations and housing starts, can be affected by changes in the rate of interest. (6)

Essay questions

1   **a**   Explain how commercial banks are able to create credit.   (10)

   b   Discuss the limitations on commercial banks' ability to create credit.   (15)

2   **a**   What can cause a fall in the rate of interest?   (10)

   b   Analyse the effects of a fall in the rate of interest on consumption, investment and the exchange rate.   (15)

PART TEN

Unemployment and inflation

Introduction

In answering the questions in this part you may find it useful to consult Chapters 44, 49 and 50 in *Introductory Economics* or appropriate chapters in other textbooks.

The questions in this part seek to test and improve your understanding of inflation, unemployment and the relationship between the two.

The specific objectives are to develop your ability to:

- define inflation
- differentiate between the main measures of inflation
- analyse the causes of inflation
- discuss the effects of inflation
- use aggregate demand and supply diagrams in investigating inflation
- define unemployment
- recognise the problems of measuring unemployment
- discuss the types and causes of unemployment
- analyse the effects of unemployment
- identify the main costs of unemployment
- define (NAIRU) the non-accelerating inflation rate of unemployment
- distinguish between equilibrium and disequilibrium unemployment
- apply aggregate demand and supply analysis in investigating unemployment
- explain the traditional Phillips curve
- understand the expectations-augmented Phillips curve.

Short questions

1 What are the main features of the economic condition described as stagflation?

2 Distinguish between the headline and underlying rates of inflation.

3 What would be the economic costs of zero inflation? Is zero inflation desirable?

4 Is government borrowing inflationary?

5 What effect is inflation likely to have on a country's balance of trade?

6 Explain what is meant by full employment.

7 Why might the official unemployment figure understate the true unemployment figure?

8 Are there any benefits of unemployment?

9 Distinguish between equilibrium and disequilibrium unemployment.

10 Compare the effectiveness of reducing income tax and reducing job seekers' allowance as methods of reducing unemployment.

Multiple choice questions

1 Which of the following is a possible cause of cost push inflation?

    A a budget deficit

    B a reduction in direct taxes

    C an increase in bank lending

    D an increase in the price of imported raw materials.

2 The diagram shows the price level and real national income operating in an economy.

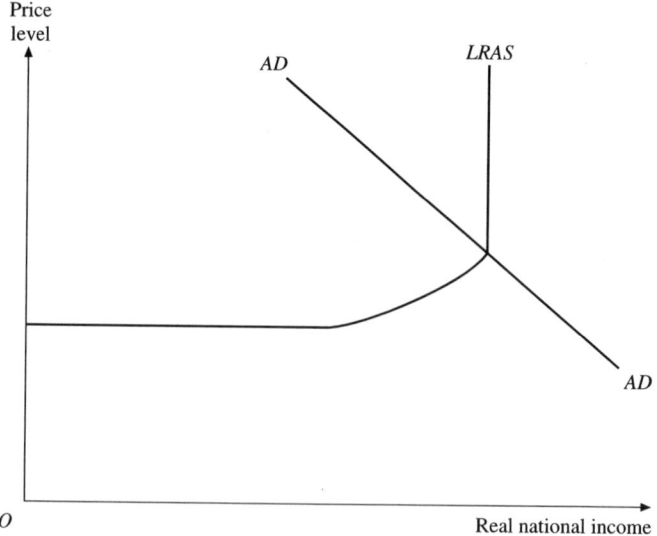

Fig. 10.1

What effect will an increase in consumer expenditure have?

    A increase aggregate supply

    B increase the general price level

C reduce the level of unemployment

D reduce the level of real national income.

3 What is the non-accelerating inflation rate of unemployment? The level of unemployment which will exist:

A when the labour market is in equilibrium

B after adjustment for seasonal variations

C when the rate of unemployment is falling

D when technological and frictional unemployment are excluded.

4 What is the main cost to society of unemployment?

A the value of job seekers' allowance and other benefits paid to the unemployed

B the output which those unemployed could have produced if they had been in employment

C the reduction in wages resulting from the increase in competition among the labour force for jobs

D the increase in the size of the public sector borrowing requirement arising from the fall in tax revenue.

5 In a situation of full employment level of national income, which of the following would be most likely to cause inflation?

A a fall in exports

B a fall in taxation with unchanged government expenditure

C an increase in the average propensity to save

D an increase in labour productivity without a corresponding increase in wages.

6 According to new classical school economists, which of the following policies would reduce the natural rate of unemployment?

A an increase in the money supply

B an increase in government expenditure

C the introduction of new training initiatives

D the introduction of a statutory incomes policy.

7 The following diagram shows the aggregate labour market in which the wage rate is OW.

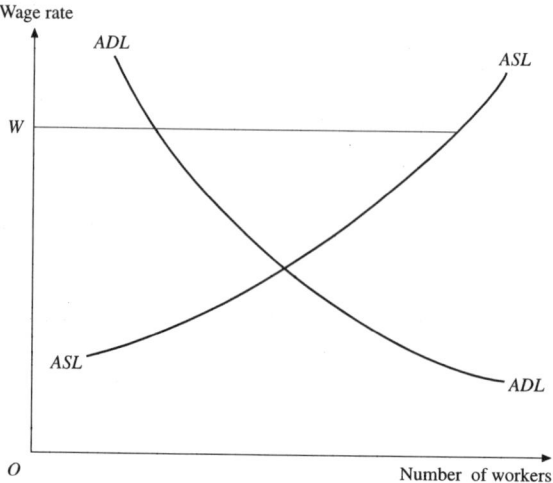

Fig. 10.2

What type of unemployment is shown?

A   seasonal unemployment

B   structural unemployment

C   disequilibrium unemployment

D   the natural rate of unemployment.

8   The diagram shows a long-run Phillips curve (LPC) and three short-run Phillips curves (SPC). The economy is initially at the natural rate of unemployment (OX) with an inflation rate of 5 per cent.

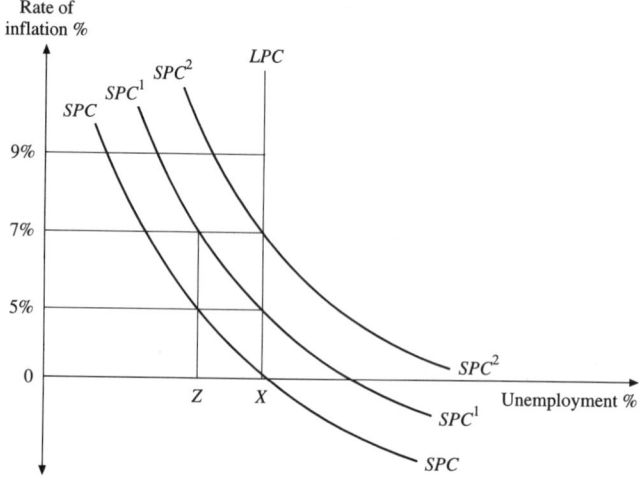

Fig. 10.3

If the government seeks to reduce unemployment to OZ, what will be the effect on the rate of inflation?

A   reduce it to 0 per cent

B   leave it unchanged at 5 per cent

C   raise it to 7 per cent

D   raise it to 9 per cent.

9   If the prime aim of the government is to reduce inflation and it believes the cause of inflation is cost push, which of the following would it be likely to introduce?

A   a revaluation of the exchange rate

B   a reduction in government spending

C   an increase in the rate of interest

D   an increase in the general level of taxation.

10   The table shows unemployment figures expressed as a percentage of the total labour force.

	USA	Japan	Germany	UK	OECD average
1989	5.2	2.3	5.6	6.9	6.2
1990	5.4	2.1	5.0	6.9	6.1
1991	6.7	2.1	4.3	8.8	6.8
1992	7.3	2.1	4.7	9.9	7.4
1993	6.8	2.5	5.8	10.3	7.8
1994	6.0	2.9	7.2	9.6	7.8
1995	5.6	3.1	8.2	8.7	7.5

Source: Table 14, *National Economic Review*, No. 156, May 1996, National Institute of Economic and Social Research

What can be concluded from the data shown?

A   Output fell in Japan from 1993 to 1995.

B   The number of people employed rose in the USA and the UK from 1993 to 1995.

C   In the period 1992–93, unemployment rose by the greatest percentage in Germany.

D   Germany and Japan had unemployment rates below the OECD average throughout the period shown.

Data response questions

1

Year	UK unemployment (%)	Retail prices (annual % change)	Exchange rate (sterling–DM)
1986	11.2	3.4	3.14
1987	10.0	4.1	2.96
1988	8.1	4.9	3.14
1989	6.3	7.8	3.03
1990	5.9	9.5	2.87
1991	8.1	5.9	2.91
1992	9.9	3.7	2.73
1993	10.4	1.6	2.48
1994	9.3	2.5	2.47
1995	8.3	3.4	2.24

Source: Tables 5, 6 and 10, *National Institute Economic Review*, No. 156, May 1996, National Institute of Economic and Social Research

  a   Analyse the relationship between changes in unemployment and in the rate of inflation for the period shown.   (5)

  b   Do your findings in **a** accord with what you would expect from economic theory?   (5)

  c   Analyse the relationship between changes in the sterling–DM exchange rate and changes in the rate of inflation for the period shown.   (5)

  d   Do your findings in **c** accord with what you would expect from economic theory?   (5)

  e   Identify and briefly comment on any two factors, other than unemployment and the exchange rate, which may influence changes in the rate of inflation.   (5)

2

Britain's jobless total could be set to fall sharply over the coming years as rising job security and the growth in part-time work keep the lid on pay increases, the Bank of England said yesterday.

The Bank's quarterly inflation report flatly contradicted claims by government ministers that job insecurity was 'a state of mind' but stressed that the changing face of the labour market could help to cut the dole queues.

Although the official unemployment total has already dropped by more than 750 000 since its peak of almost 3 000 000 in late 1992, the Bank believes that its 'natural' – or non-inflationary rate – is well under two million.

> Mervyn King, the Bank's economics director, said yesterday that provided Britain avoided the boom-bust cycle, there was evidence that the natural rate could be similar to that in the US, thought to be around 6 per cent of the workforce.
>
> Mr King was reluctant to be drawn on how low the Bank thinks unemployment could go without triggering a surge in pay inflation, but a 6 per cent jobless rate in the UK would imply a jobless total of around 1 500 000.
>
> Treasury officials also believe that the deregulation of the labour market has made this feasible because workers are 'pricing themselves back into work' by being willing to accept lower wage increases. The Inflation Report said: 'Real (inflation-adjusted) earnings growth continues to be surprisingly low, raising the possibility that the natural rate of unemployment is lower than in the 1980s.'
>
> Source: 'Dole Queue to Shrink, Says Bank', Larry Elliott, *The Guardian*, 15 May 1996

a   What reasons are given in the extract for expecting unemployment to fall in the future?   (4)

b   Explain the difference between the official unemployment total and the natural rate of unemployment.   (5)

c   Discuss why a fall in unemployment might trigger 'a surge in pay inflation'.   (5)

d   Explain why a fall in the growth of earnings may mean that the natural rate of unemployment is now lower than it was in the 1980s.   (5)

e   Discuss two other possible causes of a fall in the natural rate of unemployment.   (6)

Essay questions

1   a   Explain what is meant by inflation and unemployment and how they are measured.   (5)

    b   Compare the relative costs of inflation and unemployment.   (20)

2   a   Discuss whether it is possible to reduce unemployment without increasing the rate of inflation.   (17)

    b   What disadvantages may policies designed to reduce unemployment have?   (8)

PART ELEVEN

International trade

Introduction

In answering the questions in this part you may find it useful to consult Chapters 51–58 in *Introductory Economics* or appropriate chapters in other textbooks.

The questions in this part seek to test and improve your understanding of the nature of international trade, protectionism, trade blocs, terms of trade, balance of payments, exchange rates, international liquidity and development economics.

The specific objectives are to develop your ability to:

- explain the basis of international trade

- identify the benefits of international trade

- describe the pattern of trade between the UK and the rest of the world

- distinguish between absolute and comparative advantage

- provide a written, diagrammatic and numerical explanation of comparative advantage

- describe the methods of protection

- discuss the reasons for, and effects of, protecting domestic industries from foreign competition

- distinguish between economic unions, common markets, customs unions and free trade areas, and give examples

- evaluate the argument for monetary union in Europe

- recognise the sources of possible conflict between the European Union and other trading blocs

- explain how the terms of trade are measured

- interpret movements in the terms of trade

- understand the balance of payments accounting conventions, particularly the current account

- explain the causes of deficits and surpluses on the current account and their effects on the economy

- use diagrams to explain the determination of the exchange rate in a free market

- explain the purchasing power parity theory

- compare fixed and floating exchange rate regimes in the light of real world experience

- explain the ways in which governments can intervene in the market for foreign exchange
- analyse the immediate and lagged effects of changes in the exchange rate
- recognise the significance of the Marshall-Lerner condition
- discuss the role of international organisations in international trade
- show awareness of the main differences between developed and developing countries.

Short questions

1 What are the differences between international trade and trade between regions?

2 Why might countries not benefit from specialisation and trade?

3 What effect will an adverse movement in the terms of trade have on the balance of trade?

4 Does a deficit on the current account of the balance of payments matter?

5 Explain what is meant by the term 'the effective exchange rate'.

6 Discuss the effect a rise in the effective exchange rate may have on the rate of inflation.

7 What is meant by the term 'hot money'?

8 What determines the rate of growth of a country's exports?

9 Outline the aims of the IMF and the WTO.

10 Discuss two trade strategies a country can implement to increase its economic performance.

Multiple choice questions

1 The basis of international trade is that countries have:

   A similar patterns of demand

   B different economic systems

   C similar balance of payments positions

   D different endowments of factors of production.

2 The following table shows the output per worker in two economies, X and Y, when each economy divides its resources equally between the two products.

| | Units of output | |
	Country X	Country Y
TVs	50	32
Cars	10	4

Which of the following exchange rates will benefit both Country X and Country Y?

A 1 car for 2 TVs   **B** 1 car for 5 TVs   **C** 1 car for 7 TVs
D 1 car for 8 TVs

3   The diagram shows the production possibility curves of two countries, each producing only two types of commodities.

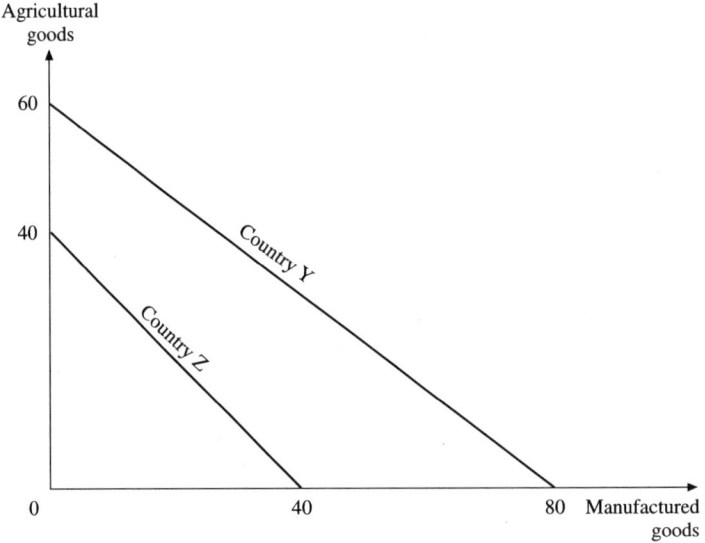

Fig. 11.1

What can be concluded from the diagram?

A   Country Z has a comparative advantage in the production of agricultural goods.

B   Country Y will export agricultural goods and import manufactured goods.

C   Country Z has an absolute advantage in the production of both agricultural and manufactured goods.

D   It is not possible for Country Y to benefit from trading with Country Z.

4   What is an adverse movement in the terms of trade?

   A   the movement of the balance of trade from a surplus to a deficit

   B   a fall in the volume of exports relative to the volume of imports

   C   a fall in the total value of exports relative to the total value of imports

   D   a fall in the average price of exports relative to the average price of imports.

5   If the price elasticity of demand for UK exports is 2.5, what effect would a 5 per cent depreciation of the pound sterling have? It would cause:

   A   a 0.4 per cent rise in the value of exports

   B   a 0.4 per cent rise in the volume of exports

   C   a 12.5 per cent rise in the value of exports

   D   a 12.5 per cent rise in the volume of exports.

6   Which of the following items would appear in the transactions in the liabilities section of the UK balance of payments accounts?

   A   the investment by a UK company in a foreign subsidiary

   B   a South Korean firm building a motor assembly plant in the UK

   C   the purchase of a US television series by a UK television station

   D   the payment of interest by a UK company on a loan from a French bank.

7   The diagram shows the domestic market for a good. With free international trade the price is OP and world supply is WS. The country then imposes a tariff on imports of the good, causing the domestic price to rise to OP1.

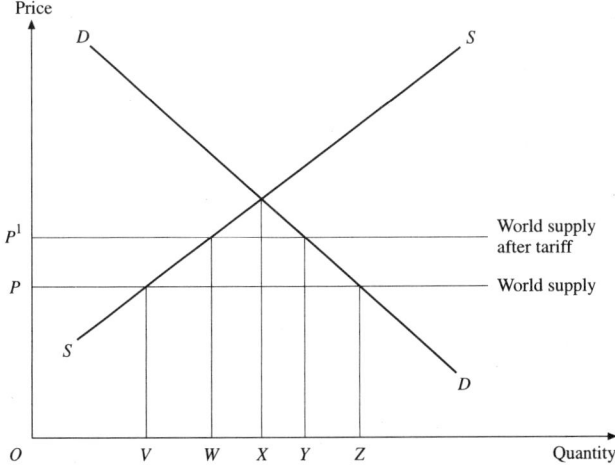

Fig. 11.2

What will be the change in the quantity of goods imported as a result of the tariff? A fall from:

A VZ to VX **B** VZ to WY **C** OZ to OY **D** OZ to OX

8 The diagram shows the domestic demand and supply for pounds sterling in international money markets.

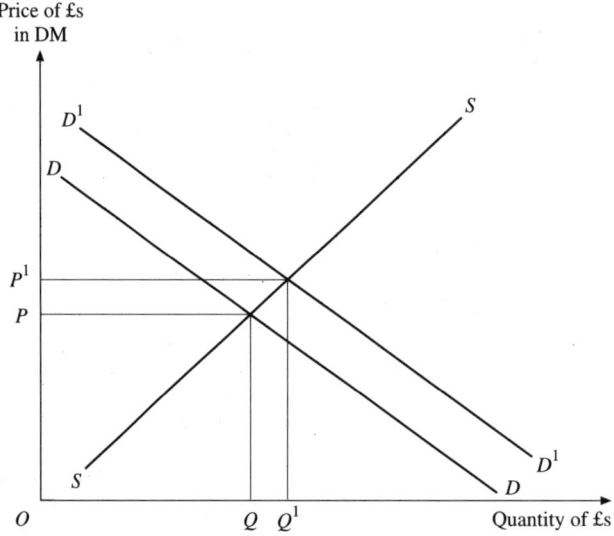

Fig. 11.3

What could have caused the rise in the value of the pound?

A an increase in the quality of German goods

B a rise in the marginal propensity to consume in the UK

C a higher rate of inflation in the UK than in Germany

D a rise in UK interest rates relative to German interest rates.

9 What will be the effect of the value of the pound sterling changing from 1490 to 1629 Italian lire?

A The pound will be overvalued.

B UK exports to Italy will become cheaper.

C Italian exports to the UK will become dearer.

D The Italian lira will be cheaper in terms of the pound.

10 The following table shows data relating to the 1995 UK balance of payments.

	£ million
Exports	152 671
Imports	164 221
Services	5713
Investment income	6638
Transfers	−7471
Transactions in assets	116 889
Transactions in liabilities	121 687

Source: Tables 16.1 and 16.2, *Monthly Digest of Statistics* April, 1996, Office for National Statistics (ONS)

What can be deduced from these data?

A the balancing item was £1872 million

B the balance of trade was −£6670 million

C the invisible balance was £12 351 million

D the current account balance was £4798 million.

Data response questions

1

> **'A Much Devalued Theory**
>
> Whether you are an American exporter selling computers in Japan, or a Briton planning a skiing holiday in France, you have good reason to care about exchange rates. But much nonsense is talked about them. One common mistake is to see possession of a strong currency as a policy goal in its own right, as if a strong currency denoted a strong economy. It is better to consider the exchange rate as an instrument rather than a goal of policy. And even that role is more limited than is commonly believed. Many people think that devaluation is a painless way to boost exports and output, and so create jobs. At the other extreme, some economists claim that devaluation only generates inflation and is powerless to affect real economic activity. The truth lies somewhere in between. Under certain conditions, devaluation can be a useful policy tool. It is not, however, a soft option.
>
> Source: 'A Much Devalued Theory', *The Economist*, 20 January 1996

a Explain why an American exporter selling computers in Japan and a Briton planning a skiing holiday in France should care about exchange rates. (6)

b Define devaluation. (2)

    c Discuss, in your own words, one advantage and one disadvantage of devaluation for the domestic economy. (6)

    d Explain under what conditions 'devaluation can be a useful tool'. (6)

    e Discuss whether the exchange rate is an instrument of government policy or a goal of policy. (5)

2

Year	Visible balance (£ million)	Current balance	GDP (£ million) 1990 prices
1986	−9559	−871	424 214
1987	−11 582	−4983	443 817
1988	−21 480	−16 617	465 746
1989	−24 684	−22 512	476 228
1990	−18 809	−19 035	478 886
1991	−10 284	−8176	468 913
1992	−13 104	−9831	466 456
1993	−13 378	−11 042	476 946
1994	−10 831	−2080	496 414
1995	−11 550	−6670	508 298

Source: Tables 1 and 11, *National Institute Economic Review*, No. 156, May 1996, National Institute of Economic and Social Research

    a Calculate the invisible balance for the years shown. (4)

    b Compare and contrast the visible balance and the invisible balance for the period shown. (5)

    c Discuss the relationship between the current balance and GDP shown in the data. (5)

    d Is the relationship you found in **c** the one which economic theory would predict? (5)

    e Discuss three causes of a deficit on the UK current balance apart from a change in UK GDP. (6)

Essay questions

1 **a** Discuss the forms that import restrictions may take. (10)

    b Evaluate the arguments for and against protectionism. (15)

2 **a** Distinguish between fixed and floating exchange rates. (5)

    b What can cause a fall in the exchange rate? (12)

    c Briefly analyse the effects of a fall in the exchange rate of a country on its external and internal economy. (8)

PART TWELVE

Government policy

Introduction

In answering the questions in this part you may find it useful to consult Chapters 59–64 in *Introductory Economics* or appropriate chapters in other textbooks.

The questions in this part seek to test and improve your understanding of the nature of government policy, fiscal policy, monetary policy, measures to reduce balance of payments deficits, unemployment and inflation.

The specific objectives are to develop your ability to:

- identify the key objectives of government policy

- distinguish between targets, instruments and policies

- discuss conflicts in objectives

- show an awareness of changes in objectives and priorities

- explain why government intervention may not increase economic welfare

- show an awareness of the constraints on UK macro-economic policy in the context of moves towards greater economic integration in the EU

- define fiscal policy

- discuss changes in the size and composition of public expenditure

- distinguish between progressive, proportional and regressive taxes and direct and indirect taxes

- evaluate the relative merits of direct and indirect taxes

- distinguish between discretionary fiscal policy and automatic stabilisers

- identify the aims of taxation

- examine the effects of fiscal policy on aggregate demand, aggregate supply, the public sector borrowing requirement (PSBR), the money supply and interest rates

- appreciate the relationship between the budget position and the PSBR

- discuss the significance and the size of the PSBR

- define monetary policy

- explain the underlying principles behind the use of monetary policy

- define and evaluate monetary policies

- evaluate the 'crowding out' argument

- discuss the measures which can be taken to reduce a deficit on the current account of the balance of payments

- distinguish between expenditure-reducing and expenditure-switching methods of correcting a current account deficit
- discuss the measures which can be taken to reduce unemployment
- discuss the measures which can be taken to reduce inflation
- compare Keynesian and new classical approaches to the selection and use of government policy measures
- assess the effectiveness of government policy.

Short questions

1 Define monetary and fiscal policy.

2 Explain what is meant by the incidence of taxation.

3 Why is the PSBR likely to change during a recession?

4 Why might a reduction in taxation increase employment?

5 Discuss two arguments for and two arguments against the introduction of an incomes policy.

6 How does the UK government attempt to reduce inequalities in the distribution of income?

7 What measures might the government adopt to raise the level of investment in the economy?

8 What are the causes of government economic failure?

9 Discuss two fiscal policy measures a government may take to promote growth.

10 Explain what is meant by supply side policies.

Multiple choice questions

1 Which of the following measures, designed to reduce a deficit on the current account of the balance of payments, would be described as an expenditure-reducing measure?

A devaluation

B the imposition of quotas

C an increase in direct taxes

D the granting of subsidies to domestic producers.

2 What does an expansionary fiscal policy seek to reduce?

A imports

B inflation

C unemployment

D the rate of economic growth.

3 A tax is regressive when:

A marginal tax rates exceed average tax rates

B there is a wider range in pre-tax than post-tax incomes

C the cost of collecting the tax exceeds the tax revenue raised

D low income earners pay a higher proportion of their income in tax than high income earners.

4 Which of the following is an instrument of monetary policy?

A interest rates

B value added tax

C national insurance contributions

D government expenditure on higher education.

5 Which of the following produces an automatic reduction in government expenditure during a period of rising national income?

A child benefit

B state pensions

C student grants

D job seekers' allowance.

6 An economy has a budget deficit, low economic growth, unemployment and a surplus on the current account of the balance of payments. It decides to raise income tax. What does this suggest its main macro-economic objective to be?

A to reduce unemployment

B to reduce the budget deficit

C to increase the rate of economic growth

D to restore an equilibrium on the current account.

7 Which of the following economic policies will tend to increase aggregate demand?

A an increase in the rate of interest

B a reduction in government investment subsidies

C the purchase of government bonds by the Bank of England

D the replacement of a progressive tax by a regressive one which raises the same total revenue.

8 An economy is experiencing a balance of payments deficit and demand pull inflation. Which of the following measures is likely to reduce both the balance of payments deficit and the rate of inflation?

A raising income tax

B reducing interest rates

C raising government expenditure

D reducing the value of the currency.

9 The diagram shows the level of national income (Y) and the general price level (P) in an economy.

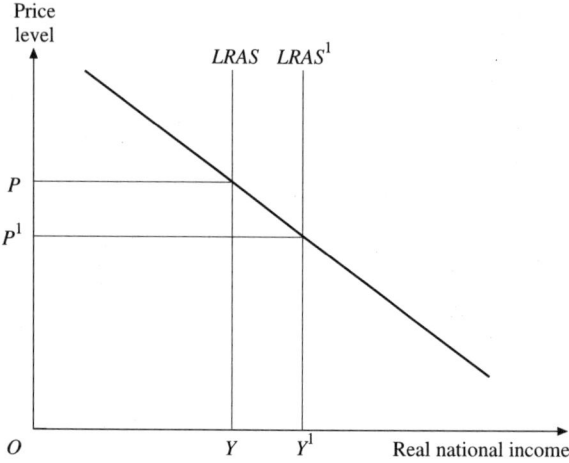

Fig. 12.1

What could have caused a rise in real national income to OY1 and a fall in the price level to OP1?

A an increase in demand for imports

B an increase in government expenditure

C a reduction in the state retirement age

D the successful application of supply side policies.

10

Year	PSBR (£ million)
1988	−12 423
1989	−9802
1990	−1850
1991	8807
1992	30 269
1993	43 794
1994	38 656
1995	35 377

Source: Table 10, *National Institute Economic Review* No. 156 May 1996, National Institute of Economic and Social Research

What can be deduced from the data shown?

A   Government revenue exceeded government expenditure from 1988 to 1990.

B   The government was adding to aggregate demand from 1988 to 1990.

C   The budget was in surplus from 1991 to 1995.

D   The government was pursuing a deflationary fiscal policy from 1991 to 1995.

Data response questions

1

General government expenditure as a percentage of GDP[1]

United Kingdom
Percentages

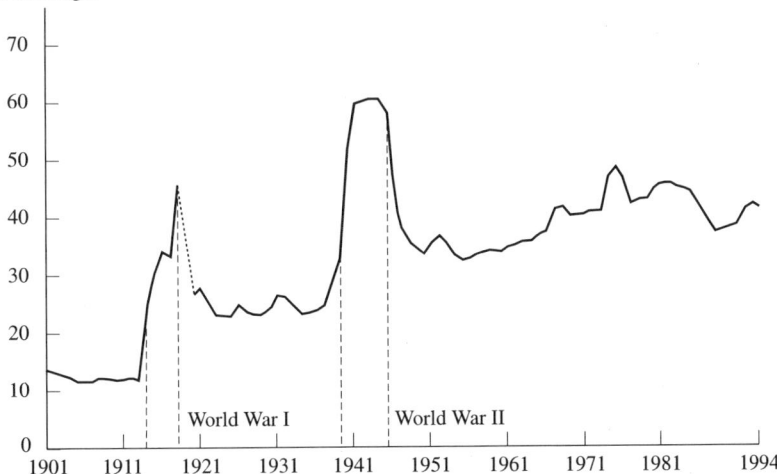

1 GDP adjusted to take account of change from rates to community charge. Data for 1919 are not available.
Source: Central Statistical Office

Fig. 12.2

United Kingdom

	Percentages					
	1981	*1986*	*1989*	*1992*	*1993*	*1994*
Social security	27	31	32	33	34	34
Health	11	12	14	14	13	14
Education	12	12	13	13	12	13
Defence	11	12	10	10	9	8
Public order and safety	4	4	6	5	5	5
General public services	4	4	5	5	4	4
Housing and community amenities	6	5	4	4	4	4
Transport and communication	4	2	3	3	2	2
Recreational and cultural affairs	1	2	2	2	2	2
Agriculture, forestry and fishing	1	1	1	1	2	1
Other expenditure	19	16	11	11	12	13

All expenditure (= 100%)
(£ billion in real terms[1])   224.6 241.0 250.9 268.1 278.3 285.7

1 Adjusted to 1994 prices using the GDP market prices deflator.
Source: Central Statistical Office

Fig. 12.3

Source: *Social Trends 26*, 1996, Central Statistical Office

   a Comment on the trend in public spending shown in the graph. (6)

   b Discuss two reasons why a government may increase public spending. (4)

   c Comment on the changes in the pattern of government expenditure shown in the table. (6)

   d What factors influence government expenditure in the largest item by function of government expenditure? (5)

   e Discuss two benefits government expenditure on higher education provides for university students. (6)

2

Economic pundits talk about 'slaying' inflation as if inflation fighting were like elephant hunting: first find your elephant, then fire. This is how policymakers tend to behave; they shoot only when they see inflation rising. But by then it is almost always too late, because monetary policy takes up to two years to have its effect. Instead, central bankers need to squeeze the interest-rate trigger well before inflation rises. That requires skill, luck and a tough political hide; for if they succeed in killing inflation before everyone can see that it is an obvious threat, they will get little credit for it. Indeed, they will often be accused of needlessly holding back a growing economy. Thus central bankers' recent success in curbing inflation may now make it harder for them to raise short-term interest rates – as most should soon do.

In America, for instance, the fact that inflation has remained below 3% for most of the past three years has been hailed by many as evidence that inflation is dead. The Federal Reserve has therefore been criticised for raising interest rates in early 1994, and so slowing economic growth sharply last year. Some critics now advise the Fed to cut interest rates again to boost growth; others say it should certainly hold back from any early rise. Yet the slowdown in growth in 1995 was exactly what America needed. The economy is operating at close to full capacity; had growth been brisker last year, inflation would now be climbing.

Another example to ponder is Germany. Its GDP has fallen for two consecutive quarters, which on some definitions means it is in recession; and its inflation rate is only 1.7%. On the surface this would seem to argue for a cut in interest rates. But underneath the economy is already picking up speed. Unemployment fell in May, and industrial production and business confidence are starting to perk up. This means that German interest rates do not need to be cut; previous cuts are having their effect.

One big difference for Europe and Japan is that they both have more economic slack than America; in neither is higher inflation immediately imminent. But their economic recoveries raise the inflation risk for America if, with its economy already at full employment, the rest of the world enjoys a robust expansion.

Source: 'Shooting at Inflation', *The Economist*, 18 July 1996

a   What market failure is discussed in the first paragraph of the extract? (5)

b   Why may raising short-term interest rates slow economic growth? (5)

c   Explain why the slowdown in its growth was beneficial to the American economy. (4)

d   Does the definition of recession given in the extract agree with the usual definition of recession? (2)

   e What is meant by 'economic slack'? (3)

   f Explain why economic recovery in some countries might cause inflation in another country. (6)

Essay questions

1 **a** Discuss the policies that a government may use to reduce inflation. (15)

   b Explain how the existence of inflation could make it difficult for a government to achieve other objectives of macro-economic policy. (10)

2 **a** What are the functions of taxation? (7)

   b Giving examples, distinguish between direct and indirect taxes. (3)

   c Discuss whether the government should raise a larger proportion of tax revenue from indirect taxation than it does currently. (15)

Section 2
Answers

Answers to short questions

1 In deciding whether to go to university or not a student has to consider what he or she will be giving up, not only by choosing to go to university but also by choosing not to. The opportunity cost of proceeding to HE may be full time employment for three years, whereas the opportunity cost of not proceeding may be higher future income.

2 A production possibility curve illustrates scarcity, choice and opportunity cost. The curve indicates the combinations of two products that can be produced by an economy using all of its existing resources as fully and efficiently as possible. People are likely to want more, e.g. 15 million consumer goods and 6 million capital goods, but the curve shows that this is not possible because there are not enough resources. It also shows that the economy has to make choices. For example, it can produce 10 million consumer goods and 6 million capital goods or 11 million consumer goods and 4 million capital goods. The opportunity cost of producing 1 million more consumer goods is, in this case, 2 million capital goods.

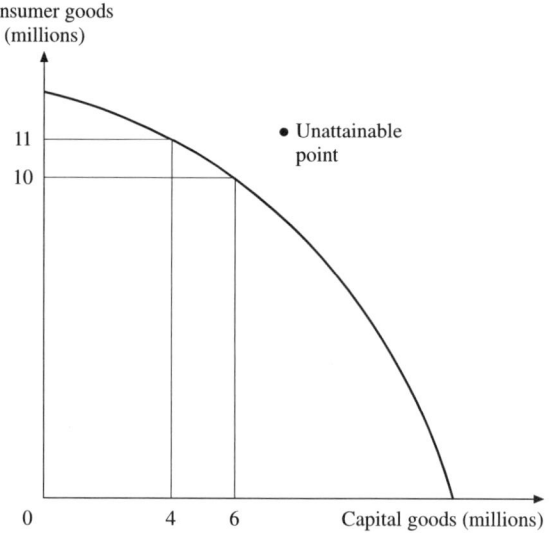

Fig. 1.5

3 A famine will reduce the size of the population, including the size of the working population, damage the productivity of the land and, due to under-use or use by inexperienced workers, may also damage capital equipment. All of these will reduce the country's productive capacity and cause the production possibility curve to shift inwards to the left.

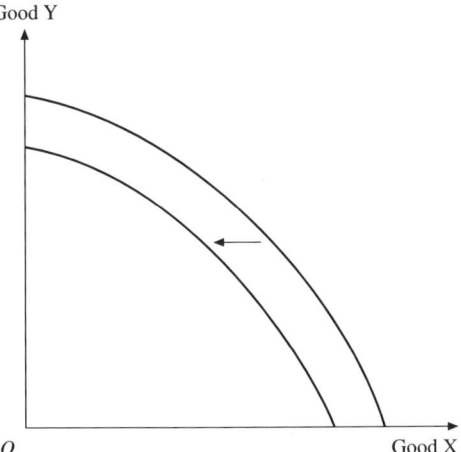

Fig. 1.6

4 The three fundamental questions which all economies face, whatever economic system they operate, are what to produce, how to produce it and how to distribute the goods produced.

5 During the period of the Second World War, the UK operated a planned economy. The government decided what to produce, how to produce and how to distribute the goods produced. There was state planning of output, state direction of labour (i.e. people were told what jobs to do) and rationing.

6 There are a number of methods which planners can use to assess consumers' demand in a command economy. They can conduct surveys, take note of queues or make (at least some) use of the price mechanism. Goods which are becoming more popular will be picked up in surveys, will result in longer queues and/or will rise in price.

7 Most command economies do make some use of the price mechanism. However, they usually do not allow prices to be determined completely by market forces. There are usually limits set on price changes, particularly of essential goods. In moving towards a market economy these limits are likely to be removed. As a result the general price level is likely to rise.

8 If the demand for tea falls, its price will also fall, whereas if drinking coffee becomes more popular, its price will rise. The profitability of tea production will decline while the profitability of coffee production will rise. This will encourage at least some resources to move from tea to coffee production.

9 Land is any natural resource used in production, e.g. fishing grounds, farm land and forests. Labour is all human effort used in production, e.g. the work of teachers, professional footballers and carpenters. Capital is a man-made resource used in production, e.g. a builder's delivery van, an insurance company's photocopying machine and a paper mill.

10   Entrepreneurs bear the uncertain risks which may arise in production. While risks whose probability can be assessed, e.g. fire, theft and flooding, can be passed on to an insurance company and so represent a cost, uncertain risks must be borne by the entrepreneur. These uncertain risks of production include the possibility that costs of production may rise, that the government may impose a tax on the product, that new competitors may enter the market and that the product may become unpopular.

Answers to multiple choice questions

1   Answer **B**
A normative statement is a value judgement. It is a matter of opinion and it cannot be tested. Some people believe student grants should be increased and student loans phased out, whereas others do not.
Options **A**, **C** and **D** are all positive statements and can be tested.

2   Answer **B**
An economic good is one which takes resources to produce it. As these resources could have been used to produce alternative goods, its production involves an opportunity cost. The vast majority of goods are economic goods.
A, **C** and **D** are not defining characteristics. Indeed, economic goods may be sold at a profit or loss, can be produced under conditions of increasing or decreasing costs, and are supplied by both the public and private sectors.

3   Answer **B**
The existence of scarcity means that economic agents cannot obtain all the goods they would like. They have to make choices. For example, with all its resources employed, an economy may be able to produce 20 million units of consumer goods and 10 million units of capital goods or 15 million units of consumer goods and 14 million units of capital goods. It cannot, however, produce 20 million units of consumer goods and 14 million units of capital goods.

   A   Most, but not all, goods are economic goods. A few goods are free goods, i.e. they require no resources to produce them.

   C   Scarcity can be illustrated by means of a production possibility curve. A production possibility curve shows that maximum potential is limited by resources. However, in the longer run resources can be increased, e.g. by improved technology or a rise in the working population. This would be illustrated by a shift to the right of the production possibility curve.

   D   Scarcity exists wherever production occurs and wants exceed potential output.

4   Answer **C**
Any point on or inside a production possibility curve is attainable. However, any point outside is not as there are insufficient resources to produce it.

5 Answer **C**
A straight line production possibility frontier shows a constant rate of substitution of opportunity cost, i.e. the same amount of one good has to be given up to obtain one more unit of the other good, whatever the respective quantities being produced.

6 Answer **C**
The movement from R to S is a movement from one production possibility curve to another one, further to the right. This shows an increase in productive potential affecting both types of goods.
An improvement in technology affecting both consumer and capital goods would achieve this.

A This would be illustrated by a movement from on to inside a curve or a movement from in the curve to further inside.

B Production possibility curves show potential output. They do not indicate whether or not inflation exists.

D This would be illustrated by a movement inside the curve towards or on the curve.

7 Answer **B**
If the economy devotes all its resources to producing manufactured goods, it could produce OZ amount. Similarly, if it devotes all its resources to producing agricultural goods then it could produce OX amount. If it chooses to produce OY amount of manufactured goods then it is limiting its output of agricultural goods to OW. It is forgoing the opportunity to produce WX amount of agricultural goods.

8 Answer **D**
In a market economy the price mechanism is the main mechanism for allocating resources. If consumers demand more of a product, its price will rise which will encourage more firms to produce it.

A and B refer to a planned economy.

C The private sector will not produce pure public goods and underproduces merit goods.

9 Answer **C**
In a market economy consumers are said to be sovereign. They determine what is produced by voting with their purchases. If they demand more of one product and less of another, firms, motivated by profit, will shift their resources towards the more popular product.

10 Answer **D**
One potential disadvantage of a planned economy is the possibility that bottlenecks may occur. The output of one firm may be held up because of a shortage of components produced by a supplier.

A and C In a planned economy the state will determine what is produced and will control the price level.

B   Planned economies may be slow to respond to changes in consumer tastes. This may result in firms failing to produce the goods that consumers want. However, the question concerns the failure to reach output targets and not failure to satisfy consumers' wants.

Answers to data response questions

1 a   Economic resources can also be called inputs or factors of production. They are used to produce economic goods and services. Land, labour, capital and the entrepreneur are all economic resources. For example, to produce a film requires a location or locations, a film crew, actors, a director and film equipment.

b   Scarcity arises because economic resources are insufficient to satisfy people's wants. People want more goods and services than all the workers, machinery, etc. are capable of producing. As countries are not able to produce all that their inhabitants want, choices have to be made about what to produce. For example, should a group of workers be employed in building houses or offices? When a decision is made to produce one type of good a decision is also, in effect, being made not to produce another type. In the example mentioned above, if it is decided to build houses the opportunity to build offices will have been lost. This is the opportunity cost, i.e. the best alternative forgone. These three concepts can be shown on a production possibility curve. In the diagram below current resources limit output to any point on the curve AB or inside.

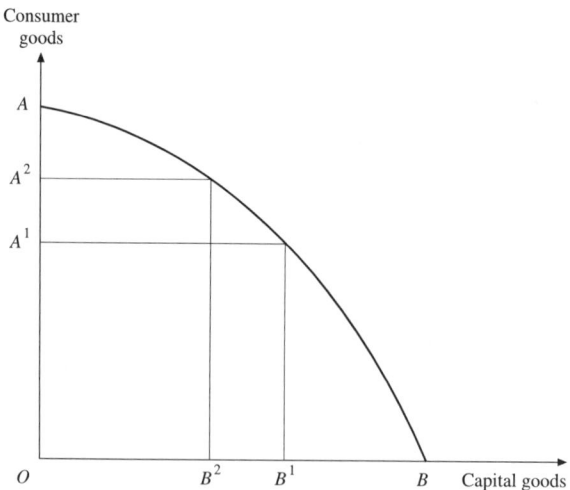

Fig. 1.7

The economy can choose to produce OA1 amount of consumer goods and OB1 amount of capital goods. A decision to increase output of consumer goods to OA2 will involve forgoing B1B2 amount of capital goods.

c   All economic agents have to make choices. Consumers have to decide what to buy, owners of the factors of production how to use their resources, producers what to make, workers which jobs to undertake and the government has to decide what to spend its revenue on. These choices have to be made because resources are scarce. There are not enough resources to produce everything that consumers want. The goods and services produced are rationed out by the government in a planned economy and by the price mechanism in a market economy. So, for example, in a market economy those consumers with the highest incomes are able to buy the most products. Nevertheless, they still have to make choices as they are unlikely to be able to afford to buy everything they want. Time is also in limited supply and if a person chooses to spend the week working for one company, they cannot use the same time to work for someone else. In using land for houses, a landowner cannot use it for offices. Similarly, if a producer decides to use their workers and equipment to make one type of good, they are forgoing the opportunity to make another type. For example, if a college decides to use the services of a lecturer and a classroom on a Thursday afternoon to deliver an A Level economics lecture, it cannot use these same resources to deliver an A Level geography lecture at the same time. In using resources, e.g. to educate students, a government is forgoing the opportunity to use those same resources for defence or other programmes.

d   It would be possible to increase output without incurring an opportunity cost if the economy is producing within its production possibility frontier. This would occur if not all resources are being employed or if resources are being used inefficiently. In both cases the country will not be producing as many goods as it is capable of doing with existing resources. By employing unemployed resources or allocating resources more efficiently, output can be increased. The production possibility curve below illustrates that the utilisation of previously unemployed resources moves the economy from inside to on the curve. No goods are sacrificed and more capital and consumer goods are produced.

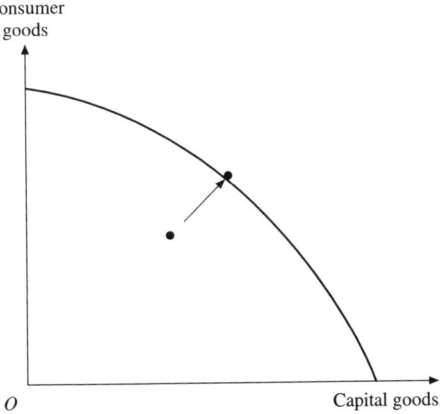

Fig. 1.8

e   A number of factors influence the products which firms produce. These include the level and changes in demand, profit levels, ability to enter and exit markets and availability of factors of production. An increase in demand for a product is likely to cause those firms already producing it to make more and for firms making other products to switch resources to its production. This is because the higher demand will result in higher prices and increased sales which will raise profitability. High profit levels may also be earned if costs of production fall. Lower costs of production will also make it viable for more firms to produce a product. Indeed, high costs of production are one of the most common barriers to entry into an industry. Private sector firms will only produce those products which will generate a revenue in excess of the costs of production. They must also have access to raw materials, be able to purchase equipment and attract workers with the right skills, have no legal restrictions on producing the products and not face too great an attachment of consumers to the products of other producers.

f   When a government spends money on building a new hospital it makes use of resources which could have been used for alternative purposes. One possible opportunity cost is expenditure on education. For example, more teachers could be employed or more computers purchased. Another possible opportunity cost is expenditure on the road network.
    If a government decides to maintain its current level of expenditure on other items and to raise extra revenue or borrow to finance the building of a new hospital there is still an opportunity cost. If income tax is raised, the opportunity cost is forgone expenditure by taxpayers. In the short run, government borrowing will reduce the expenditure of lenders and, in the long run, will reduce the expenditure of taxpayers as interest payments are made.

2 a i   Economic efficiency occurs when resources are used in such a way that it is not possible to make one person better off without making someone else worse off. This is sometimes referred to as *social efficiency* or *Pareto optimality*. It is achieved when an economy operates on its production possibility frontier.
           Economists also discuss *allocative efficiency* (which is achieved when production occurs where price equals marginal cost) and *productive efficiency* (which exists when a given output is produced at the lowest possible cost).

   a ii A market economy is an economic system in which the allocation of resources is determined by the price mechanism. Economic agents, acting in their own self-interest, produce an outcome which, in theory, benefits them all. Consumers are sovereign and determine what is produced. Producers respond to changes in consumer demand, switching resources from goods which are becoming less popular to those which are becoming more popular.

   b   A number of conditions have to be met for a market economy to work efficiently. One is that there is perfect competition, i.e. a high number of buyers and sellers acting independently. Firms operating under conditions of perfect competition will be responsive to changes in consumer demand. If consumers want more of a product, they will be prepared to pay a higher price. This will cause existing producers to earn supernormal profits. They will produce more and the high profits will attract new firms into the industry. The long-run increase in supply will lower price. So, resources are moved in response to the decisions of consumers. Perfectly competitive firms always achieve allocative efficiency, i.e. they devote sufficient resources to the production of a good to meet the quantity consumers want to buy.

Another necessary and connected condition is perfect mobility of factors of production. Producers, wishing to expand output in response to an increase in consumer demand, must be able to attract additional factors of production. Similarly, those producers wishing to reduce output must be able to shed factors of production.

c   A market clears when all goods offered for sale are sold. Demand and supply are equal. There are no shortages and no surpluses. The Soviet planners found no sign of shortages or surpluses. The absence of queues and shortages indicates that consumers could obtain all they wanted at the going market price. The absence of stocks of decaying vegetables provides evidence that producers could sell all they wanted to supply at the going market price.

d   In theory, the free interaction of demand and supply should ensure that all markets clear. If price is initially set above the equilibrium level, supply will exceed demand and price will be driven down to where demand and supply are equal.

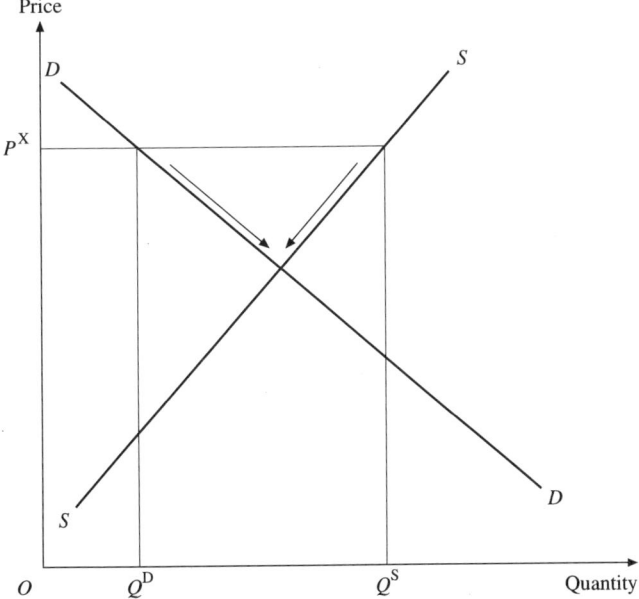

Fig. 1.9

Conversely, if price is initially below the equilibrium level, demand will exceed supply and price will be driven up.

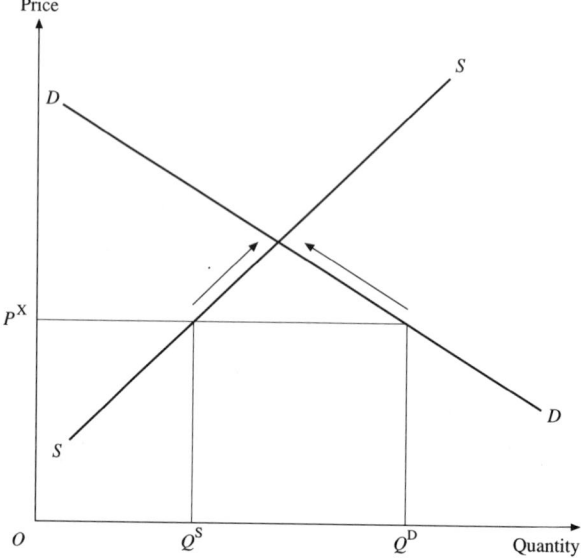

Fig. 1.10

If demand or supply conditions change, price will move from one equilibrium level to another one. For example, an increase in demand will cause price to rise and supply to extend.

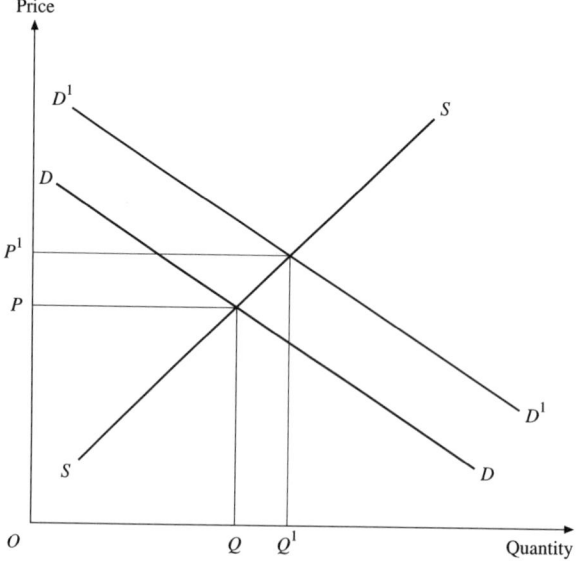

Fig. 1.11

In the long run supply will increase as new firms are attracted into the industry.
In a market system price determination is left to the forces of demand and supply and, in theory, markets should clear.

e   In the former Soviet Union planners played a considerable role. The Soviet Union was a planned economy in which the state decided what to produce, how to produce and how the goods produced were distributed. The planners decided what to produce by looking at the country's resources and assessing consumers' wants. They then issued directives to state-owned firms as to what to produce and how to produce. However, managers of state concerns were given some discretion as to the methods they used to meet the target output set for them. The state determined the distribution of goods and services by setting wage and price levels and providing some goods and services free at the point of consumption.

Answers to essay questions

1   a   A production possibility frontier shows all the possible combinations of two types of goods which can be produced with the full and efficient employment of all resources. It can also be referred to as a production possibility curve, boundary or transformation curve. The diagram below shows that if a country devotes all its resources to producing consumer goods, it can make OY quantity. If it concentrates on capital goods, it can make OX quantity. It can also make any combination of consumer and capital goods on or inside the curve, e.g. OY1 quantity of consumer goods and OX1 quantity of capital goods.

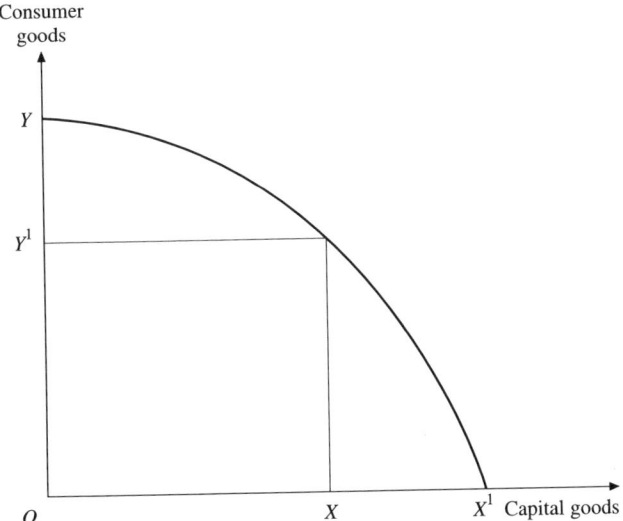

Fig. 1.12

A production possibility frontier shows that the quantity of goods a country is capable of producing is restricted by the scarcity of resources. It also indicates that a country has to make choices and that a decision, e.g. to produce more consumer goods, may involve a cost in terms of forgone capital goods.

b i A movement from inside to on a production possibility frontier can result from the employment of previously unemployed resources or from the more efficient use of resources. Such a movement will mean that more goods are produced. The diagram shows that, initially, the country produces 90 million consumer goods and 40 million capital goods. After the movement the country produces an extra 30 million consumer goods and 10 million capital goods.

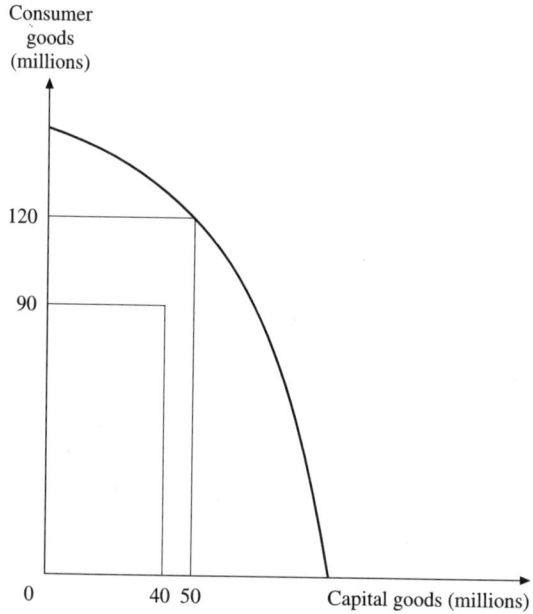

Fig. 1.13

b ii A movement along the frontier will result in an increase in the output of one category of good and a decrease in the output of the other category. The following diagram shows that the output of capital goods rises from 50 million to 60 million and the output of consumer goods falls from 120 million to 100 million.

As the economy is operating on the production possibility frontier it must be using its resources fully and efficiently. So it is only possible to make more of one good by making less of the other good. In choosing to produce more capital goods, it is forgoing consumer goods. In the example used the opportunity cost of 10 million capital goods is 20 million consumer goods.

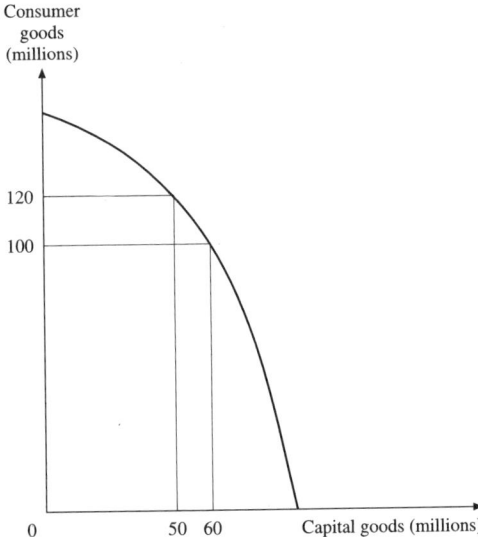

Fig. 1.14

b iii A movement from one frontier to another one further to the right will probably mean that more of both categories of goods are produced. The diagram below shows that the output of consumer goods increases from 100 million to 130 million and the output of capital goods increases from 60 million to 80 million. The economy might also choose to produce, for example, 100 million consumer goods and 90 million capital goods.

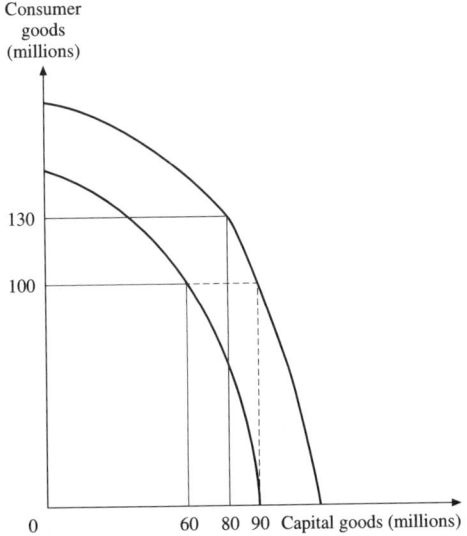

Fig. 1.15

When an economy moves from a point on one frontier to a point on a frontier to the right, actual growth will have occurred. The economy will be making full use of a greater quantity or a greater quality of resources.

c A production possibility frontier will shift to the right if the production potential of the economy increases. Land, i.e. natural resources, may be increased as a result of, for example, the discovery of oil fields or mineral deposits and the reclamation of land. Capital will increase as a result of net investment. A number of factors can result in an increase in the supply of labour. For example, these include net immigration, an increase in the birth rate some years previously, a fall in the death rate and an increase in the retirement age.

Increased productive potential can also arise from an improvement in the quality of resources. The application of fertilisers, irrigation, the introduction of new mining methods may all improve the quality of land. Advances in technology are a significant factor in improving the quality of capital. The main factors in improving the quality of labour are education and training.

2 a Economic systems can be distinguished by examining how they answer the three fundamental questions, i.e. what to produce, how to produce it and who should receive what is produced?

In a planned economy the state makes all the main decisions, deciding what shall be produced, the methods of production and how the goods are distributed. The means of production are owned by the state which issues directives to the managers of state firms, setting out production targets. The state determines the output of goods, taking into account social costs and benefits.

Whereas state planning is the means of allocating resources in a planned economy, in a market economy it is the price mechanism. There is private ownership of the means of production. Consumers decide what is produced by voting with their purchases. Producers respond by making those goods which people want to buy. They seek to produce goods as cheaply and efficiently as possible. Those who own the factors of production which are in the greatest demand will gain the highest income and those with the highest incomes will be able to buy the largest quantity of goods.

In a mixed economy there is use of both the price mechanism and state planning in the allocation of resources. Some resources are owned by the state and some by private individuals. So in this case the three fundamental questions are answered by both the state and individuals.

b The price mechanism plays a central role in a market economy. One function is to ration goods. All economic systems face the fundamental problem of scarcity. In a market economy price rations the sale of scarce goods to those who can afford to pay the price charged.

For example, if oil, or another commodity, begins to run out, fewer people will be able to obtain it. The price mechanism will automatically determine who these people are and will set in motion the search for an alternative. The decrease in supply will raise the price of oil which will reduce the number of people who can afford it. The market will clear and there will not be a shortage. The high price will also encourage consumers to switch to other fuels. This, in turn, will stimulate producers of existing fuels to increase output and for entrepreneurs and scientists to search for new sources of fuel. Another and connected function of the price mechanism is to act as a signal to producers and consumers. An increase in demand causes price to rise. This rise in price acts as a signal to producers to divert resources to the production of the good. Figure 1.16 below shows demand increasing, price rising and supply extending.

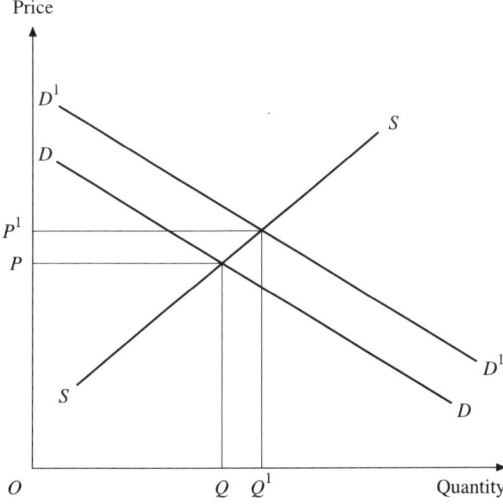

Fig. 1.16

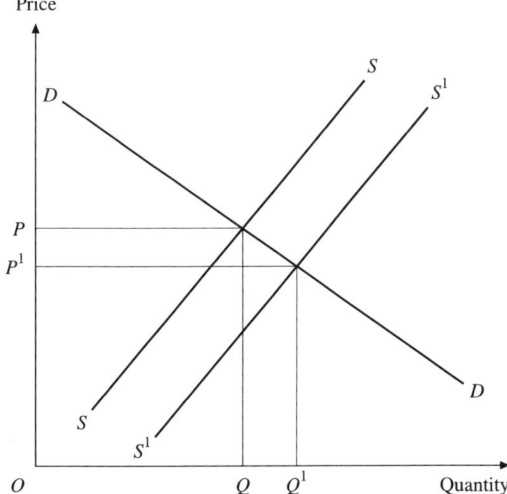

Fig. 1.17

In contrast, an increase in supply will lower price. This signals to consumers that the product is more affordable and more consumers will enter the market. Figure 1.17 shows supply increasing, price falling and demand extending.

c   A planned economy may experience a number of problems in moving towards a market system. In a planned economy some goods may be provided free at the point of consumption and others are likely to be sold at prices held below the equilibrium level by government price controls. As the role of the state declines and more goods are sold by private enterprises, prices are likely to rise and inflation may occur. Indeed, a high rate of inflation may be encountered as the new entrepreneurs, lacking experience, may set prices above the equilibrium level The lack of entrepreneurial experience may also cause other problems. The most efficient methods of production may not be employed and labour relations may not be handled well. Indeed, there is likely to be industrial unrest as workers, operating in a new and strange environment, seek to maintain their real purchasing power and job security.

In a planned economy the state determines the output of goods. Although it is likely to seek to discern what consumers want, the pattern of output will probably differ from that which will prevail in a market economy where the consumer is sovereign. Some industries will decline and some will expand. Not all resources will be mobile. This will mean that some resources will become unemployed while there will be a shortage of other resources. The economy will be producing inside its production possibility curve.

The reduction in government intervention and the increase in power which individuals gain to act in their own self-interest may result in undesirable consequences. Taking into account only private benefits, consumers are likely to demand fewer merit goods and to demand demerit goods. For example, the demand for education may decline while a market for pornography may be created.

There may be a time gap before a new framework of government controls can be developed to offset the disadvantages of a market economy. In this period firms seeking to keep their costs low may create pollution by disposing of their waste in an unsafe manner. Imperfect competition is also likely to develop, with consequences for prices, output, quality and consumer sovereignty.

The weaker members of society, e.g. the old and the disabled, who had previously been protected by state provision of basic necessities, will become vulnerable in a system in which the goods are distributed on the basis of effective demand. It will take time to develop a new system of welfare provision. There may also be a disruption in the provision of police and other public services. This may result in a rise in crime and other social problems.

Answers to short questions

1   The size of the market refers to the demand for the product. The extent to which a firm can employ specialised labour and machinery will depend, to a large degree, on how many products it can sell. If a firm's output is large, each of its workers may perform specialised tasks, whereas if a firm employs only a few workers, each worker may have to perform a range of tasks.

2   The geographical mobility of labour refers to the ability of workers to move from a job in one part of the country to one in another region, e.g. from Sheffield to London, whereas occupational mobility is the ability of workers to move from one occupation to another, e.g. from working as an estate agent to working as a baker.

3   Initially, as more capital is used with a fixed supply of labour, the marginal product of capital is likely to rise. However, after a certain point is reached, diminishing returns are likely to set in and marginal product will fall. The proportions between capital and labour become less efficient.

4   A firm's fixed costs are those which have to be met even if output is zero and which do not change as output changes, whereas its variable costs are the direct costs of production which change as output changes. A magazine publishing firm's fixed costs include the rent of the premises, business rates, advertising, pensions and insurance. Among its variable costs are the purchase of paper, delivery costs and payments to freelance writers for articles.

5   The short-run average cost curve is assumed to be U-shaped because, initially, as output increases, overheads will be spread over more units and increasing returns to variable factors of production will be enjoyed. However, after a certain point is reached average cost will rise as diminishing returns set in.

6   As a car manufacturer grows in size a range of internal economies of scale become available to it. For example, a large car manufacturer may be able to take advantage of buying economies. As it will order in bulk it may be given discounts on the purchase of tyres and other inputs. It may also be able to enjoy research and development economies. It could employ a team of research engineers and designers to work on improving existing models and developing new ones.

7   The two main motives behind horizontal mergers are to reduce competition and to take greater advantage of economies of scale. Horizontal mergers are mergers between companies at the same stage of production and producing the same type of product. Merging with another company in the same industry is a direct way of reducing competition. Merging also creates a larger company and, as the product is the same, plant and firm economies may increase.

8   There are a number of reasons why, despite all the advantages large firms have, small firms survive. These include the ability to provide personal services, to provide products in markets where demand is low, and because they are relatively easy to set up. Owners of small firms can know the requirements of their customers and can respond to them in a flexible manner. A small firm may also survive because the market is small and so may not be attractive to larger firms. The economy will contain a large number of small firms although the composition of these firms will change from year to year. A small amount of capital is needed to set up a small firm and, each year, new firms are set up. Although approximately one third go out of business, they are replaced by new ones.

9   The three main sources of finance for firms are retained profits, borrowing and the issuing of new shares. Retained profits are internal finance, i.e. obtained from within the firm, and are the most common source of funds. Borrowing and the issuing of new shares bring in funds from outside the firm and so are known as external finance.

10   A bulk increasing industry is one where the finished product is bulky relative to its raw materials. It will probably be located near to its market to reduce transport costs. A bulk reducing industry is one where the finished product is compact relative to its raw materials. In this case it will probably be located near to the source of its raw materials.

Answers to multiple choice questions

1   Answer **D**
Diminishing returns set in when the addition of a variable input causes marginal product to fall. This means that total output increases at a diminishing rate and it becomes more costly to produce extra units.

2   Answer **C**
To answer this question it is necessary first to calculate total variable cost which is total cost minus total fixed cost. In this case the total fixed cost is £15 000, i.e. the cost incurred when output is zero. Once total variable cost is found, average variable cost is calculated by dividing total variable cost by output.

Output	Total cost	Total fixed cost	Total variable cost	Average variable cost
0	15 000	15 000	–	–
10	20 000	15 000	5000	500
20	23 000	15 000	8000	400
30	24 000	15 000	9000	300
40	27 000	15 000	12 000	300
50	35 000	15 000	20 000	400

3   Answer **C**

Marginal cost is the change in total cost resulting from changing output by one unit. In this case the total cost of producing 200 conservatories is £800 000 (200 × £4000). The average cost of producing 201 conservatories is £4000 – £15 + £12 = £3997. So the total cost of producing 201 conservatories is £3997 × 201 = £803 397. The marginal cost is £803 397 – £800 000 = £3397.

Answer **A** is the change in average cost, answer B is the change in variable cost and answer **D** is the new average cost.

4   Answer **C**

Marginal product falls before average product and the two are equal where average product is at a maximum as shown in the diagram below.

Output

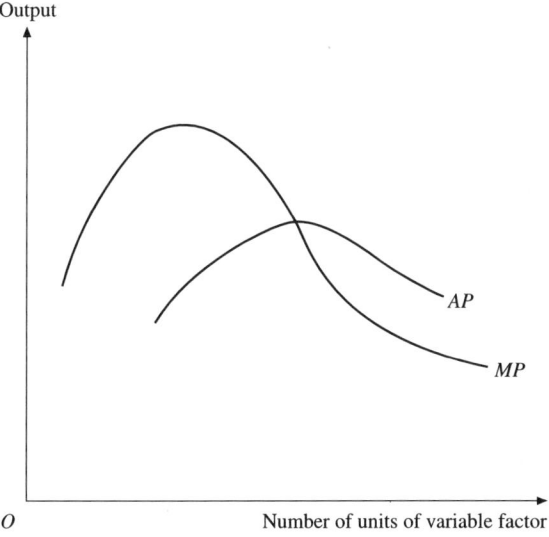

O   Number of units of variable factor

Fig. 2.3

5   Answer **C**

At output OQ total cost is QZ, total fixed cost is XQ and total variable cost is XZ. Average variable cost is variable cost divided by output, i.e. XZ/OQ. Answer **A** XQ is total fixed cost. Answer **B** shows only a proportion of variable cost. Answer **D** is average fixed cost.

6   Answer **C**

To answer this question it is necessary to calculate short-run average costs and long-run average costs.

Output	*1*	*2*	*3*	*4*	*5*
Short-run average cost	10	9	8	7	6
Long-run average cost	10	11	12	13	14

The short-run average costs are falling whereas the long-run average costs are rising. Diseconomies of scale are associated with rising long-run average costs.

7   Answer **A**
Financial economies of scale are the benefits that a firm gains as it grows in size, in the form of the increase in sources of finance open to it and the more favourable terms on which funds can be raised.
Answer **B** describes buying economies, answer **C** economies of scale which can be experienced by financial institutions and answer **D** is an example of managerial economies.

8   Answer **B**
The two companies are producing unrelated products and so the merger is a conglomerate one.

9   Answer **C**
External economies of scale are the benefits firms gain from the industry growing in size. These benefits, including, for example, specialised courses run in colleges, are particularly likely to arise if the firms are located close to each other. If the firms are located in the same area, external economies of scale can be referred to as economies of concentration. Answer **A** is a general description of internal economies of scale. Answer **B** describes internal risk-bearing economies and answer **D** describes technical economies of scale.

10   Answer **D**
The data show that most enterprises are ones which employ a small number of workers. The data do not provide any information on output (answer **A**). While many enterprises have only self-employed people or only a few employees, answers **B** and **C** cannot be deduced. For example, a country might have 98 firms employing three people each and two firms employing 500 each. In this case, while the majority of firms employ a small number of workers, most workers are employed in large firms.

Answers to data response questions

1   a   1 is the marginal cost curve. It is tick-shaped and cuts the average total cost and average variable cost curves at their lowest points. 2 is the average total cost curve which is also known as the unit cost curve. It is U-shaped and is composed of average variable cost and average fixed cost. 3 is the average variable cost curve. It is again U-shaped and is below the average total cost curve. 4 is the average fixed cost curve. It declines continuously with output.

   b   Average fixed cost falls as output increases. This is because total fixed cost does not change with output so the same figure is divided by a higher figure as output increases. For example, if total fixed cost is £500 then the average fixed cost of producing five units would be £500/5 = £100 and the average fixed cost of producing ten units would be £500/10 = £50.

As average fixed cost plus average variable cost equals average total cost, average fixed cost represents the distance between average total cost and average variable cost.

c

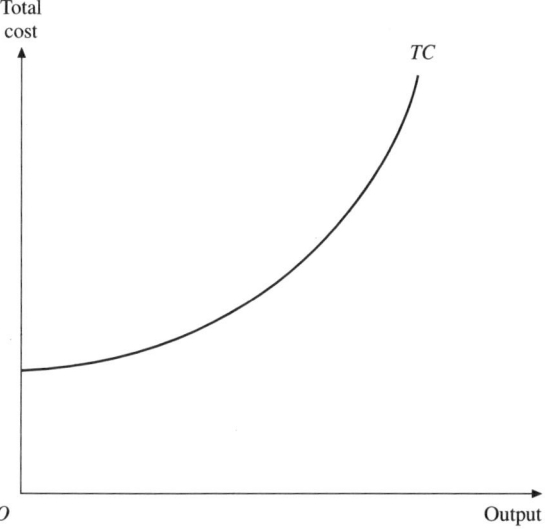

Fig. 2.4

The total cost curve does not start at zero as the diagram shows the short-run position of a firm with fixed cost. As average total cost falls and then rises, the firm experiences increasing returns and then diminishing returns. So total cost rises slowly at first and then rises more quickly.

d Marginal cost cuts average total cost at the lowest point on the average total cost curve. When average total cost is falling, marginal cost is below it. When average total cost is rising, marginal cost is above it. Changes in marginal cost lead to changes in average total cost.

e Both diminishing returns and diseconomies of scale result in rising marginal and average total costs. However, diminishing returns is a short-run situation arising from an inefficient combination of resources. In contrast, diseconomies of scale occur in the long run and arise from the scale of operation becoming too large and unwieldy. Diminishing returns set in when the marginal product of a variable input combined with a fixed input starts to decline. Diseconomies of scale occur when an increase in inputs results in a smaller percentage increase in output and average total costs start to rise.

2 a The three mergers mentioned are examples of horizontal mergers because they involve firms at the same stage of production and producing the same good or service. British Airways is and British

Caledonian was involved in civil aviation and at the tertiary stage of production. Ford and Jaguar are involved in car production and produce at the secondary stage of production. The Hong Kong and Shanghai Banking Corporation and Midland Bank are both in the banking industry, providing a service.

b   While horizontal integration involves a merger between two firms producing at the same stage of production, vertical integration is a merger between two firms producing at different stages of production. Forward vertical integration involves a firm merging with or taking over a firm nearer the market, e.g. a film production firm taking over a chain of cinemas. Backward vertical integration occurs when a firm merges with or takes over a firm nearer the source of the supply of the product, e.g. a supermarket buying a number of farms. A conglomerate merger differs from a horizontal merger in that it involves firms in different rather than the same industry, e.g. a book publishing firm merging with a pharmaceutical firm.

c   Plant and firm economies are both forms of internal economies of scale and so represent the benefits, in the form of lower average costs, arising from a growth in size. However, plant economies arise from the growth of individual workplaces, e.g. offices, factories or farms. They include the benefits of using specialised workers and machines, the use of large machines operating at full capacity and savings in stocks. Firm economies, on the other hand, arise from the growth of a firm. A firm may grow either from operating larger plants or from opening more plants. Firm economies include marketing economies, financial economies, research and development economies and risk-bearing economies.

d   A horizontal merger between two firms, each operating a number of plants, may enable production to be concentrated in a smaller number of larger plants which can be worked to full capacity. With each plant producing a larger output, it may be possible to take greater advantage of plant economies. For example, workers can specialise to a greater extent. The principle of multiples may also apply, with a larger output enabling a team of machines to work to full capacity in line with each other. For example, suppose a plant needs to use three types of machines to produce a product and one type can produce 30 units per hour, another 10 units per hour and a third 20 units per hour. If the plant is only large enough to operate one of each type of machine, the maximum output per hour would be 10 units and two of the machines would work below full capacity. The lowest common multiple of 30, 10 and 20 is 60. So if the plant was large enough to operate two machines of the first type, six of the second and three of the third, the machines could be worked at full capacity and output per hour could be 60 units. The engineers' rule refers to the ability of large plants to take advantage of increased dimensions. A large plant can use capital equipment and transport facilities of greater capacity without an increase in costs of the same proportion. For example, a juggernaut lorry may carry three times the volume of a standard size lorry but still only needs one driver, and a more powerful personal computer also still only requires one operator.

e The extract refers to buying economies, managerial economies and financial economies, so a number of firm economies are not mentioned. These include risk-bearing economies and staff facilities economies. As a firm grows in size it can diversify its product range and thereby reduce the impact of a fall in demand for any one of its products. Also, a large firm can provide a range of facilities for its staff including canteens and sports facilities, which may reduce staff turnover and increase staff motivation and productivity.

f Horizontal mergers will result in a fall in unit (average) cost if greater advantage can be taken of economies of scale. However, there is a danger that horizontal mergers can give rise to diseconomies of scale if the new firms created are above the optimum size. In particular, a new large firm may experience problems of management. A large firm will have a number of plants and departments which have to be coordinated. Managers will have more sections to control, checking that all decisions are being carried out effectively. There may be problems of communication, with more people to inform and consult. Indeed, large firms can be slow to respond to changes in consumer demand and supply conditions because of the layers of bureaucracy which may develop. Labour relations may also be less good than in smaller firms. Workers may feel more remote from management and it may take longer to resolve any problems. A number of academic studies have found that profits decline after horizontal mergers, in part because the resulting decrease in competition reduces pressure on the new firms to keep their costs low.

Answers to essay questions

1 a Division of labour is the specialisation of workers. A production process can be split into a number of separate operations and each one assigned to a different worker. Division of labour was described by Adam Smith in his book *The Wealth of Nations*, published in 1776. He studied the effect of division of labour in a pin factory where specialisation led to a considerable increase in output.

b The extent to which car manufacturers can take advantage of division of labour depends on the level of demand for the cars they produce, the number of models they make, the extent to which market conditions change and the way their workers respond to specialisation. The higher the level of demand the more workers will be employed and the more they can specialise. Demand for standard family cars will be high, whereas demand for expensive sports cars will be lower and so, in the latter case, less specialisation can take place. The fewer the models made, again the more specialisation that can occur. If market conditions change frequently, workers will have to be more flexible. For example, consumers' greater concern with safety has resulted in new cars being fitted with air bags. Changes in technology also require workers to learn and apply new skills. Car manufacturers may choose not to take full advantage of division of labour if they believe that having a team of workers who carry out a variety of tasks will result in greater efficiency and lower costs.

c i There are a number of advantages which a firm may gain from division of labour, all of which should result in a fall in the firm's unit (average) costs. If workers specialise, they can concentrate on the job they are best at and should become very proficient at it as practice makes perfect. Less time should be spent on moving around on the job and less equipment will be needed as workers will only have to be given the equipment needed to carry out their particular tasks. Less time and money will be spent on training as workers will have to learn only one or a few tasks. In addition, the breaking down of the production of a good or service into a series of separate operations may make it easier to mechanise the process.

However, the firm may also experience disadvantages from division of labour which can result in a rise in unit costs. Workers who undertake the same tasks each day may become bored. This may result in a reduction in motivation, high absenteeism, high labour turnover and a deterioration in industrial relations. Quality of output may decline and it may become necessary to employ quality inspectors. If workers are specialised there may also be a decline in flexibility, making it difficult to cover for workers off sick or undergoing training. By training workers in just one or a few tasks a firm may not find out which tasks workers are best at and it may mean that workers do not gain an overview and so are less likely to make suggestions about how to reduce costs and/or raise revenue.

c ii Division of labour may mean that workers find it easier to gain employment as they will require little training in order to carry out the jobs on offer. Some people may prefer to undertake work which is of a less demanding nature. In addition, some workers who become very skilled at particular tasks may be able to command high wages. New jobs may be created for those involved in quality control and those who design and operate machinery.

However, division of labour may make it possible to replace workers by machines or by unemployed workers. Major disadvantages of division of labour, from the worker's point of view, are boredom and loss of job satisfaction which can result from undertaking the same task day after day.

2 a Internal economies are the benefits, in the form of lower unit (average) costs, gained as a result of growing in size. These can be divided into plant and firm economies.

Plant economies arise from the growth of individual workplaces, e.g. offices, factories and farms. As workplaces become larger, more specialised and larger capital equipment can be used and workers can also become more specialised. Costs can be reduced by running machines at full capacity, cutting down on stocks and selling or converting by-products.

Firm economies occur as firms grow in size. An increase in the size of a business unit may enable greater advantage to be taken of buying economies. When large orders are placed with firms supplying raw materials, discounts may be given. Large firms may also be able to employ specialised buyers, get reduced rates for advertising and save money in transporting goods as large lorries and ships are cheaper to operate in terms of goods transported. A large firm is likely to be able to raise finance more easily and more cheaply than small firms. For example, a bank usually charges lower rates of interest to large, well-known firms than to small firms. Firms operating on a large scale can employ specialist staff, including accountants and personnel officers, provide facilities for their staff, including staff canteens and transport, and operate research and development departments. They can also spread their risks by producing a diversified product range and may be able to operate plants which specialise in particular products.

In contrast to internal economies of scale, diseconomies of scale are the disadvantages in the form of higher unit (average) costs that firms experience as they grow too large. Firms which grow past their optimum size may experience management problems in the form of difficulty in coordinating and controlling a large organisation. Increased bureaucracy may hinder communication and large plants tend to have poorer industrial relations than small ones. Large firms will increase demand for inputs which may increase their prices and thereby raise unit costs.

b A downward-sloping long-run average cost curve means that firms continue to experience falls in unit (average) costs as output rises.

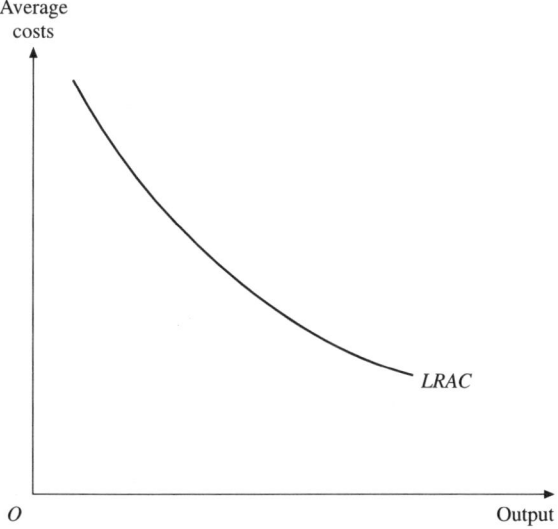

Fig. 2.5

This will occur in industries where the optimum size of the firm or plant is large. These industries are likely to be ones in which technical economies of scale are significant and offset any managerial and administrative economies which may be experienced. Examples of industries which may experience a downward-sloping long-run average cost curve are car manufacturing and oil production.

c   External economies of scale refer to the fall in average costs that firms in an industry can gain as a result of the industry they are in growing in size. A computer firm may gain a number of advantages from the computer industry growing in size. More courses on computing may be put on in schools, colleges and universities, providing computer firms with a supply of skilled labour and generating demand for computing hardware and software. More firms may be set up to provide ancillary services for the computer industry, including those providing computer paper. Computer firms may cooperate in funding research and development programmes in universities. Service industries may grow, for example, those providing specialised advertising and insurance facilities. Trade fairs may also be organised where computer firms can advertise their models and take orders. However, if the industry grows too large, a shortage of skilled workers may develop which will increase wages. Raw material costs, e.g. the cost of microchips, may increase as demand rises. If the computer firms are based in one place, growth in the industry may give rise to congestion.

Answers to short questions

1　Effective demand is the willingness and ability to buy a product at any given price. An extension in demand for a product can only be caused by a change in the price of the product itself. For the vast majority of products a fall in price will cause an extension in demand as shown in the diagram below.

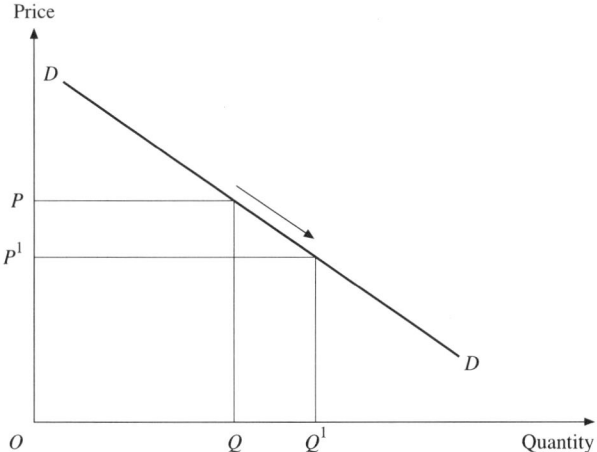

Fig. 3.5

A lower price will enable people to buy more and will encourage people to buy more. It is only in the case of exceptional goods, e.g. Veblen goods, that a rise in price will cause an extension in demand.

2　An increase in demand for apples means that more apples are being demanded at each and every price. Among the possible reasons why people may demand more apples are an advertising campaign, a rise in the price of pears and an increase in real incomes. A successful advertising campaign will encourage existing buyers to buy more and will attract new buyers. Pears are a substitute for apples and if they rise in price some people may switch from pears to apples. An increase in real incomes will enable people to buy more goods, including apples.

3　A rise in the price of pork will cause demand for pork to contract. A rise in price means that people's purchasing power falls. They are able to buy fewer goods and so are likely to buy less pork and less of some other goods. A higher price for pork is also likely to make people switch to substitute meats, e.g. chicken. So people will be less able and willing to buy pork.

4　Price is determined by demand and supply. Demand is influenced by marginal utility. For example, as shown in the diagram below, people will buy extra units of a good only if its price falls, as they value these units less than the first ones.

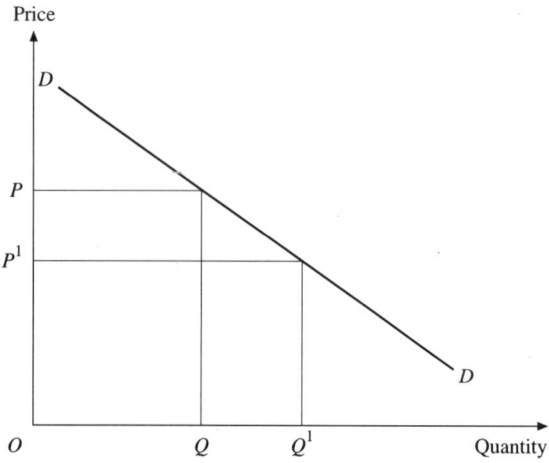

Fig. 3.6

Water has a high total utility as it is essential for people to have a certain quantity of water for drinking, washing, cooking, etc. Diamonds are less essential. However, consumers' decisions are made at the margin. People consume water to the point where its marginal utility is relatively low and so would be prepared to pay only a low price for water. People buy fewer diamonds so the marginal utility they derive, and the price they are prepared to pay, are higher.

5   **i**   Most goods have negative price elasticity of demand, as, in most cases, a rise in price will cause a contraction in demand. For example, a rise in the price of perfume is likely to cause a fall in demand for perfume.

ii   Complements, i.e. goods and services which are used together, have negative cross elasticity of demand. For example, a rise in the price of strawberries is likely to cause a decrease in demand for cream.

iii   Inferior goods, e.g. bus travel, have negative income elasticity of demand. A rise in income will cause demand for these goods and services to fall.

6   Cigarettes have a low price elasticity of demand. A rise in price will cause a smaller percentage fall in demand. The two key reasons why cigarettes have inelastic demand are that they are addictive and that they are perceived by a number of smokers as having no close substitutes.

7   A decrease in the supply of cabbages means that fewer cabbages will be offered for sale at each and every price. There are a number of reasons why supply may fall. These include a period of bad weather, an increase in the cost of producing cabbages and the imposition of an indirect tax on cabbages. A period of bad weather may reduce the crop of cabbages and hence

those offered for sale. An increase in, for example, farm workers' wages, not matched by a rise in labour productivity, and the imposition of VAT on cabbages will make it more expensive to produce cabbages and thereby reduce their supply.

8 Among the determinants of the elasticity of supply of televisions are the quantity of stocks held, time and the production period. If large stocks of televisions are or can be stored, entrepreneurs can adjust supply by signicant amounts in response to a change in price. For example, if price rises, televisions taken from stocks, in addition to newly produced ones, can be offered for sale. Over time, supply of most products becomes more elastic. In the long run, television manufacturers can adjust all their factors of production in response to a change in price. The shorter the production period, the easier it is to adjust supply and, again, the more elastic supply is.

9 Complements, for example, football shirts and football shorts, and bread and butter, are bought to be used together. They have negative cross elasticity of demand. A change in the price of one of the goods will cause a change in demand, in the opposite direction, for the other good.

Goods which are produced together are in joint supply, e.g. beef and leather and lamb and wool. An increase in the demand for one of the goods will lead to a rise in price and an extension in supply of that good and an increase in the supply of the other good.

10 A rise in demand for duvets will increase their profitability and output. If people are buying duvets they are likely to be buying fewer blankets which are a substitute for duvets. The decrease in demand for blankets will cause a fall in their price and a contraction in supply. As fewer blankets are produced, demand for blanket workers will fall. This will cause a fall in their wages and employment.

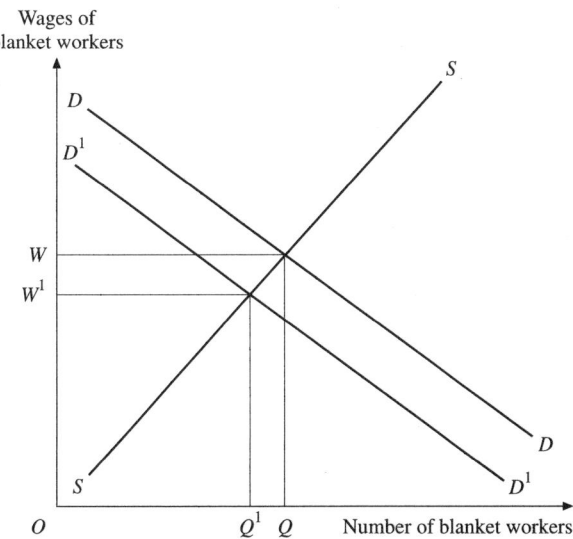

Fig. 3.7

Answers to multiple choice questions

1   Answer **C**
A shift to the left in the demand curve for a good illustrates a decrease in demand. If a substitute becomes cheaper people will buy more of the substitute and less of this good. **A** would cause a contraction in demand. **B** and **D** would cause a fall in price and an expansion in demand.

2   Answer **B**
Marginal utility is the change in total utility resulting from a change in consumption of one unit. Diminishing marginal utility occurs when marginal utility falls and hence total utility rises more slowly or, in some cases, actually falls. In this example the marginal utility of cabbages and peas falls, while the marginal utility of carrots stays constant.

| | *Marginal utility (utils)* | | |
Units consumed	*Cabbages*	*Carrots*	*Peas*
2	8	7	7
3	7	7	5
4	5	7	2
5	2	7	−1

3   Answer **A**
Total utility reaches a maximum when marginal utility is zero. It increases when marginal utility is positive and falls when marginal utility is negative. Answer **B** is incorrect as the person is gaining utility from the good. **C** cannot be concluded as we do not know the price of Z nor the prices and marginal utilities of other goods the person purchases. **D** is incorrect as disutility occurs past point OQ.

4   Answer **B**
Consumer surplus is gained when consumers pay less for a good than they are willing to pay. It is represented by the area above the price line and below the demand curve. Before the increase in supply the area of consumer surplus is PAB. After the increase in supply it rises to P1AC which is a rise of P1PBC.

5   Answer **A**
When a good has unit price elasticity of demand, a change in price will cause an equal percentage change in quantity demanded, usually in the opposite direction. This means that total expenditure (revenue) will not change as price changes. A rise in price will cause an equal percentage fall in demand.

   B   An increase in price will cause an increase in quantity supplied which can also be referred to as an extension in supply.

   C An increase in the price of a good will cause an increase in demand for, and expenditure on, substitute goods.

   D When price elasticity of demand is unity, expenditure on the good will remain constant.

6 Answer **A**
Complements have negative cross elasticity of demand. This means a rise in the price of one of the goods will cause a decrease in demand for the other good. This is illustrated in figure **A**. **B** illustrates positive cross elasticity of demand which is experienced by substitutes. **D** illustrates zero cross elasticity of demand which is the relationship independent goods have. **C** shows the quantity of a good changing when the price of another good remains unchanged.

7 Answer **D**
The formula for income elasticity of demand is:

$$\frac{\text{percentage change in quantity demanded}}{\text{percentage change in income}}$$

In this case YED = $\dfrac{10\%}{5\%}$ = 2

8 Answer **D**

$$PES = \frac{\%\Delta QS}{\%\Delta P} \quad \text{So } 0.8 = \frac{?}{25\%}$$

So the %ΔQS = 20 per cent. Supply was originally 600. An increase in price will cause a rise in supply: in this case from 600 to 600 + 20 per cent, i.e. to 720. With 720 being sold at £50, the firm's revenue will be 720 × £50 = £36 000.

9 Answer **A**
The diagram shows that the fall in price to P1 has been caused by an increase in demand to D1 and an increase in supply to S1. An increase in real incomes will cause an increase in demand and a fall in raw material costs will cause an increase in supply.

   B A subsidy granted to producers will increase supply but an increase in the price of a complement will cause a decrease in demand.

   C An increase in income tax will decrease demand while the introduction of improved technology will increase supply.

   D An increase in population will increase demand but an increase in value added tax will cause a decrease in supply.

10 Answer **B**
In 1983 expenditure on food formed 14.8 per cent of total consumers' expenditure. It fell to 12.6 per cent in 1993.

A   Expenditure on clothing and footwear rose by a greater percentage than expenditure on transport and communication – 45.5 per cent compared to 37.7 per cent.

C and **D** The data do not provide any specic information on prices, supply or demand.

Answers to data response questions

1 a   The two main sections of the personal computers (PC) market in the UK are the home market and the professional market. The home market covers the demand for personal computers for personal use. In this market PCs are seen mainly as a consumer good. The professional market covers the demand for PCs for use in business and education. In this market PCs are mainly a capital good.

b   The fall in price, the improved performance and facilities and advertising have led to an increase in demand for PCs. The reduction in price has increased the ability and willingness of consumers and entrepreneurs to purchase PCs. The improved performance has resulted in more businesses using PCs in preference to mini computers and the development of, for example, CD-ROM and the Internet have encouraged more consumers to buy PCs. The increased competition created by the rise in the number of firms producing PCs has led to an increase in expenditure on advertising which, in turn, has generated more customers.

c   The extract suggests that computers and televisions are complements. They are used together in multimedia packages.

d   The extract discusses falling production costs and increased competition causing the price of PCs to fall. One major cause of the lower production costs is advances in technology. The fall in set up and average cost of producing PCs, resulting from advances in technology, has increased the number of firms selling PCs. Both the lower production costs and increased competition have shifted the supply curve to the right, thereby causing price to fall and demand to expand as illustrated below.

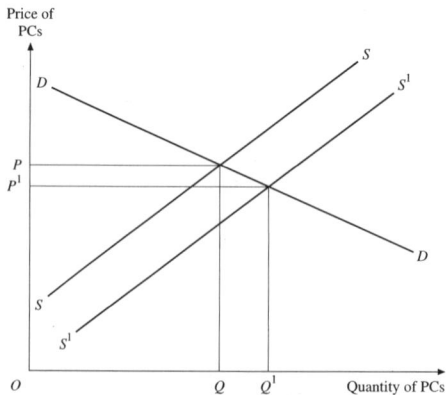

Fig. 3.8

e The increase in demand for PCs is likely to increase demand for computing magazines. They are complementary goods. Some of the people who buy PCs will also buy magazines, some on a casual basis and some on a regular basis. The 1990s have witnessed a large-scale increase in the number of computing magazines on sale.

f The extract mentions the price of PCs, consumer confidence, substitutes and complements to PCs. A change in income, population size and advertising will all influence demand for PCs. PCs have positive income elasticity of demand, so a rise in income will result in an increase in demand. A rise in population size and an increase in advertising expenditure will also tend to lead to an increase in demand for PCs.

2 a Supply of newspapers increased in the 1980s in terms of the number of titles (*The Independent* started in 1986) and in terms of the number of papers sold. This higher supply resulted from improvements in technology and an increase in demand.

b Two causes of a change in the supply of newspapers, not mentioned in the extract, are the imposition of a tax and a change in raw material costs. In the 1980s the government considered imposing VAT on newspapers. This would have caused a decrease in supply, shifting the supply curve to the left in a non-parallel way. In the mid-1990s the price of paper rose significantly, which pushed up the costs of producing newspapers and again shifted the supply curve to the left.

c The extract suggests that newspapers have positive income elasticity of demand. It mentions sales rising when the economy was booming and incomes were rising in the late 1980s. It also discusses sales falling during the recession in the late 1980s and sales increasing as a result of the upturn in incomes in 1993/94.

d The newspapers used both price and non-price competition to attract buyers. In 1993 and 1994 there was a price war, started by News International cutting the price of *The Sun* and *The Times*. This led to cuts in the price of other papers, including *The Daily Telegraph* and *The Independent*. *The Guardian* and *The Daily Telegraph* sought to maintain existing readers and to attract new readers by developing features including, in *The Guardian's* case, its tabloid section. *The Daily Telegraph* tried to gain new young readers by, for example, providing the *Young Telegraph* on Saturdays. There are a number of other ways in which newspapers seek to capture a larger share of the market, including running competitions and publishing exclusive stories.

e Newspaper owners must have believed that demand for their newspapers was elastic so that a fall in price would result in a greater percentage rise in demand and hence an increase in revenue. This was contrary to the belief of some economists that demand was inelastic because of brand loyalty.

f A number of factors influence the price elasticity of demand for a particular newspaper. One is the availability of substitutes. In addition to other newspapers, television and radio are substitutes. The closer people perceive other newspapers and alternative media to be to a particular newspaper, and hence the more willing they are to switch, the more elastic demand will be. The extent to which reading a particular newspaper can become something of a habit is another factor. The more 'addictive' it is, the greater the brand loyalty will be and the more inelastic demand will be. The smaller the proportion of income which has to be spent on a newspaper, the more inelastic demand will be.

Answers to essay questions

1 a   The three main factors which influence the demand for any good are the price of the good, the price of related goods and real disposable income. Demand will extend from OQ to OQ1 as a result of a fall in price from OP to OP1.

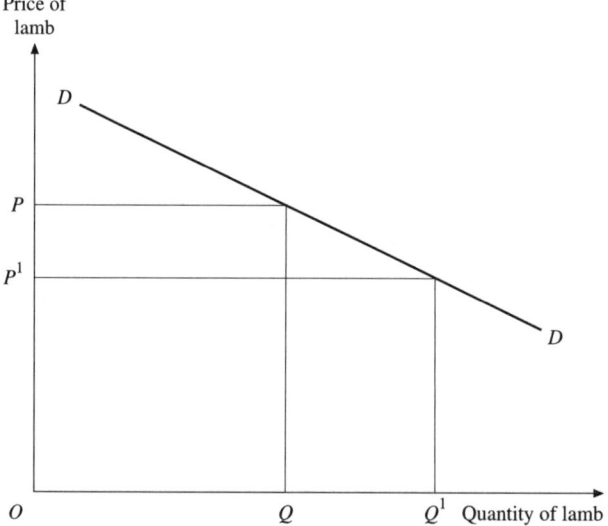

Fig. 3.9

The lower price will mean that people will be more able and willing to buy lamb. Demand for lamb is relatively price elastic as it has a number of substitutes in the form of alternative foods. For example, a rise in the price of chicken or any other substitute will cause an increase in demand for lamb. In contrast, a rise in the price of a complement, e.g. mint sauce, will cause a decrease in demand for lamb. A fall in real disposable income would also reduce demand. Lamb is a normal good with positive income elasticity of demand.

There are a number of other factors which affect demand for lamb. One is advertising. A successful advertising campaign would be expected to raise demand for lamb, whereas a change in tastes, for example, away from eating red meat, would reduce demand for lamb. A decrease in population size would also reduce demand. Changes in the distribution of income and age structure of the population may also affect demand for lamb.

b i An increase in the price of lamb would cause a contraction in demand for lamb as shown in the diagram below.

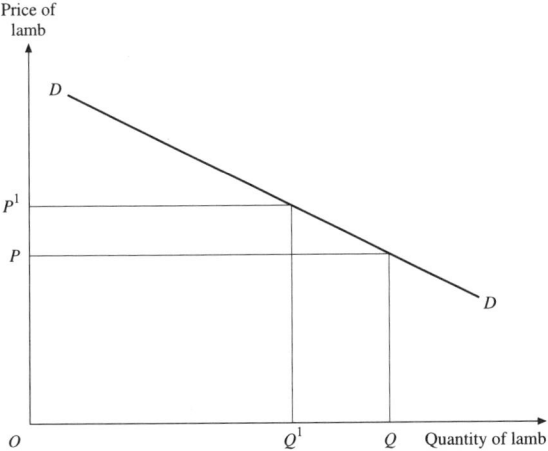

Fig. 3.10

As demand is relatively elastic, a rise in price will result in a greater percentage contraction in demand and revenue will fall.

b ii As noted earlier, lamb and mint sauce are complements. A rise in the price of lamb will cause a decrease in demand for mint sauce. The extent of the fall in demand will depend on the amount by which the price of lamb rises and the degree to which lamb and mint sauce are substitutes.

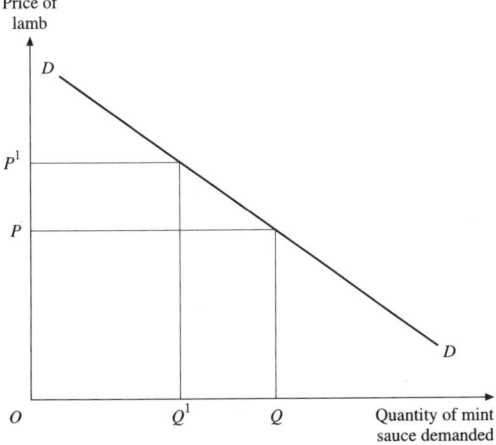

Fig. 3.11

A decrease in demand for mint sauce will cause its price to fall and supply to contract. Demand for mint sauce is relatively elastic as it is something of a luxury. Although mint sauce has a natural ingredient it does not take long to grow and process and it can be stored so its supply is also relatively elastic.

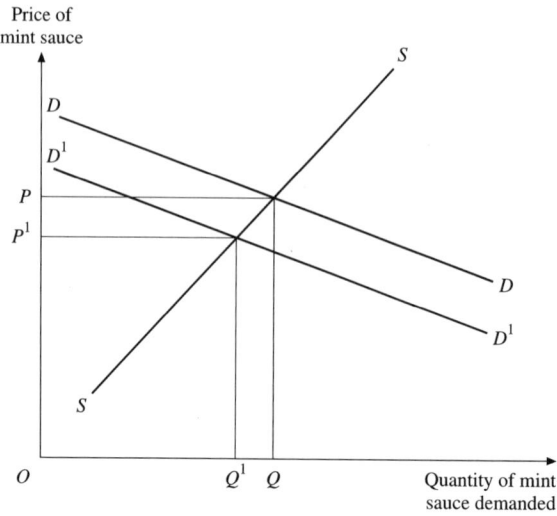

Fig. 3.12

b **iii** Beef is a substitute for lamb. An increase in the price of lamb is likely to result in an increase in demand for beef, as shown in the diagram below.

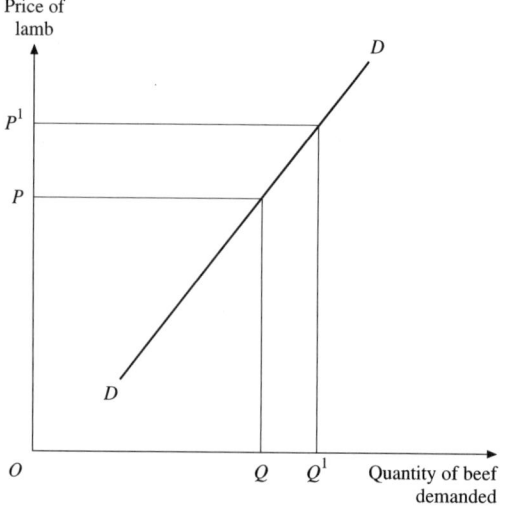

Fig. 3.13

Demand for beef is relatively elastic as it has substitutes and is regarded by some as something of a luxury. As with lamb, supply of beef is relatively inelastic. It is a natural, agricultural product which cannot be adjusted quickly to changes in price. An increase in demand for beef would cause its price to rise and supply to extend.

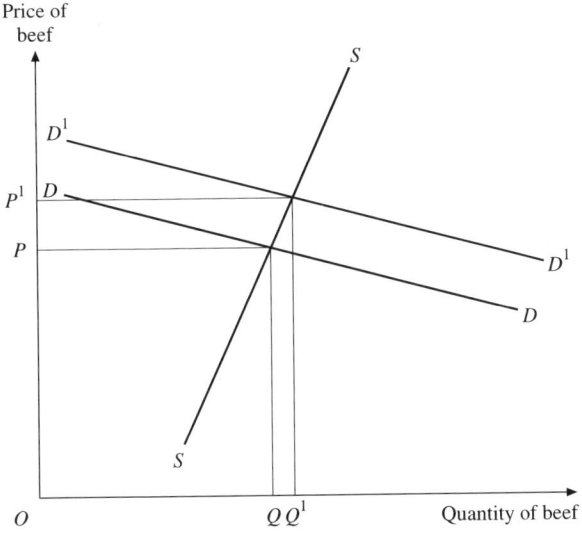

Fig. 3.14

The greater impact is likely to be on price rather than on quantity.

b iv Demand for shepherds is a derived demand. The effect of a rise in the price of lamb will depend on its cause. If it has resulted from an increase in costs of production, the supply of lamb is likely to decrease. Fewer sheep will be kept and demand for shepherds is likely to decrease. Demand for shepherds is relatively inelastic, at least in the short run. The number of shepherds employed is relatively low in terms of the number of sheep kept and shepherds' wages do not form a high proportion of the total costs of producing lamb. Supply is relatively elastic as a high level of qualifications is not required.

The decrease in demand for shepherds will cause their wages to fall and supply to contract. Some of those who were shepherds will seek alternative employment as the wage rate falls.

Wage rate of
shepherds

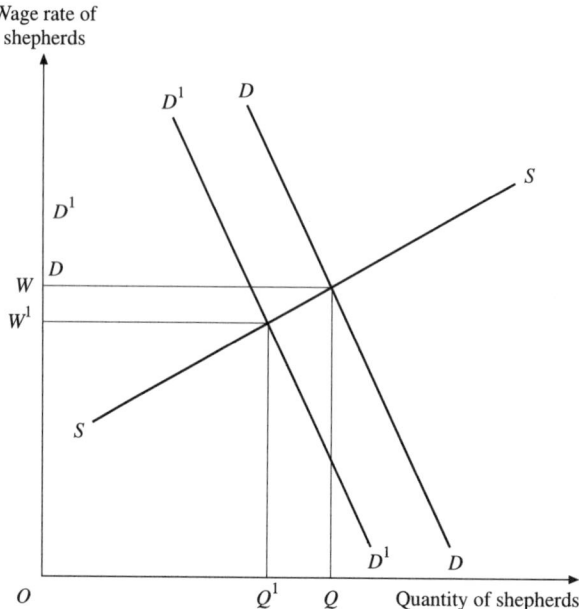

Fig. 3.15

2 a Price, cross and income elasticities of demand are all concerned with the extent to which demand responds to change in a key variable. Price elasticity of demand measures the response of demand to a change in the price of the good. The formula is PED = %ΔQD

$$\frac{}{\%\Delta P}$$

Most products have negative price elasticity of demand which means that, for example, a rise in price will cause a fall in demand.

The extent to which the quantity demanded changes in response to a change in price can vary from zero to infinity. In practice, though, most goods have either elastic demand or inelastic demand. In the case of elastic demand, a change in price will cause a greater percentage change in demand. So a rise in price will be accompanied by a greater percentage fall in demand and hence a fall in total expenditure (revenue). In contrast, a rise in the price of a good in inelastic demand will cause a smaller percentage change in quantity and a rise in total expenditure. The following diagram illustrates inelastic demand.

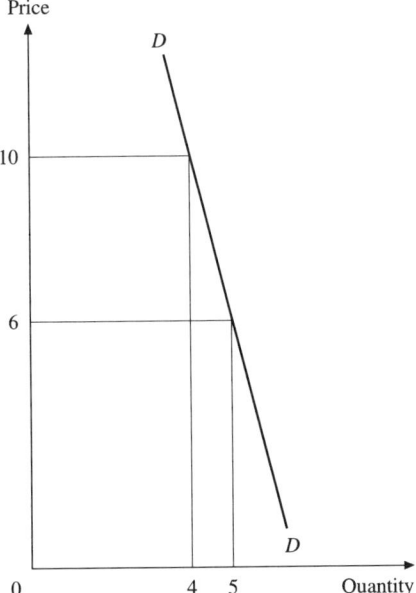

Fig. 3.16

The factors which influence the price elasticity of demand a good has are the availability of close substitutes, how necessary the good is perceived to be, whether it is addictive, whether its purchase can be postponed and what proportion of income is taken up purchasing the good. A luxury, non-essential good with a range of close substitutes, which takes up a large part of income and the purchase of which can be postponed, will have elastic demand.

Cross elasticity of demand measures the response of demand for one good to a change in the price of another good. The formula is:

$$XED = \frac{\%\Delta QD \text{ of good A}}{\%\Delta P \text{ of good B}}$$

Substitutes have positive cross elasticity of demand. A rise in the price of one good will cause an increase in demand for the substitute good. This is illustrated in the following diagram.

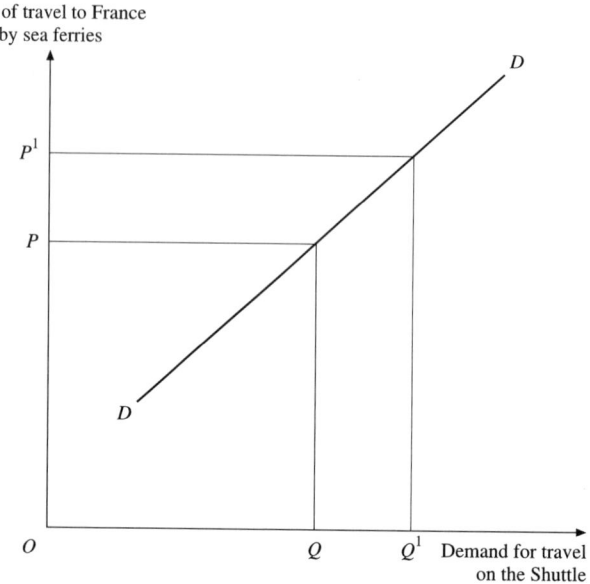

Fig. 3.17

Complements have negative cross elasticity of demand. A rise in the price of a good will cause a decrease in demand for complementary goods. The diagram below shows the effect of a rise in the price of parking in a car park near to a theatre on the demand for theatre tickets.

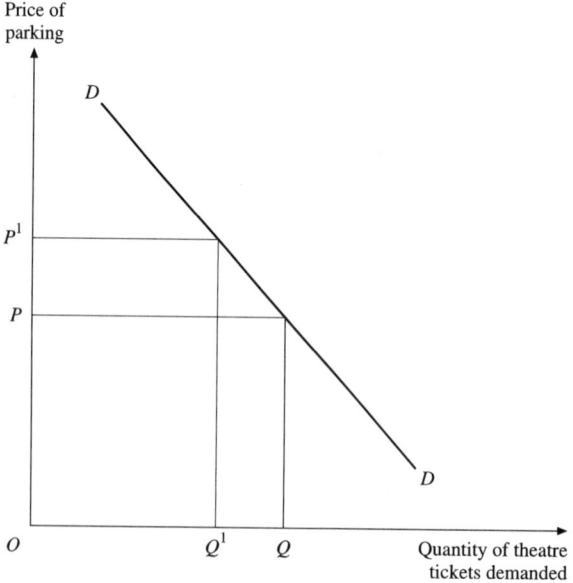

Fig. 3.18

Independent goods have zero cross elasticity of demand. For example, a rise in the price of cameras is unlikely to have a direct effect on demand for bread. This is shown in the diagram below.

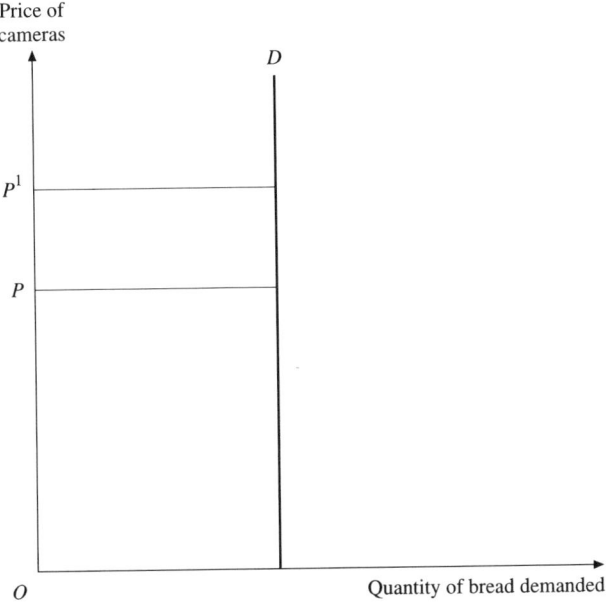

Fig. 3.19

Income elasticity of demand measures the response of demand to a change in income. The formula is $\text{YED} = \dfrac{\%\Delta QD}{\%\Delta Y}$

Income elastic demand means that a change in income will cause a greater percentage change in demand, whereas income inelastic demand means that a change in income will cause a smaller percentage change in demand. Most goods have positive income elasticity of demand. This is why they are called normal goods. A rise in income will cause an increase in demand and a fall in income will cause a decrease in demand. Positive income elasticity of demand is illustrated in Figure 3.20.

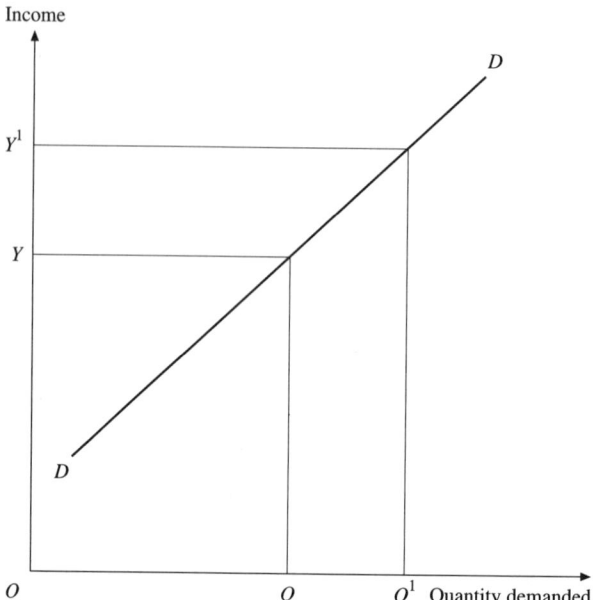

Fig. 3.20

Goods which have positive income elasticity of demand greater than 1 (elastic) are sometimes referred to as superior goods.

A few goods have negative income elasticity of demand, e.g. bus travel. In this case income and demand will move in opposite directions as shown below.

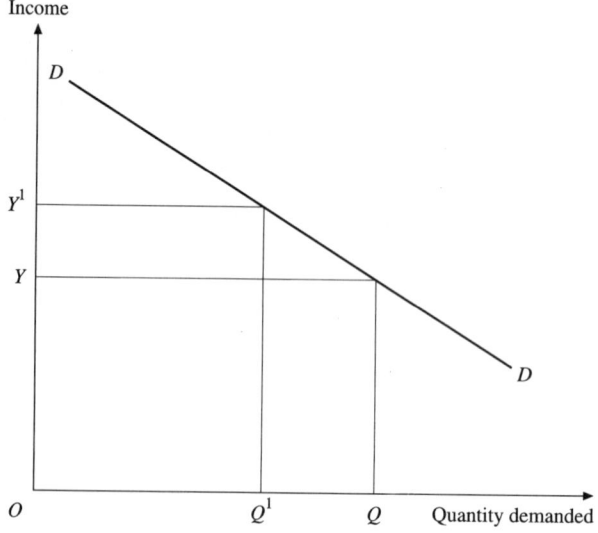

Fig. 3.21

b If a coach firm competes with a number of other coach firms or other forms of transport on the same route, it is likely to have price elastic demand. If it is aware of this, it will know that it will be able to gain an increase in total revenue by lowering its price. The rise in quantity demanded will be greater than the fall in price. However, the coach firm will also be concerned with profit. A fall in price will increase total revenue but also total cost. The effect on profit will depend on their relative rises.

The concept of cross elasticity of demand can be used by a coach firm in its bid to raise its revenue in a number of ways. If positive cross elasticity of demand exists between the coach firm's services and the services of other coach firms and other forms of transport, a rise in the price of the other firms' services will increase demand for travel with the coach firm and raise its revenue. It will also mean that a fall in the price of the coach firm's travel will attract consumers away from its rivals. The higher cross elasticity of demand is, the fiercer competition is. Negative cross elasticity of demand will exist between the firm's service and its complements. Reducing the price of meals served on the firm's coach trips may raise revenue. If demand for holiday packages is increasing, the coach firm may have the potential to expand.

Knowledge of income elasticity of demand may prove to be very significant for a coach firm. Coach travel may have negative income elasticity of demand. If this is the case, as income tends to rise over time, a coach firm will be in danger of falling demand. It then has two basic choices. It could leave the industry or try to change the image of coach travel and transform it into a normal good. A number of coach firms have taken the second option. The standard of coaches has improved and the facilities offered have increased, including the provision of hostess services and toilets.

Answers to short questions

1 The essential feature which determines the structure of a market is the degree of competition in the market. This, in turn, is influenced by a number of factors, e.g. how easy it is to enter or leave an industry. The existence of barriers to entry and exit will limit the number of firms in the industry and hence the level of competition. The level of demand is another influencing factor. If demand is low, only one firm may exist in the market. For example, in a small town there may be only one cinema. Also, where long-run average costs are lower if an industry operates under monopoly than if it is shared by a number of firms, only one firm may exist. Its dominant position will mean that it can undercut any potential rival firm. This is an example of a natural monopoly.

2 Perfect competition provides a number of benefits to consumers. They are given a choice of producers who respond quickly to any changes in demand. The firms always achieve allocative efficiency and, in the long run, produce at the lowest point on the average cost curve and earn normal profits.

3 In both perfect competition and monopolistic competition there is an absence of barriers to entry. Firms in both markets seek to maximise profits and produce where $MC = MR$. In the long run, firms in both market conditions will earn only normal profits, i.e. $AC = AR$.

However, differences do exist between the two market structures. A firm operating under conditions of monopolistic competition influences price by changing its output. Such firms are price makers; increasing output lowers price and hence AR exceeds MR. In contrast, each firm producing under conditions of perfect competition is a price taker and one firm changing its output has no effect on price, $AR = MR$. The products produced by firms operating under conditions of monopolistic competition are similar but not identical and may be advertised on a small scale. However, in perfect competition the products are homogeneous and no advertising takes place.

4 Game theory suggests that oligopolists' behaviour is influenced by assumptions about their rivals' behaviour. In deciding their own strategy they will take into account how other firms in the industry will react. This may mean that they will, for example, seek to reduce uncertainty by colluding with other firms or perhaps by opting not for maximum profits but for a satisfactory level of profits.

5 Commercial banks and civil airlines within the UK operate under conditions of oligopoly. In both cases the market is dominated by a few large firms. There are barriers to entry into both markets. Supernormal profits are earned by some firms in both the short and long run and non-price competition is a significant feature. In the case of civil airlines there have also been examples of price wars.

In a village a public house may enjoy a monopoly position. However, in most towns and cities public houses operate under conditions of monopolistic competition. There are no significant start-up costs, the pubs provide a similar but not identical service, there is non-price competition, the pubs can influence price but the market is not usually dominated by a few large pubs.

6 There are a number of ways a discriminating monopolist can separate markets. It may be done, for example, on a regional basis. Some car producers sell models more cheaply on the continent of Europe than in the UK. A market may also be separated on the basis of time. Telephone calls are cheaper to make at off peak periods, for example.

7 A producer will gain higher profits from price discrimination if three conditions are met. The producer must have a degree of monopoly power, face different elasticities of demand in the markets and must be able to keep the markets separate. Some consumers may gain if they are in markets where the product is sold cheaply. Indeed, in the short run, at least, they may benefit from a good being sold at less than cost price. They will also benefit if, in the absence of price discrimination, the product would not be financially viable and would be withdrawn from the market. If price discrimination generates additional profits, the government will gain extra corporation tax revenue.

However, consumers in markets where demand is less elastic will pay more than consumers who are in markets where demand is more elastic. If price discrimination is used to drive out rival producers by dumping, in the long run consumers will have less choice and face higher prices.

8 There are a number of forms of non-price competition which firms may engage in.
   a   Car firms, for example, spend a considerable amount on advertising. The intention behind this is to persuade potential customers that their model is superior to rival models.
   b   Firms may also seek to attract customers by running competitions. This is a particular feature of the tabloid press which operate, for example, bingo and lottery competitions. Here the intention is to attract new customers and also to ensure that existing readers continue to buy the newspapers.
   c   This motive of maintaining customer loyalty is also behind the introduction of loyalty cards in supermarkets. These encourage shoppers to return to the same supermarket to gain increasing discounts.
   d   After sales service is also used to attract and maintain customers. This is a feature particularly of the electronic goods market where different lengths of free guarantees are offered.

9 The total revenue curve of a firm producing under monopoly slopes up initially. This is because, at a low output, demand is elastic and marginal revenue is positive. It reaches a peak when demand is unity and marginal revenue is zero. It falls when demand is inelastic and marginal revenue is negative. This is illustrated in the following diagram.

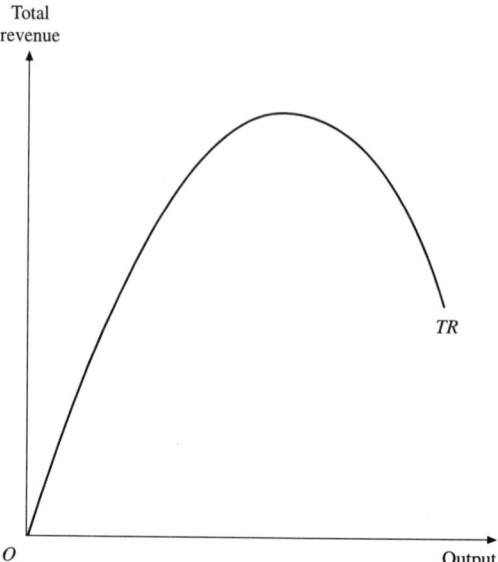

Fig. 4.5

In practice a monopolist will seek to produce on the upward-sloping part of the total revenue curve (where demand is elastic and marginal revenue is positive).

The total revenue curve of a firm producing under conditions of perfect competition is a straight upward-sloping line as illustrated below.

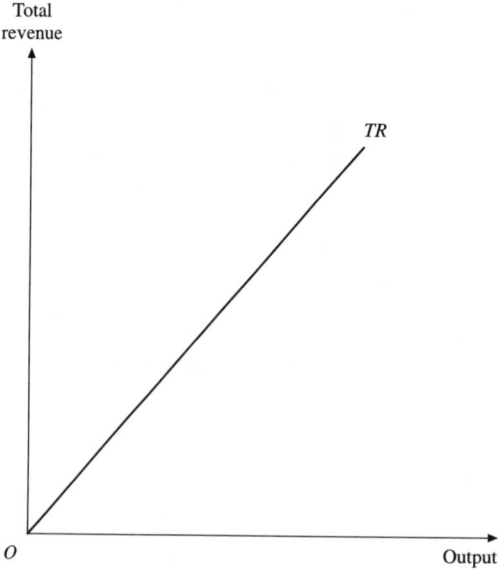

Fig. 4.6

The shape of the total revenue curve is accounted for by the fact that, under perfect competition, marginal revenue is constant. So total revenue rises by constant amounts. For example, if marginal revenue is £5, total revenue from selling one good will be £5, two goods £10, three goods £15, etc.

10 Firms will produce at minimum average cost under conditions of perfect competition in the long run or under any other market conditions if forced by the government to do so. The high degree of competition, with free entry and exit, ensures that firms producing under conditions of perfect competition in the long run earn only normal profits and produce where $MC = MR = AC = AR = P$. Where $MC = AC$ is the lowest point on the AC curve, a state-owned firm may be instructed to produce at the lowest point on the AC curve. A regulator of a private sector firm, e.g. OFGAS, may also require it to follow a particular output strategy, such as producing at the lowest AC, although, more commonly, conditions are set down more in relation to pricing.

Answers to multiple choice questions

1 Answer **D**
To stay in production in the short run a firm producing under conditions of perfect competition must be able to cover its average variable costs. If it cannot it will not be able to cover its running costs and will make more of a loss by continuing in production than in closing down immediately.

2 Answer **D**
A firm maximises profit when it produces where $MC = MR$. So in this case, it is necessary first to calculate MC and MR.

Output	MR	MC
11		
	10	2
12		
	10	4
13		
	10	6
14		
	10	10
15		

3 Answer **B**
Sales revenue is maximised when marginal revenue is zero. Output **A** is profit maximisation output ($MC = MR$), **C** is the productively efficient output – the lowest point on the AC curve ($MC = AC$) and **D** is normal profit output ($AC = AR$).

4 Answer **A**
The supply curve is based on the marginal cost curve. Firms operating

under conditions of perfect competition produce not only where MC = MR but also where MC = AR (price). So when price is £4, Firm R will supply 6, Firm S 7 and Firm T 7, a total market supply of 20. When price rises to £6 Firm R supplies 7, Firm S 9 and Firm T 8, a total of 24.

Price elasticity of supply is $\dfrac{\%\Delta QD}{\%\Delta P}$

Which in this case is $\dfrac{20\%}{50\%} = 0.4$

5   Answer **A**
It is a monopoly because the total revenue curve first slopes up and then down. It is a short-run situation as there are costs, which must be fixed costs, when output is zero.

6   Answer **C**
Firms producing under conditions of monopolistic competition produce similar but not identical products. The firms are price makers, make normal profits in the long run and there is free entry and exit.

7   Answer **B**
The kinked demand curve suggests that prices will be relatively stable under conditions of oligopoly. Firms are discouraged from raising their price for fear of losing market share and revenue if their rivals do not raise their price. They are also reluctant to lower their price as if their rivals follow suit, they will gain few, if any, extra customers and, with lower prices, are likely to experience a loss of revenue.

8   Answer **B**
The monopolist will maximise profits by producing where MC = MR. Drawing a line across to show the marginal cost and checking where this cuts marginal revenue gives the output in the two markets. Then, to find the respective prices, a line is drawn up to the average revenue (price) line and across.

9   Answer **D**
Normal profit is included in costs of production. The total cost of producing output OQ is represented by the area OVYQ. The area VWXY (answer **C**) shows supernormal profit.

10   Answer **C**
The data indicate that the UK car industry is operating under conditions of oligopoly. It is stated that the industry is dominated by seven groups which, together, supply 99 per cent of the market.

Answers to data response questions

1 a i Sunk costs are expenditure by a firm on producing a good which cannot be recovered if the firm decides to stop producing the good. For example, spending on an advertising campaign or the sinking of a mine shaft may involve expenditure which cannot be recouped on the exit of the firm from the industry.

a ii Hit and run entry occurs when firms enter an industry in search of high profits with the intention of staying in for a short period of time and leaving before profit levels fall. It will occur when there are no or low barriers to entry and exit and when supernormal profits are being earned.

b Traditional theory of price and output states that the structure of a market and the behaviour of firms in that market are influenced principally by the number of firms in the industry. An industry containing a large number of firms is likely to be highly competitive, with firms being price takers, achieving allocative efficiency and making normal profits. Traditional theory suggests that the fewer the firms in an industry the more market power they will have, the more likely it is that there will be barriers to entry and exit and the more likely it is that the firms will enjoy supernormal profits and fail to achieve allocative efficiency.

The theory of contestable markets, in contrast, suggests that what is important in determining how firms behave is not the actual number of firms in an industry but the potential number of firms. For example, an industry may currently contain only a few firms but if there are barriers to entry and exit the firms are likely to behave in a competitive manner.

c A monopoly can also be a contestable market. There may be only one firm in a market but if there are no barriers to entry and exit, the firm may behave in a competitive way, keeping profits low and producing efficiently. However, if there are barriers to entry and exit then a monopoly will not be a contestable market and the monopolist will not behave in a competitive manner.

d The passage mentions the high costs of new firms entering a market. This is a reference to economies of scale as a barrier to entry. It also mentions sunk costs and brand loyalty. Other barriers to entry include legal barriers and concentration of raw materials. For example, the granting of a patent to a firm will protect it from competition from other firms for a given period. If the ownership of raw materials is concentrated in the hands of a few firms, it will make it difficult for other firms to compete on equal terms.

e The existence of supernormal profits will have the same effect in a perfectly contestable market as in a competitive market. New firms will be attracted into the industry by the existence of supernormal profits. With the absence of barriers to entry, they will be able to come into the industry. This will increase supply, lower price and return profits to the normal profit level.

f Although the UK telecommunications industry is becoming more competitive with the entry of some new firms, it is not a contestable market. While some firms have, indeed, entered the market, they have had to overcome barriers to entry which may have discouraged other firms from seeking to come into the market. The advanced technology and expensive capital equipment used in the telecommunications industry mean that there are considerable economies of scale. So new firms will start at a cost disadvantage compared to well-established firms. Another barrier to entry is brand loyalty. Existing firms have built up relationships with customers and advertise on a very large scale.

2 a In the context of the extract, excess profits mean supernormal profits, i.e. profits in excess of what is necessary to keep the firm in the industry. Monopolies are able to earn supernormal profits in the long run because the existence of barriers to entry prevents the entry of new firms into the industry.

b Monopolists are likely to seek to maximise profits. This will mean producing where MC = MR. This output is below the allocatively efficient output and is also likely to be below the output which would ensure minimum average costs. This is illustrated in the diagram below.

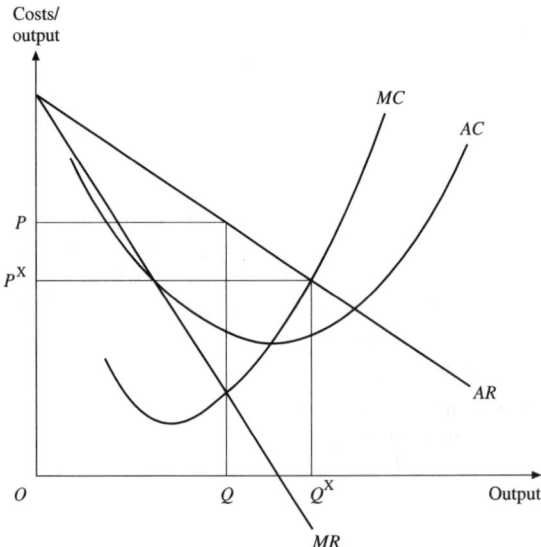

Fig. 4.7

The lack of competition means that monopolists can be inefficient and still survive in the market. They are not forced to lower costs for fear that their prices will be undercut by more efficient rival firms.

c Predatory pricing occurs when a firm sets a relatively low price, sometimes below production cost, with the intention of forcing rival firms out of the industry. Limit pricing occurs when a firm sets a low price with the intention of deterring the entry of new firms into the industry. So predatory pricing seeks to reduce existing competition, whereas limit pricing seeks to reduce potential competition.

d The extract mentions predatory pricing. Another example of anti-competitive behaviour is vertical price squeezing, where a firm which controls the supply of an input charges rival firms a high price to put them at a competitive disadvantage. Resale price maintenance is also a form of anti-competitive behaviour. This involves a firm insisting that retailers charge a set price for its goods. The intention is to ensure that there is a sufficient number of outlets so that no one outlet can dictate the amount they will pay to the firm for its goods.

e A natural monopoly occurs when one producer can produce a product at a lower average cost than any other number of firms. In this case the most efficient situation is to have one firm in the industry. There are two main reasons why a natural monopoly situation may exist. One is where economies of scale are very significant. In this situation an output which is as great or greater than the total market demand may need to be produced to take full advantage of economies of scale. The second reason is where the existence of more than one firm would involve a wasteful duplication of resources. For example, it would be disruptive and not a good use of resources to have different firms laying different series of gas pipelines to houses in the same area. So industries which involve national or local network systems with high fixed costs may efficiently sustain only one firm.

f A monopolist is likely to earn supernormal profits and so produce where P (AR) exceeds AC and MC. On the other hand, a perfectly competitive firm will produce, in the long run, where P (AR) equals AC and MC. So it might appear that a monopolist will charge a higher price than a perfectly competitive firm. The diagram below is often used to illustrate this view.

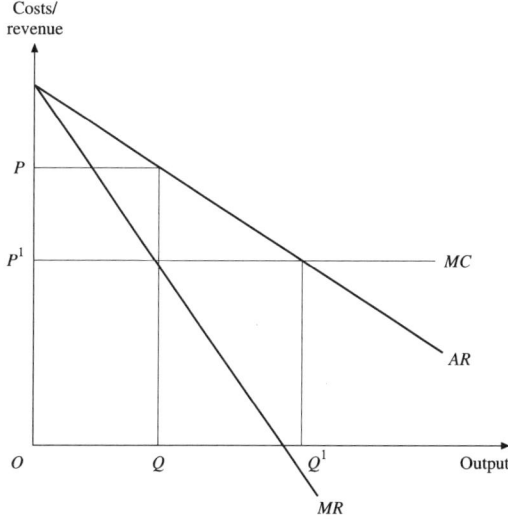

Fig. 4.8

The monopolist produces an output of OQ, charging a price of OP. Under conditions of perfect competition AR = MR. So output is OQ1 and price is OP1. However, this assumes that costs of production will be the same under perfect competition and monopoly, whereas it may be the case that in industries where economies of scale are significant, a monopolist may be able to produce at a much lower cost. Even when supernormal profits are added to that cost, the price may be lower than under conditions of perfect competition.

Answers to essay questions

1 a Normal profit is earned when average revenue equals average cost. Normal profit is included in costs of production and is the minimum needed to be earned by a firm for it to stay in the industry in the long run. It is equivalent to opportunity cost and transfer earnings. Supernormal profit is experienced when the profit level is above the normal profit level. In this case average revenue exceeds average cost. It is a bonus above what is needed to keep the firm in the industry in the long run. Under conditions of oligopoly and monopoly it is equivalent to economic rent as it can be earned in the long run. However, under conditions of perfect competition and monopolistic competition, it is equivalent to quasi-economic rent as it will exist only in the short run.

   b A firm producing under conditions of perfect competition may earn supernormal profit in the short run if there is a fall in the costs of production or an increase in demand. For example, a change in tastes may increase demand for the product. The diagram below shows the effect an increase in demand has on the industry.

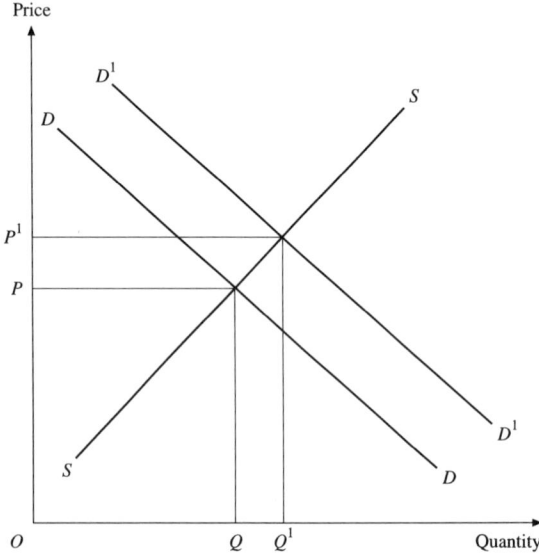

Fig. 4.9

The shift to the right in the demand curve raises price and causes an extension in supply. Each firm in the industry now faces a higher price and, in response, produces more. The diagram below shows the effect on an individual firm.

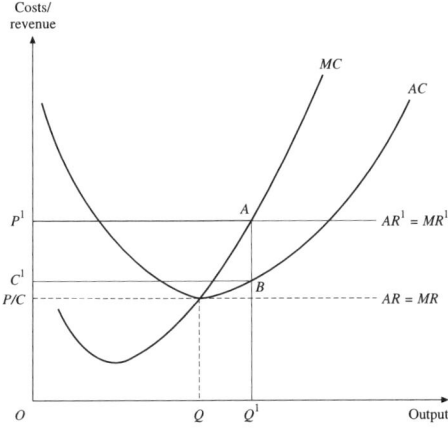

Fig. 4.10

The firm initially produced where MC = MR and where AC = AR and hence where it was experiencing normal profit. The increase in demand pushes price up to P1 and the firm now produces where MC = MR1. The firm experiences supernormal profit shown by the area P1ABC1. It is also no longer producing at the lowest point on the AC curve.

However, in the long run this supernormal profit will be competed away. The existence of perfect information attracts the attention of firms outside the industry to the supernormal profit being earned. The absence of barriers to entry permits the entry of new firms into the industry. This increases supply which, in turn, causes a fall in price as shown below.

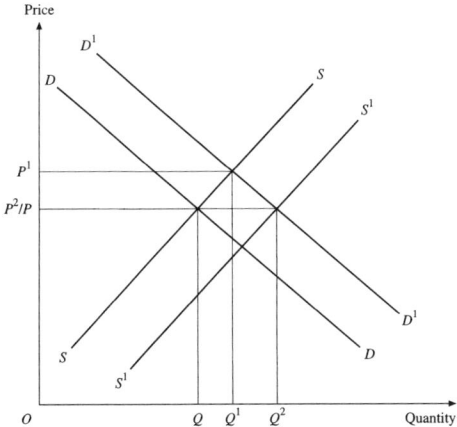

Fig. 4.11

New firms continue to enter the industry until the resulting rise in output lowers price to a point where normal profit is earned again. The diagram below shows the firm producing where MC = MR = AC = AR = P. This is its long-run equilibrium position. It is earning normal profit and producing at minimum average cost.

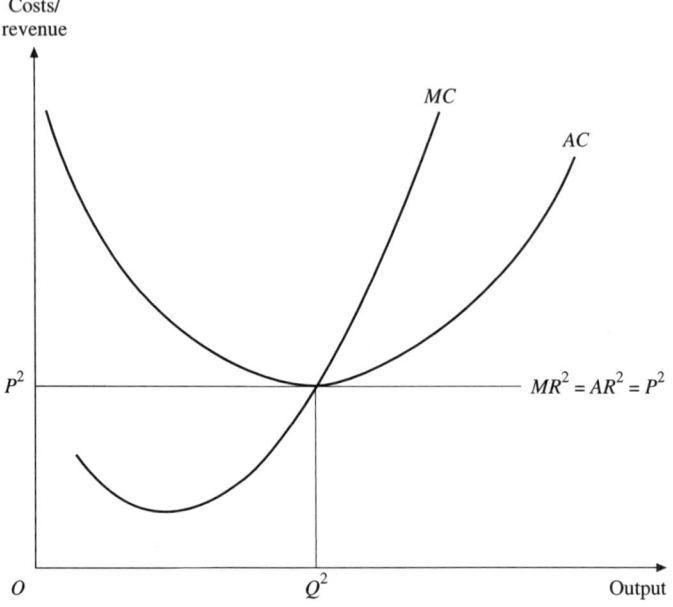

Costs/revenue

MC

AC

P^2

$MR^2 = AR^2 = P^2$

O

Q^2

Output

Fig. 4.12

c A perfectly competitive industry is in long-run equilibrium if market demand is equal to market supply. Any short-run changes in market conditions would have been fully adjusted to. For example, as in the case above, supply would have increased in response to an increase in demand. More resources would have been switched to the industry to reflect the change in consumer preferences. Each firm in the industry will be in long-run equilibrium earning normal profit. There will be no incentive for firms to enter or leave the industry.

2 a Oligopoly is a market structure in which the industry is dominated by a few large firms. There may be any number of firms in the industry but, for example, the largest four may account for 85 per cent of all the goods sold.
In oligopoly there are barriers to entry and exit, high technology may be important in the industry, supernormal profit may be earned in the long run, firms are very concerned about the behaviour of their rivals and non-price competition is often a significant feature. Examples of oligopolistic industries are commercial banking, the car industry and the pharmaceutical industry.

b i A firm's market share is threatened by both rival firms inside the industry and by potential rival firms outside the industry. Although there are barriers to entry into oligopolistic markets, firms outside may seek to overcome these. So, to maintain their market share, oligopolistic firms may engage in limit pricing. This involves setting price below the maximum profit level in order to discourage the entry of new firms. When new firms enter an industry they may initially have higher average costs because their output is not high enough for them to take full advantage of economies of scale. So while existing firms may be able to earn supernormal but not maximum profit at a certain limit price, potential new firms might not be able to cover their average costs.

Firms are also likely to be keen to maintain other barriers to entry, e.g. keeping advertising expenditure high to reinforce brand loyalty and add to the high start-up costs any new firms would face.

An oligopolistic firm may also try to maintain its market share by 'playing safe' and keeping its price stable. The firm may fear that if it raises its price, its rivals will not follow suit and so it will lose a large number of its customers, whereas if it lowers its price, its rivals may cut their prices so it would gain only a little, if any, extra custom. Each customer would also be paying a lower price. This 'price trap' is illustrated by the kinked demand curve.

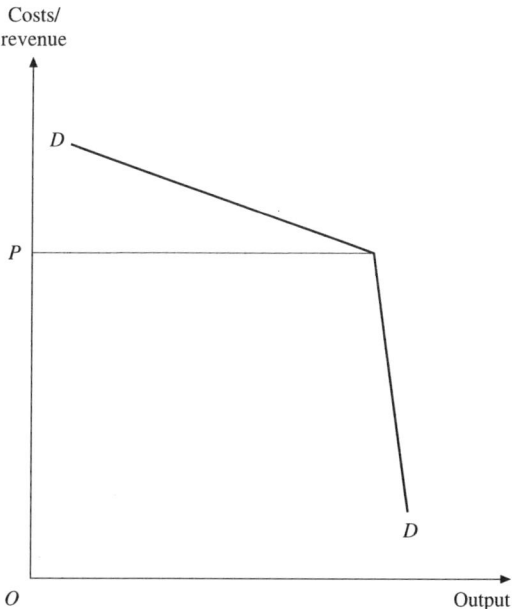

Fig. 4.13

Raising the price level above P will cause a significant fall in demand. Above P demand is relatively elastic so a rise in price will cause a fall in revenue. On the other hand, lowering the price below

P would cause only a relatively small expansion in demand. Below P demand is relatively inelastic and a fall in price will cause a fall in total revenue. Oligopolistic firms will also seek to respond to any initiatives introduced by rival firms, which they think will reduce their market share. For example, if a rival firm brings out a new, enlarged bar of chocolate, the other firms are likely to do the same.

Under conditions of oligopoly firms may seek to maintain market share by colluding. This may be in the form of tacit collusion, with firms following a price leader, or open collusion. The latter is more likely if certain conditions are met, e.g. there is only a small number of dominant firms, there is a willingness to share information, there are similar costs of production, and the existence of significant barriers to entry.

b   ii   To increase market share a firm may decide to lower its price. This is a high risk strategy as it may provoke a price war. A firm may be prepared to engage in a price war if it believes it will win. If it is more efficient than other firms, if it has higher retained profits or if it can cross subsidise, it may be able to keep its prices low and wait for other firms to go out of business. In the mid 1990s *The Sun* and *The Times* took on rival newspapers in a price war. They did succeed in increasing their market share in the tabloid and quality press markets respectively.

A more common way of increasing market share is by engaging in non-price competition. A number of methods may be used in an attempt to attract more custom. For example, newspapers run competitions and exclusive stories in the hope of gaining new readers. Firms selling breakfast cereals include coupons and free gifts to make their products more appealing. Supermarkets run loss leaders, some offer loyalty cards, some provide free home delivery and some provide extra facilities such as restaurants and toilets. Pepsi and Coca-Cola make strong use of their brand names and brand images. In addition to their brand names, chocolate manufacturers make use of distinctive packaging.

A major form of non-price competition is advertising. Informative advertising provides consumers with information and persuasive advertising seeks to encourage people to buy the product by creating a favourable image of the product. Large amounts are spent by oligopolistic firms to reinforce brand loyalty among existing customers and to attract new customers.

Answers to short questions

1 Public goods are non-excludable. This means that it is not possible to charge directly for them. People can act as free riders. So they have to be financed by taxation. Another defining characteristic is that a public good is non-rival. One person consuming the good does not reduce the ability of other people to consume it. Public goods also often have zero marginal cost.

Defence is an example of a public good. It is not possible to exclude those not willing to pay from enjoying the benefits of defence and one person being defended does not reduce another person's level of defence. In contrast, a private good is one for which it is possible to exclude people who do not pay from consuming it and one which is rival with one person's consumption reduces the quantity of the good that is available to other people. For example, bread is a private good. If a person wants bread but is not prepared to pay for it, a baker will refuse to give the person bread. In addition, if one person buys a particular loaf, for example, no other customer can buy that particular loaf. In practice, most goods are private goods and can be sold through the market with a price attached to them.

2 Education is a private and not a public good. Any educational establishment, if it wished, could exclude those not willing to pay from studying the courses on offer. Having an extra student in a class may also reduce the time a teacher can spend on, for example, marking each student's work. Education can be, and indeed is, sold through the market. Parents pay to send their children to so-called 'public' schools and people pay to attend evening classes. However, in the UK the state does provide free education to children from five to 18. This is because the state regards education to be a special type of private good, i.e. a merit good. If education were provided entirely through the market, the state believes it would be underconsumed. People may not fully appreciate the benefits of education for themselves, their children and society, may take a short-term view and may lack relevant information.

3 Social costs from people smoking include both private and external costs of cigarette consumption. The private cost of people smoking is the price they pay for the cigarettes. The external costs, which may also be called negative externalities, include air pollution, litter, the use of NHS resources in treating smoke-related illnesses, including those caused by passive smoking, and lost output because of people being away from work with smoking-related complaints.

4 The optimum level of pollution is that at which the marginal social cost of pollution reduction equals the marginal social cost of pollution. This means that the private and external costs of reducing pollution equal the benefit society gains from the reduction in pollution. This is unlikely to be zero. The following diagram illustrates why this is so.

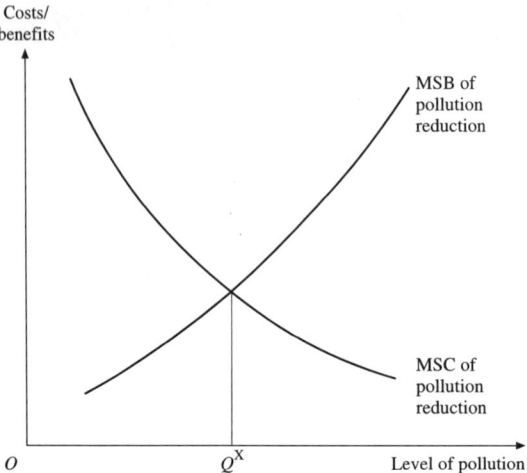

Fig. 5.4

To obtain a zero level of pollution a high number of resources would have to be devoted to pollution reduction, which could have been put to alternative uses. The marginal cost of pollution reduction would exceed the marginal social benefit society would gain.

5 An increase in tax on tobacco would, in effect, raise the cost of producing cigarettes. It would shift the supply curve to the left, which, in turn, would cause price to rise and demand to contract. If the increase in tax is an increase in excise duty, it will be a parallel shift in the supply curve as illustrated below.

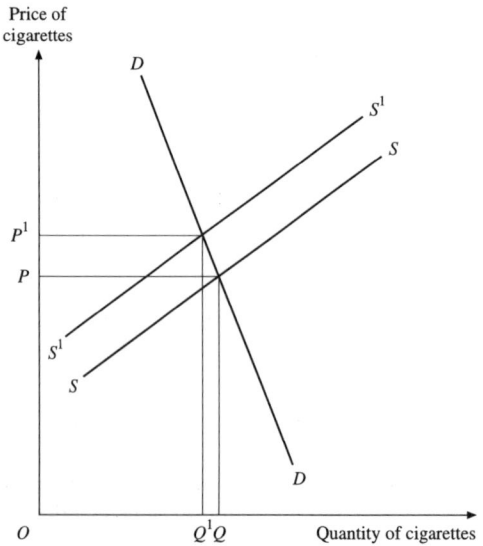

Fig. 5.5

Demand for cigarettes is inelastic as there are no close substitutes and they are addictive. So the resulting rise in price will mean that expenditure on cigarettes will rise. The government will receive more revenue with consumers bearing the main burden of the tax. A socially efficient tax on cigarettes would equal the external cost of cigarettes, thereby turning them from an external to a private cost.

6   One example of a positive external benefit of consumption is inoculation. If one person becomes inoculated against disease, other people benefit because it reduces their chances of catching the disease.
The training of workers by one firm will benefit society by improving labour productivity and output. It will also benefit other firms if they can attract trained workers to work for them.

7   A buffer stock seeks to reduce price fluctuations. The operators set upper and lower price limits and intervene in the market if the price threatens to go outside the limits. The operators will buy the good if the market price is falling below the lower limit. They will stockpile the good and draw from the stockpile to sell the good if the price is going above the upper limit.

8   It is debatable whether mergers between banks and building societies are in the public interest. They may enable greater advantage to be taken of economies of scale which are becoming more significant in an industry where greater use is being made of advanced technology. If profits are increased, the new firms may provide more services and spend money on researching and developing new techniques and services. Consumers may be faced with lower prices. However, the mergers may reduce the number of financial outlets in a town. If the new institutions are banks, they will be public limited companies as opposed to mutual societies and so shareholders will have to be paid dividends, money which could have been used to benefit customers in the form of lower interest charges to borrowers and higher interest payments to savers. The new larger firms may experience diseconomies of scale. They may also restrict output and raise price.

9   Giving people the ownership of, for example, the air in their town, the views from their houses or the ocean would mean that those who seek to damage such things would have to compensate the owners or could be sued by them. This would mean that externalities would be internalised. Indeed, externalities arise because property rights are not fully allocated.

10   Privatisation is the transfer of assets from the public to the private sector. Privatisation provides revenue for the government when it takes place. The government receives the money from, for example, selling a previously nationalised industry. A privatised company may also be forced to be more efficient as if it does not produce a good which people want, it will go out of business. It will not be 'propped up' by the government. The firms will also be freed from state control which may mean that they can make decisions more quickly.
However, in the longer term a government may lose revenue if profitable

assets are sold off as the government will lose future profits. Private sector firms base their decisions on private costs and benefits. They will not take into account externalities. There is also the risk that private sector firms will not operate efficiently. They may have monopoly power and may restrict output below, and raise price above, the allocatively efficient output.

Answers to multiple choice questions

1   Answer **D**
A demerit good is one which the government regards as harmful for people, e.g. cigarettes. The government will seek to discourage or ban its consumption. Answer **A** describes a public good.

2   Answer **A**
A tax on a good causes its supply to decrease. The new supply schedule can be calculated using the old supply schedule to see how much would be supplied at the market price minus the tax. For example, selling the good for £10 would mean that the firm would now receive £10 − £3 = £7. So the firm will now supply at £10 what it had previously supplied at £7, i.e. 600. The demand schedule and the new supply schedule are:

Price	QD	QS
10	20	600
9	60	400
8	150	150
7	260	50

So now demand and supply are equal at £8. The initial equilibrium price was £6, so price will rise by £2.

3   Answer **C**
The amount of the tax is found from the distance between the two supply curves at the point where the tax is imposed. In this case it is £5. The new quantity sold is 50 so the total tax raised is 5 × £50 = £250. Of this £2 × 50 = £100 is borne by the consumers in the form of a higher price and £3 × 50 = £150 is borne by the producers in lower post-tax revenue.

4   Answer **C**
A subsidy shifts the supply curve to the right. If it is a specific subsidy, the supply curve will make a parallel shift. **A** shows an *ad valorem* tax, **B** a specific tax and **D** an *ad valorem* subsidy.

5   Answer **A**
If a firm produces where price exceeds marginal cost, allocative efficiency is not achieved. Economic welfare would be increased by more resources being devoted to the output of the good and price being lower.

B   This is necessary to maintain firms in the industry in the short run.

C   This is normal profit output achieved in the long run under conditions of perfect competition and monopolistic competition.

D   This will result in an efficient allocation of resources.

6   Answer **C**
A private cost is one which goes through the market and which is paid by a party directly involved. The land will be purchased by the firm which will own or rent out the factory. It will pay a price for the land. **A**, **B** and **D** are all external costs (negative externalities) borne by third parties who are not financially compensated.

7   Answer **C**
A socially efficient tax is one which fully internalises external costs and which ensures that consumption is at the optimum level.

8   Answer **D**
Street lighting is a public good because it is not possible to exclude those who are not willing to pay directly for it from benefiting from the light. Also, one person's enjoyment of the light from a street light does not reduce someone else's light. The service is non-rival.

9   Answer **A**
The allocatively efficient output is where P = MC. In this case it is an output of OQ3, giving a price of OP3. However, to maximise profits the firm will produce where MC = MR, i.e. an output of OQ, and charge a price of OP.

10   Answer **D**
In a cost benefit analysis all costs and benefits are taken into account, both private and external, i.e. social costs and benefits.

Answers to data response questions

1   **a**   The Office of Fair Trading carries out initial investigations into alleged uncompetitive practices. It operates in three main areas: checking on competition policy, consumer credit and consumer affairs. The Monopolies and Mergers Commission investigates current and proposed mergers referred to them to check that they are acting in the public interest.

   b   Anti-monopoly legislation may have a detrimental effect on the economy in circumstances where the benefits of monopoly exceed the costs. For example, natural monopolies may be able to take full advantage of economies of scale and may avoid wasteful duplication. Monopolies may also engage in research and development in the knowledge that any extra profits they earn can be protected by the barriers to entry into the industry. Because they operate on a large scale and can take advantage of economies of scale, monopolies may be able to compete more effectively than non-monopoly firms with overseas competitors.

c   i   Restraints to competition are any restrictions which prevent firms competing on equal terms. For example, barriers to entry reduce the ability of new firms to compete with existing firms. Price fixing and collusion may reduce competition among existing firms.

c   ii Cartels are organisations of producers who, while producing separately, sell through a central agency, for example OPEC (the Organisation of Petroleum Exporting Countries). The aim of a cartel is to increase members' profits by raising prices. Supply is restricted by the use of quotas.

d   Competition between firms brings a number of benefits. If consumers have a range of producers to choose from, each one will have to seek to produce the products which consumers want in an efficient way. Prices may be driven down to the lowest viable level. The search to attract extra customers may also raise quality and availability. Firms will be sensitive to changes in consumer demand, seeking to devote resources to the goods which are in high demand.

e   A government can promote competition in a number of ways. It can seek to prevent existing monopolies and oligopolies from abusing their market power. For example, OFLOT monitors the behaviour of the National Lottery and can influence prices. The government can also investigate proposed mergers to assess whether the newly created firms will act in the public interest and/or outlaw restrictive practices such as cartels and tacit collusion.

2 a i   The government (or local authority) could charge drivers to enter cities by placing tolls on roads into cities. However, the way currently being tested is to fit an electronic device into cars, which registers not only when the cars enter a city but also the time they enter. This enables differential pricing to be used. The city of Cambridge experimented with a system where local cars, according to their number plates, could enter the city free on certain days of the week and be charged on the other days. The government could also use area licensing which involves charging drivers for permits which have to be displayed by cars which are being driven in certain areas.

a ii   The government (or local authority) can ban cars from using certain roads, e.g. those in town centres. It can also ban cars from using certain lanes, e.g. bus lanes. It may also restrict access by removing parking rights, limiting the parking time and introducing traffic-calming schemes.

b   The use of cars for short journeys may cause a number of external costs. The extract refers to pollution and this comes principally in the form of air and noise pollution. It also mentions congestion which will affect people's mental and physical health and reduce working hours. In addition, high volumes of cars can disfigure and damage buildings. Car travel also results in accidents which cause distress and place a burden on the NHS and emergency services.

c   Carrot measures, in this case, are measures which seek to encourage people not to use cars, particularly in cities, by making alternative forms of transport more attractive, e.g. subsidising rail transport, bus transport and/or park and ride schemes. The stick measures are those which penalise the use of car travel, e.g. reducing parking spaces in city centres, charging more for parking in city centres, increasing the price of petrol, and road charging.

d   The extract refers to the need to double cycle use but does not discuss the main means by which this may be achieved, i.e. the widespread introduction of cycle lanes. One of the main reasons why people do not cycle is fear of accidents caused by cars which are driven too close, drivers who cut in front of cyclists and/or who fail to notice cyclists. Another reason why cyclists do not like cycling among cars is the air pollution they experience.
Another measure not mentioned in the extract is taxing non-residential parking. This should discourage the use of cars by people driving to and from work instead of using public transport.

e   The last sentence is referring to the need to reduce the volume of car traffic in cities without reducing the level of economic activity. Restricting car use without providing attractive alternative forms of transport may reduce shopping in cities and may cause companies to move out of cities. In both cases employment and income levels would fall.
Reducing bus fares and improving the service, including reliability, for example, should reduce traffic congestion and maintain the level of economic activity. It may even increase it if, as a result of reduced congestion, people enjoy leisure activities and working in cities more. Companies may also be encouraged to open new plants in cities where costs have been reduced by lower congestion.

Answers to essay questions

1 a i   There are private and external costs of both consumption and production. Private costs are costs which go through the market and which have a price attached to them. They are incurred by those who buy products and who produce products. For example, the private cost of buying a ghetto blaster is the price paid for it. External costs (which may also be referred to as negative externalities) are costs which are borne by third parties, i.e. those not directly involved in the consumption or production of the product. People may be adversely affected by the purchasers of ghetto blasters playing them in public areas. They will suffer from noise pollution. Private costs plus external costs equal social costs which are the full costs to society of the consumption or production of a product.

   a ii   There are private and external benefits, again, of both consumption and production. Private benefits are the benefits enjoyed directly by those who consume a product or directly by those who produce a product. These benefits go through the market and have a price attached to them. For example, the private benefit a bus company derives from operating a service into a city centre is the ticket revenue it gains. External benefits (which may also be referred to as positive externalities) are beneficial side effects. They are enjoyed by those not directly involved in the production or consumption of the product. Those travelling into a city centre by bus create benefits for others by reducing congestion, pollution and accidents. Private benefits plus external benefits equal social benefits which are the full benefits a society derives from the consumption or production of a product.

b i There are a number of policies which a government may use to reduce external costs, including imposing taxes, imposing regulations, selling licences, giving people property rights and providing information.

A tax can be placed on the production or consumption of goods which generate negative externalities. This has the advantage of internalising the externalities so that price and output decisions reflect the full costs and are borne by those directly involved. The revenue raised could be used to compensate third parties who suffer harmful effects. However, in practice it is difficult to place a monetary value on the external costs so the tax may be too high or too low. The tax may be regressive, falling more heavily on the poor and may have an inflationary impact on the economy.

A government may also impose regulations, e.g. about the 'acceptable' level of noise in a residual area, the age at which people may smoke and the amount of waste a firm may emit into a river. Regulations are not particularly popular. However, they are more popular than taxes. While regulations should reduce external costs, they may be difficult and expensive to enforce. There is also the problem that it is difficult to calculate what level of external costs should be permitted. For example, how loud should a party held at 2 a.m. be allowed to be and at what age should people be allowed to smoke. Regulations also fail to provide an incentive to reduce external costs below the legally acceptable level.

Expanding on the idea of regulations, a government could set permitted levels of negative externalities arising from production and then issue or sell licences, e.g. permitting firms to pollute up to these levels. This method allows a government to set precise levels for external costs and may generate revenue if the licences are sold. It may, for example, also encourage firms to reduce their pollution below the set amount so that they can sell their licence. However, this would merely redistribute the source of the external cost and not reduce its overall level. Again, it may be difficult and expensive to monitor this system and those who suffer the external costs may not be compensated.

Another possible policy approach is to extend property rights.

People can protect what they own. For example, if someone damages your car, they or their insurance company have to pay for it to be repaired. However, when people do not have clearly defined property rights they cannot prevent others from imposing costs on them. Indeed, externalities occur because property rights are not fully allocated. For example, people do not own the air so an individual cannot prevent a firm from polluting the atmosphere near their home. If they were given ownership of the air around their home, they could stop the firm polluting or charge the firm for polluting. The first would prevent negative externalities and the second would internalise them. While extending property rights has considerable potential, it also has practical problems. When there are many people involved, it would be difficult to get agreement about what would be an acceptable solution to all. In some cases it may be difficult to determine who are the victims and who are the culprits. Linked to this is the problem of deciding whether minor inconveniences should be taken into account. Also, while giving people the right to sue those who create externalities, the cost of litigation means that the rich will be more able to exercise the right than the poor.

The government can also inform, or force producers to inform, people about the external costs created. For example, cigarette producers are required to include a government health warning on packets of cigarettes and the government also runs anti-smoking campaigns itself. Providing information allows consumers to make more informed choices based on social rather than private costs. However, if it is the government which provides the information, at least some of the cost will be borne by third parties. People may also respond to the information in different ways. For example, some people no longer notice the government health warning on cigarette packets and some may actually be encouraged to smoke more because of the 'danger element'.

b   ii   A government may seek to increase external benefits by subsidising output or consumption, providing the good free, passing legislation and providing information.

Subsidising the consumption or production of a good which generates external benefits will increase its output and thereby the external benefits. For example, in the following diagram, if left to market forces, consumers would buy OQ output at a price of OP. At this level of consumption no external benefits are created.

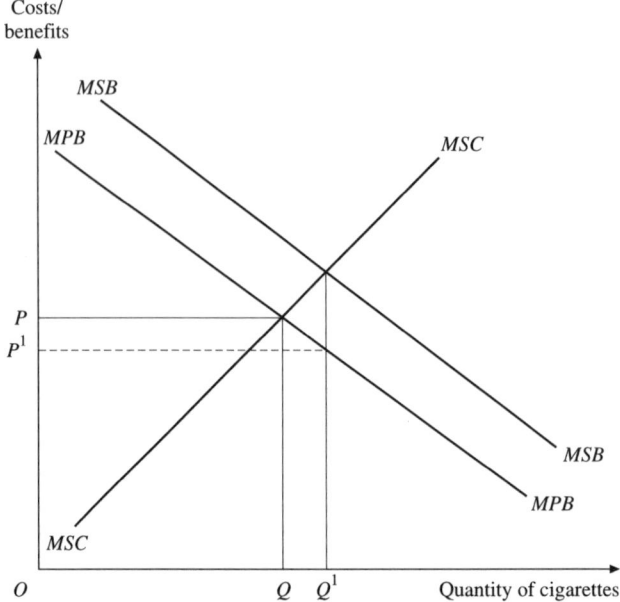

Fig. 5.6

To achieve the socially optimum output, consumers would need to buy the output where MSB = MSC, i.e. OQ1. To encourage them to do this the government would have to subsidise the good by PP1 per unit.

A government can also provide goods free to consumers at the point of sale. In the UK merit goods, such as most forms of health care, are provided free and are financed out of taxation. This encourages people to seek medical treatment which provides benefits not just to them but also to others in the form of a higher volume and quality of output.

Subsidising goods to a partial or full extent obviously involves government expenditure and the government has to try to assess the extent of the external benefits. As with external costs, this is not easy to do.

A government may also use legislation to promote external benefits. For example, in the UK car drivers have to use seat belts and parents have to send their children to school from the ages of five to 16. These measures require government expenditure to monitor and enforce them. They are based on the assumption that government officials are more capable of judging social benefit than consumers. The government could also provide information to the public about the external benefits that certain goods provide. For example, the UK government finances advertisements about the benefits of parents having their children inoculated against certain contagious diseases. This approach again involves government expenditure and it is difficult to predict how effective it is.

2 a A smoke detector is a merit good, i.e. a good which is underconsumed in a market system. There are a number of reasons why people may buy fewer smoke detectors than is economically efficient. They may not be fully informed about the benefits of installing a smoke detector. They may be prepared to take the risk of not having one in the mistaken belief that a fire could not occur in their home. The decision as to whether to buy a smoke detector is also likely to be based on private and not social benefits. Individuals decide whether the feeling of greater safety they will gain from a smoke detector is worth the price they will have to pay. They are also unlikely to consider the benefits that others will gain from their purchases. The external benefits which may occur include reduced risk of fires spreading to neighbouring homes, reduced home insurance premiums and reduced emergency service costs.

b There are a number of measures a government may employ in an attempt to increase the consumption and production of domestic smoke detectors, including setting a maximum price, providing a subsidy and cutting income tax.

To have any effect a maximum price would have to be set below the equilibrium price. One set above it would leave producers free to set the market clearing price.

However, while causing an extension in demand, a maximum price set below the equilibrium will also cause a contraction in supply. This is shown in the diagram below.

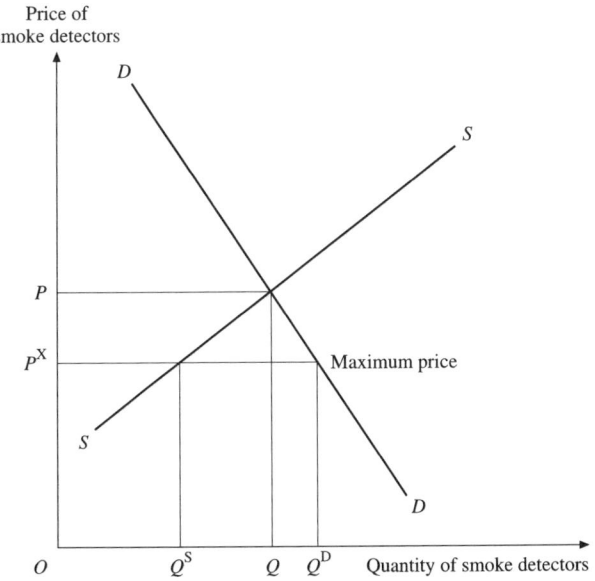

Fig. 5.7

Quantity demanded now exceeds quantity supplied, leading to a shortage. The quantity actually traded falls from OQ to OQS. So while setting a maximum price encourages people to buy more smoke detectors, it discourages producers from supplying them.

Providing a subsidy to producers will increase supply. This, in turn, will cause price to fall and demand to expand. How much of the subsidy will be passed on to the consumer will depend principally on the elasticity of demand. The more inelastic demand is, the more of the subsidy consumers will receive.

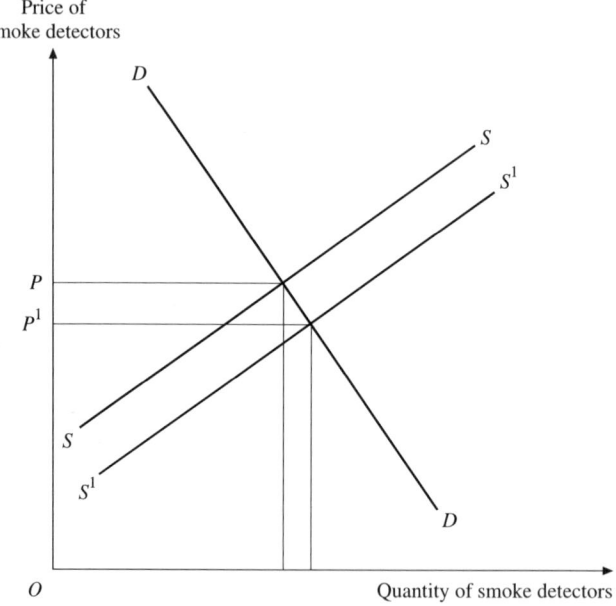

Fig. 5.8

Smoke detectors do not have close substitutes and are not particularly price sensitive so the greater impact may be on price rather than on quantity. Nevertheless, this measure does result in a rise in the quantity of smoke detectors traded.

Cutting income tax increases people's disposable income. This rise in their purchasing power may result in an increase in demand for smoke detectors, a rise in their price and an extension in the quantity supplied. However, the increase in demand is likely to be very small. Smoke detectors are normal goods but the extra disposable income may be spent on a wide range of goods. Indeed, the policy is a rather crude and indiscriminate one. Income tax may have to be reduced by a considerable amount to have only a small impact on the market for smoke detectors.

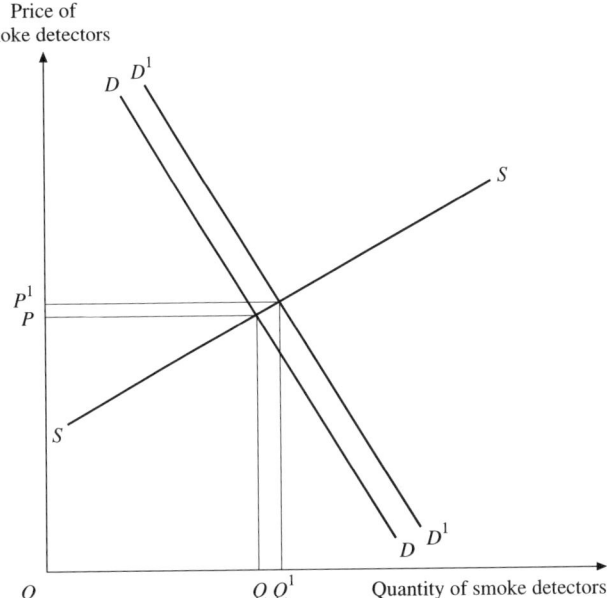

Fig. 5.9

The most effective of the three policies is likely to be subsidising the producers. This involves the use of government expenditure which has an opportunity cost. However, it directly increases the output of smoke detectors and the quantity traded, while cutting income tax will be likely to have a negligible effect on the quantity traded and setting a maximum price will actually reduce the quantity traded.

c   Two alternative government policies are legislation and providing information. The government could pass a law requiring all homes, or perhaps all new homes, to have smoke detectors fitted. This would increase demand, raise price and cause supply to extend.
A government-funded advertising campaign, explaining the advantages of having smoke detectors fitted, would also increase demand. However, it will be likely to have a smaller and less certain impact on demand than legislation.

Answers to short questions

1   The four factors of production (inputs) are land, labour, capital and the entrepreneur. The rewards are, in turn, rent, wages, interest and profit.

2   The marginal revenue productivity (MRP) of any factor of production is determined by the marginal physical product of the factor of production and the marginal revenue received from the sale of the product produced. The more productive a factor is and the more the product produced can be sold for, the higher MRP will be.

3   An economist regards normal profit as one of the costs of production. It is the reward which the entrepreneur has to earn to stay in the industry in the long run. It is earned where total revenue equals total cost, and hence average revenue equals average cost, whereas an accountant does not include normal profit in costs of production. To an accountant all forms of profit are earned where total revenue exceeds total cost.

4   Profit rewards those who bear the uncertain risks of production. Profit also encourages innovation, signals the need for expansion and provides the finance for expansion.

5   a   A firm introducing a profit-sharing scheme for its workers may increase the workers' motivation. This would, in turn, increase the workers' productivity and reduce costs of production.
    b   Lower costs may also be achieved by the reduction in labour turnover which may result from the introduction of a profit-sharing scheme. Encouraging workers to stay with the firm will reduce costs of recruitment and training.

6   Profit differs from wages, rent and interest in four key ways. It is residual, it is not known in advance, it may be negative and it may fluctuate more than the other rewards.

7   Supernormal profit is profit in excess of what is needed to keep a firm in the industry. It is a form of economic rent in the case of monopoly and oligopoly as barriers to entry mean that it can be earned in the long run. However, supernormal profit is a form of quasi-economic rent under conditions of perfect competition and monopolistic competition. This is because while it can exist in the short run it will be competed away in the long run by the entry of new firms.

8   Economic rent can be negative in monetary terms. A person may like a job so much that they are prepared to accept lower wages for it than they might earn in a less attractive job. They will be earning less than their transfer earnings and so, in effect, experience negative economic rent.

9   All of a factor of production's earnings will consist of transfer earnings when the supply of the factor of production is perfectly elastic. In this case the factor of production is being paid the minimum necessary for it to stay in its present line of employment. Any fall in earnings will cause the factor

of production to leave its current employment and transfer to alternative employment.

10   Premier league football players' pay is likely to consist of a higher proportion of economic rent than the pay of barristers. This is because the gap between their current pay and what they could earn in their next best paid job is likely to be greater than in the case of barristers. A few premier football players may be able to earn high pay in alternative occupations, e.g. as television commentators, football managers or entrepreneurs, but some who have low qualifications and few alternative skills may not be able to gain highly paid alternative employment. In contrast, barristers are highly qualified and are likely to be able to gain well-paid alternative occupations.

Answers to multiple choice questions

1   Answer **C**
Marginal physical product is the change in output which results from employing one more unit of a factor of production.

2   Answer **D**
To minimise the cost of production a firm should equate the marginal physical product of each input divided by its price. If a greater addition to output is achieved by employing an input which costs an equal amount or less than another input, it should be substituted for that other input.

3   Answer **B**
The return from labour and land exceeds that of capital and so more labour and land should be employed and less capital.

$$\frac{\text{MP of labour}}{\text{P of labour}} = \frac{\text{MP of land}}{\text{P of land}} > \frac{\text{MP of capital}}{\text{P of capital}}$$

$$\frac{15}{3} = \frac{10}{2} > \frac{18}{6}$$

$$5 = 5 > 3$$

4   Answer **D**
Normal profit is included in the costs of production as the return to the entrepreneur and hence is earned where $AC = AR$.

5   Answer **C**
Supernormal profits can be earned in the long run under conditions of monopoly and oligopoly because the entry of new firms to compete away these high profits can be prevented by the existence of barriers to entry.

6   Answer **A**
Dividends are the proportion of profits paid to shareholders.

7   Answer **A**
When a factor of production is in perfectly inelastic supply, all of its earnings will consist of economic rent.

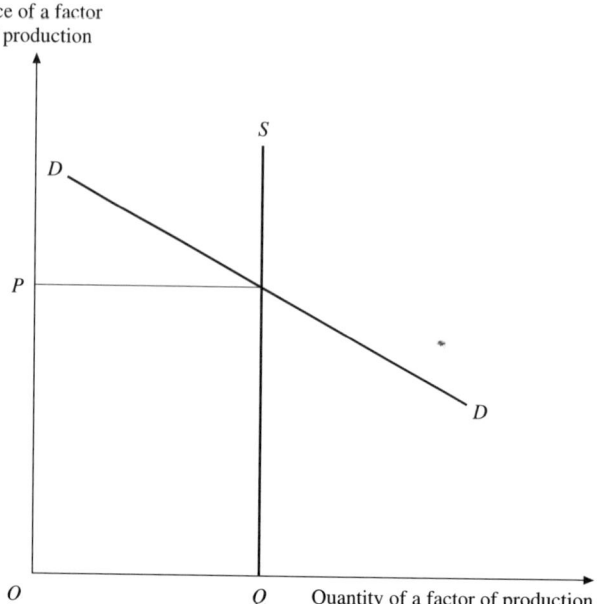

Fig. 6.2

For example, a certain quantity of land in a remote area may have only one possible use, e.g. for sheep farming. It would be used for this purpose whether the earnings are high or low.

8   Answer D

Transfer earnings are the amount a factor of production could earn in its next best paid occupation. Hence it is the minimum which must be paid to keep the factor of production in its present occupation. Answer **B** is a description of transfer payments.

9   Answer B

Economic rent is represented by the area above the supply curve and below the price line. On the other hand, transfer earnings are represented by the area below the supply curve. The change in supply from S1 to S2 shows supply becoming more inelastic, raising the area above the supply curve and reducing the area below it.

10   Answer D

Quasi-economic rent is short-term economic rent. For example, a firm may buy a specialised form of machinery. If it does not have alternative uses, all its earnings will be quasi-economic rent and none will be transfer earnings. However, in the long run the machine will only be replaced if it can earn at least enough to cover its costs. In other words, the earnings from the machine must be high enough to prevent the transfer of the machine out of its present use.

Answers to data response questions

1 a Camelot's profits were high in absolute terms. In its first full year of operation its profits were £77 million. However, its profits as a percentage of its sales were relatively small at less than 1 per cent.

b Monopoly profits are supernormal profits earned in an industry where firms have absolute, or at least a degree, of monopoly power and there are barriers to entry into the industry. In such an industry a firm can earn a profit level above that needed to keep it in the industry, i.e. above the normal profit level. New firms cannot enter easily and so the firms can continue to produce where total revenue exceeds total cost. The diagram below shows a firm earning monopoly (supernormal) profit.

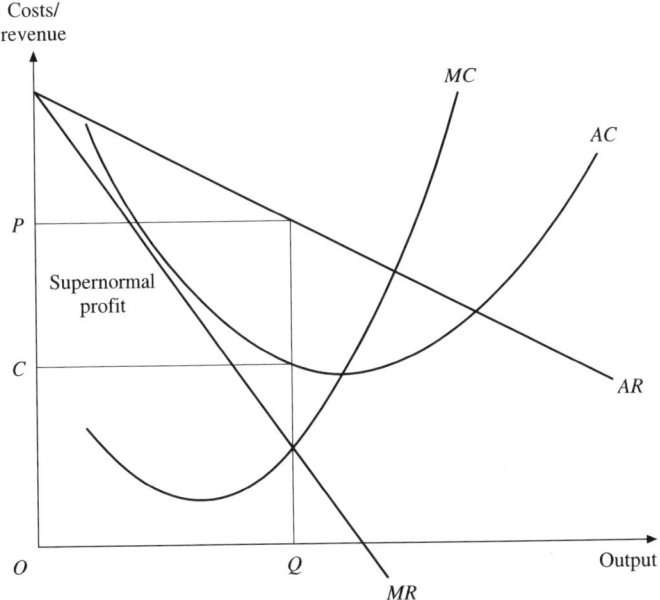

Fig. 6.3

c Camelot's first-year profits may have been higher than predicted because the level of demand had been underestimated and/or because the costs of running the operation were lower than anticipated.
Analysts may have failed to appreciate how popular the lottery would be. People who have not previously gambled now buy lottery tickets and some who have undertaken other forms of gambling, e.g. the football pools, have switched to the lottery. Buying a lottery ticket is a straightforward process and does not have a social stigma attached to it. The high prize money is attractive, holding out the opportunity to transform people's lives – albeit a remote possibility. The televising of the draw acts as a very effective form of advertising. The costs of installing and operating the lottery may also have been overestimated. While, initially,

there were some technical problems and some problems with fraud, these were soon sorted out. It was also decided to set a limit on the amount to be paid out in the case of a high number of ticket holders having three or four of the numbers drawn out.

d The extract suggests that Camelot has a moral obligation to give more money to charity. It advances three main arguments in support of this view. One is that, as a company started at a time when companies are expected to show concern for the wider community, it should set an example in giving a significant amount to charity.

The second is that while Camelot had to compete with other companies to gain the right to run the lottery, it has no competition in the operation of the lottery. Its monopoly position in a market with a high level of demand gives it the opportunity to earn high supernormal profit. This enables it to donate a large amount to charity and, by doing so, it may offset criticism of its high profits.

The last argument is that the prime reason for government support of the lottery is that it is a way of raising money for the arts, sport and good causes, so it would be in keeping for Camelot to give a sizeable proportion of its profits to charity.

e It is debatable whether Camelot's high profits have been justifiable. Profit is the reward for bearing uncertain risks. However, running the lottery has been compared to being given a licence to print money. Camelot has a monopoly position, free advertising and a market with a high demand.

On the other hand, Camelot argues that its high profits reflect its efficiency. It claims that it is maximising funds for good causes and that it is meeting a clear market demand. While it does not have a direct competitor, it does have indirect competitors in the form of the football pools, horse racing and other forms of gambling. The high profits may also enable it to improve the service to the consumer, e.g. by licensing more outlets to sell lottery tickets and by producing a range of related products such as scratch cards.

2 a 'Gross trading profits' are profits of companies before corporation tax has been deducted. These are profits expressed in terms of constant prices. This means that the figures have been adjusted by taking out the effects of inflation.

b

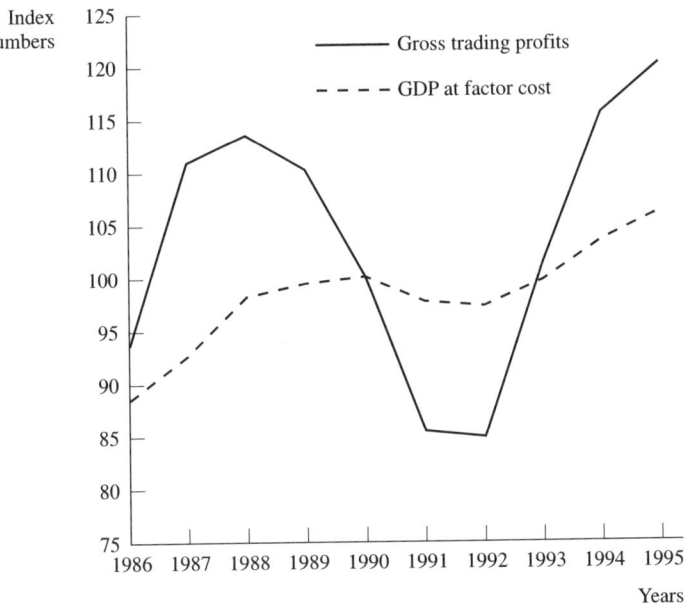

Fig. 6.4

For most of the period there was a direct relationship between gross trading profits and GDP. From 1986 to 1988 both rose. They moved in different directions in 1989 and 1990 when profits fell and GDP rose, albeit much more slowly than before. In 1991 and 1992 both fell and from 1993 to 1995 both rose. Both profit and GDP finished the period at a higher level than at the start. The graph illustrates how much more volatile profits were in the period. Profits rose by a greater percentage at the start of the period, fell by more in the middle and reached a higher peak at the end.

c The relationship found is one that economic theory would predict. When profits are rising, firms will be likely to want, and be able, to expand output. Also, when GDP is rising, sales will be rising and profits will be increasing. When GDP is falling, firms are likely to suffer falling profits. They may also cut profit margins in order to keep prices relatively low and thereby at least maintain sales volume.

Economic theory also suggests that profits can be very volatile. Profits can rise to very high levels and can be negative.

d

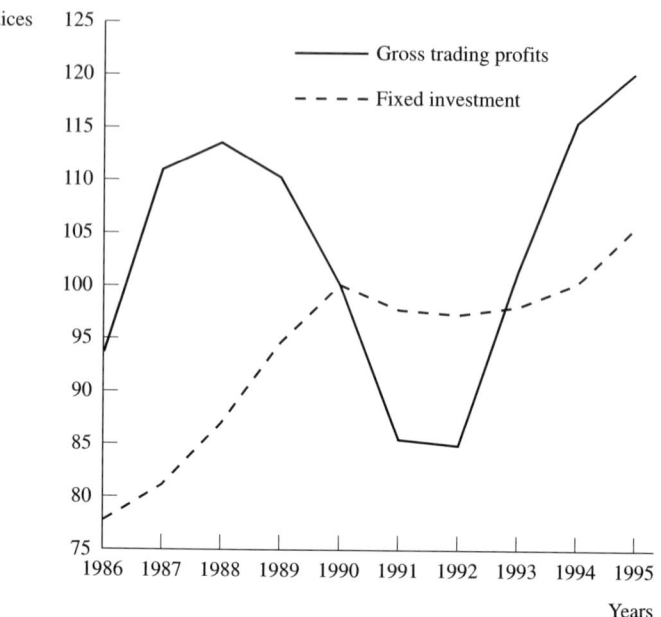

Fig. 6.5

Between 1987 and 1988 both profits and investment rose. However, between 1989 and 1991 profits fell while investment continued to rise. In 1992 both profits and investment fell and between 1993 and 1995 both profits and investment rose. For most of the period there was a direct relationship between profits and investment. At the start of the period, when there was a consumer boom, profit levels were high. For example, in 1988 profits were 13.5 per cent higher than in 1990. Investment was below the 1990 level but it was increasing. As the economy entered recession, profits fell first, followed by a fall in investment.

e A direct relationship would be expected between profits and investment. When profits are high, demand is likely to be high, so firms will want to increase output, so they will purchase additional machinery and plant. In addition to encouraging investment, high profits provide the finance to undertake the investment. Indeed, retained profits are the main source of investment finance. As suggested by the period 1990 to 1992, there may have been a time lag between changes in profits and investment. Profit levels may fall but if firms believe this is only temporary, they may continue to increase investment.

Answers to essay questions

1 **a** The marginal revenue product (MRP) of a factor of production is the amount added to a firm's revenue as a result of the firm employing one more unit of a variable factor of production. It is marginal physical product multiplied by marginal revenue.

A firm will employ a factor of production up to the point where its MRP equals the marginal cost of employing the factor. As more of a factor of production is employed, MRP is likely to rise at first. However, after a certain point is reached it is likely to fall. Marginal product (MP) begins to decline when diminishing returns set in. Marginal revenue (MR) will also fall if the firm is producing under conditions of imperfect competition.

The demand curve for a factor of production is based on its MRP. The diagram below shows that, at a payment of P, a firm will employ OQ quantity of the factor of production. A fall in the payment to the factor of production to OP1 would cause an extension in demand for the factor of production to OP1.

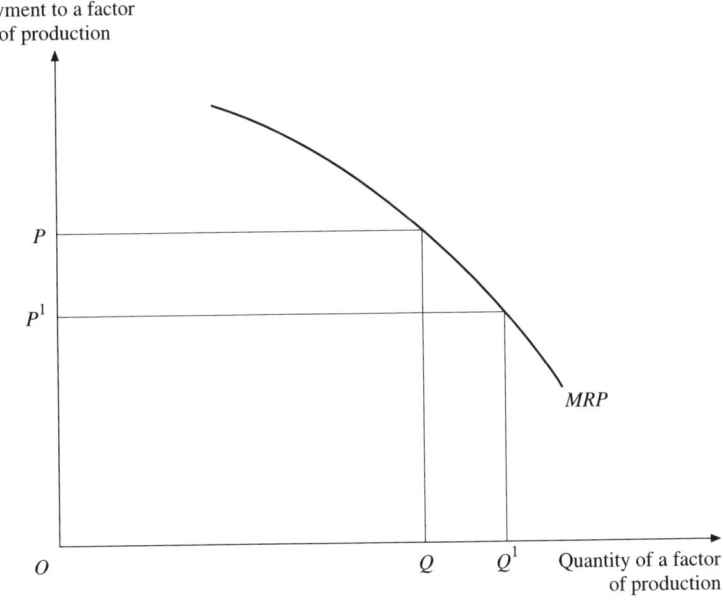

Fig. 6.6

  b The MRP of an area of farmland would increase if there is either an increase in its marginal productivity or in the price of the good it produces and hence its MR. For example, a period of good weather may increase the productivity of an area of farmland and increase the quantity and quality of the crop grown on it or the livestock raised on it. Leaving land fallow can also raise its productivity when it is brought back into use. An increase in demand for the crop or the meat from the livestock raised on the farmland will increase its price and the land's MRP.

A higher output and/or a higher financial return per unit produced will increase any factor of production's MRP. Its MRP curve (and hence its demand curve) will shift to the right and the payment received by the factor of production will increase as shown in the diagram below.

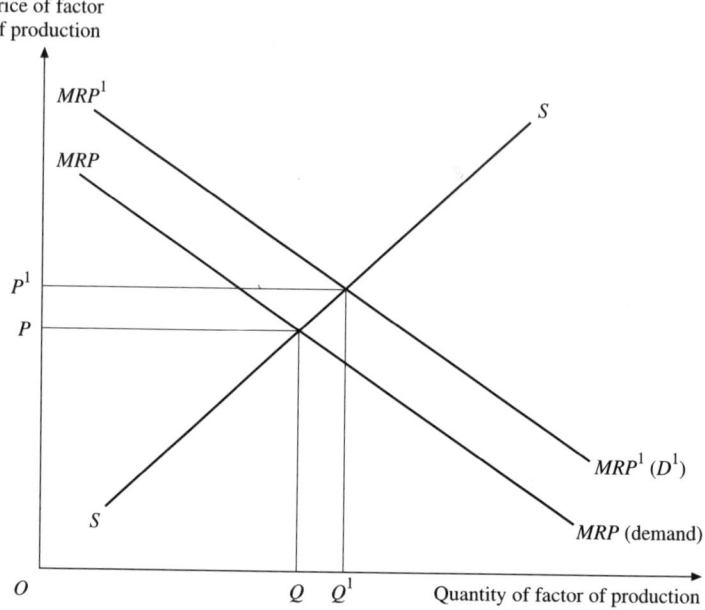

Fig. 6.7

c An area of land is geographically immobile. However, it may be occupationally mobile and the extent to which it is will influence the amount of economic rent it receives. The fewer the possible alternative uses an area of land has, the higher the proportion of its earning will be economic rent. Indeed, if the land has only one use, it will be in perfectly inelastic supply and all its earnings will be economic rent.

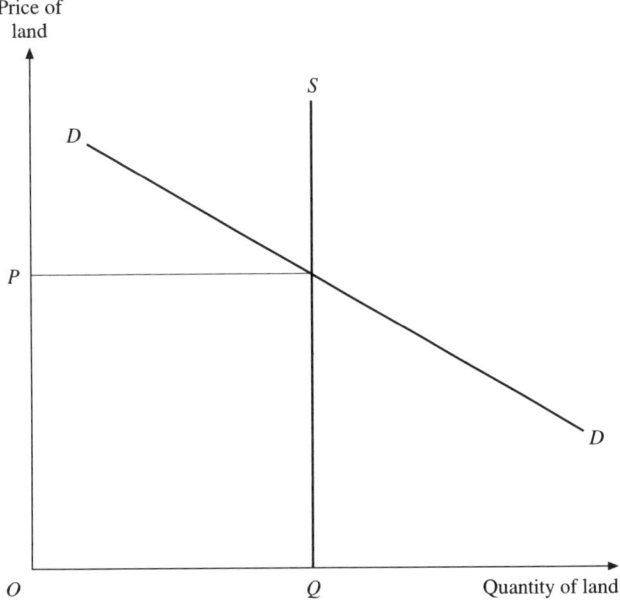

Price of land

Fig. 6.8

However, the more alternative uses an area of land has, especially if they pay similar amounts, the more elastic its supply will be in any particular use and the smaller the proportion of its earnings will be economic rent. For example, currently an area of land may be earning £10 000 per week by being rented out as a leisure park. It could earn £8000 from being rented out as farmland and £4000 from being rented out as sports fields to a company. In this case the land's economic rent would be £2000 as this is the gap between its current earnings and what it could earn in its next best paid occupation. Its transfer earnings are £8000. If payment from being used as a leisure park falls below £8000, its use will be transferred to that of farmland.

Land in the centre of cities will be in high demand, with many possible competing uses, e.g. use for houses, offices, clubs and cinemas. Its price will be high and its economic rent low.

2 a The payment to a factor of production (input) may consist of both economic rent and transfer earnings.

Economic rent is a surplus, an amount paid above what is necessary to keep a factor of production in its current employment. Transfer earnings are the minimum necessary to keep a factor of production in its current use and are equivalent to what a factor of production can earn in its next best paid occupation.

For example, a person may currently be working as an accountant earning £50 000 per annum. If their next best paid occupation would be as a manager of a small firm earning £42 000, their economic rent would be £8000 and their transfer earnings £42 000. From this it can be appreciated that transfer earnings are equivalent to opportunity cost. What the person is giving up by being an accountant is the opportunity to work as a manager and earn £42 000. Economic rent is represented on a diagram by the area (VWX) above the supply curve and below the price, whereas transfer earnings are shown by the area (OVXQ) below the supply curve.

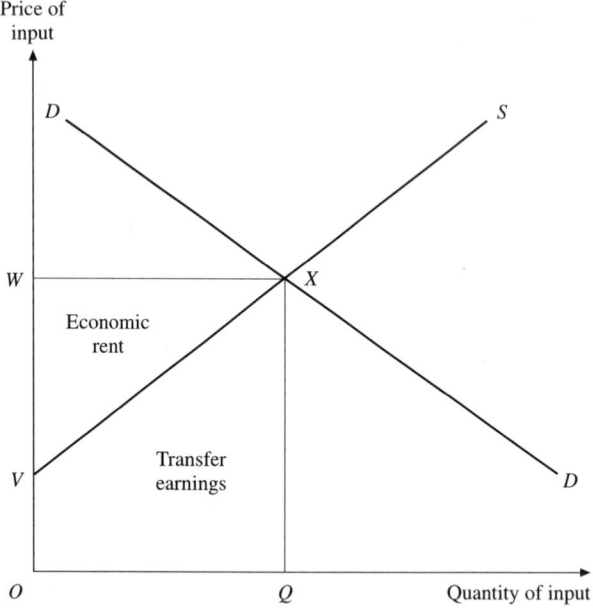

Fig. 6.9

The diagram may represent the market for a group of workers. All the workers receive a wage of OW. The last worker employed receives no economic rent. They are willing to work for OW but no less. On the other hand, the first workers employed would have worked for a lower wage and hence some of their wage is economic rent.

What proportion of an input's earnings consists of economic rent and what proportion consists of transfer earnings depends significantly on the elasticity of supply of the input. The more elastic supply is, the higher the proportion of the payment will be transfer earnings. Economic rent is more significant when supply is inelastic.

In practice it may be difficult to estimate economic rent accurately as it may be difficult to determine what is an input's next best paid occupation.

b   All factors of production can earn economic rent. As mentioned above, labour can receive economic rent. Those people who offer services which are highly specialised and in high demand, e.g. top snooker players, are likely to earn economic rent. Capital can earn economic rent. The earnings of specialised machinery, for example, may consist largely of economic rent, at least in the short run. Land can also earn economic rent. Indeed, if it has only one use, all of its earnings will consist of economic rent. Highly skilled entrepreneurs are likely to be in high demand and enjoy economic rent.

Any input may earn economic rent provided supply is not perfectly elastic. Given some degree of inelasticity of supply, an increase in demand for a factor of production will raise its price and some units of the input will receive a payment above their supply price.

c Two main arguments are advanced for taxing economic rent. One is that a tax on economic rent is, in effect, a neutral tax. It will not affect the allocation of resources. Factors of production will stay in their current employment provided their post-tax income is above their transfer earnings, e.g. if an opera singer is earning £2000 a week and could earn £600 a week in their next best paid occupation. If her economic rent of £1400 is taxed at 50 per cent, she will remain as an opera singer.

The other argument is that at least some of the economic rent may have been generated by government expenditure. For example, a highly paid worker may have benefited from higher education with at least her tuition fees having been paid by the government. An area of land may enjoy economic rent because government expenditure on infrastructure raises its earnings. A piece of machinery may have increased earning potential because of government spending on research and development. However, in practice it may be difficult to determine how much economic rent has resulted from government expenditure. It may also be difficult to calculate a factor of production's economic rent. If an over-estimate is made, the allocation of resources will be affected, possibly reducing economic welfare.

Answers to short questions

1 The factors which determine the aggregate supply of labour include the size of the total population, the age composition of the population, the school leaving and retirement ages, the working week and holidays, pay and social attitudes. The number of hours of work which are offered will be higher the larger the total population is, the more people there are of working age, the lower the school leaving age and the higher the retirement age, the longer the working week, the shorter the holidays and the more acceptable it is for married women to work.

2 There are a number of reasons why more women, particularly married women, have entered the workforce in recent years. The increase in part-time employment, the expansion of the tertiary sector and the reduction in gender discrimination have increased employment opportunities for women. More women have wanted to take up these opportunities because of rises in women's wages, increased material expectations, rising educational attainments, the invention of labour-saving household appliances and changes in social attitudes.

3 An increase in wages will not result in a firm's total wage bill if the number of workers the firm employs is reduced. Total output can be maintained or even increased if labour productivity rises. So fewer workers being paid higher wages can result in output and total labour costs remaining unchanged.

4 Firms often pay rates for overtime work which exceed standard rates because the supply of people willing to work overtime is lower than those willing to work standard hours. So a higher rate has to be paid to encourage workers to work overtime. Paying higher overtime rates is often more cost effective to a firm than recruiting more workers. This is because it saves on recruitment costs, it is flexible, as overtime can be adapted to changes in demand for the product, and it can be used to compensate for low standard wages.

5 The main three arguments a trade union can advance in support of a pay claim for its members are productivity, comparability and cost of living. If workers have increased their productivity, firms' profits are likely to have risen. So it might be argued that firms are able to pay their workers more and that the workers deserve to be paid more. The comparability (or differential) argument is that the workers' pay needs to be kept in line with that of workers in other firms in the industry or in related occupations. So if, for example, workers in the fire service get a pay rise, workers in the police service may press for a wage rise. The cost of living argument relates to the distinction between nominal and real wages. Unless nominal wages are raised in line with inflation, real wages will fall.

6 Trade unions may affect the wages of non-unionised labour in one of two different ways. If trade unions secure a pay rise for their members, firms employing non-unionised labour may give their workers a pay rise in order to dissuade them from moving to higher-paying firms. However, firms may seek to discourage their workers from joining trade unions by paying non-unionised labour more.

7   The major form of labour market discrimination not covered by legislation is age discrimination. This can also be referred to as 'ageism' and can take a number of different forms in the labour market. It can involve not hiring older workers, not training older workers and making older workers redundant ahead of younger workers. Age discrimination is inefficient. The best workers are not employed and so labour costs are higher than necessary and the labour force is unbalanced, with a lack of experience.

8   A person may take into account a wide range of factors when choosing a job, e.g. job security, danger, status, promotion prospects, working hours, holidays, qualifications and skills needed.

9   The increase in the resources devoted to training teachers is likely to result in an increase in demand for teacher trainers. This will increase the wages of teacher trainers and cause an extension in supply as shown in the diagram below.

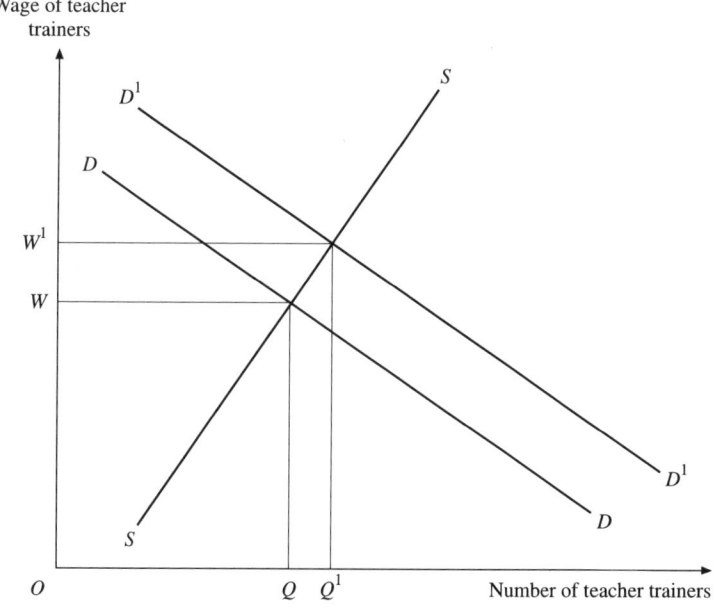

Fig. 7.5

10   The trend away from national to local pay determination is reducing the power of trade unions and increasing regional wage differentials. This is because local bargaining reduces the role of national negotiators. Wages are also more likely to rise, or rise by a greater amount, in more prosperous areas where demand for products is likely to be higher and where the com-

petition for workers is likely to be greater than in less prosperous areas. In the latter firms are likely to be able to recruit labour at relatively low wages.

Answers to multiple choice questions

1   Answer **C**
If demand for the final product becomes more inelastic, a rise in price will cause a smaller percentage change in demand. So if workers get a pay rise, causing costs and price to increase, demand will not fall significantly and so output and employment will not be reduced by much.

A, **B** and **D** would all cause demand for labour to become more elastic. A rise in wages will cause a greater percentage fall in demand for labour if it is easier to replace those workers with machines or previously unemployed workers, or if wages form a higher percentage of total costs.

2   Answer **C**
The marginal cost of employing the twenty-first worker is the change in total labour costs. When 20 workers are employed the total labour costs are $20 \times £510 = £10\,200$. When 21 workers are employed total labour costs rise to $21 \times £530 = £11\,130$. So the marginal cost of employing the twenty-first worker is $£11\,130 - £10\,200 = £930$.

3   Answer **A**
Real wages are money (nominal) wages adjusted for inflation. If money wages rise by, say, 5 per cent and the price level rises by 7 per cent, real wages will fall. Workers will have lower purchasing power.

4   Answer **B**
The diagram shows a backward-sloping supply curve for labour. When the wage rate rises above W the number of hours worked contracts. Workers decide to 'buy' more leisure and so work fewer hours.

5   Answer **C**
The higher the qualifications required to undertake a job the more inelastic supply of labour will be. A rise in wages will cause a smaller percentage extension in supply as there will not be many people with the qualifications needed to do the job.

A   The elasticity of supply of the final product will be influenced by the elasticity of supply of a specific type of labour rather than vice versa.

B and **D** This would affect the elasticity of demand for labour rather than supply.

6   Answer **D**
The wage rate equals MRP. When 2000 labour hours per day are employed, marginal physical product is 3. As the firm is operating under conditions of perfect competition, price equals marginal revenue. So MR is £5. MRP = MR $\times$ MP, i.e. $£5 \times 3 = £15$. So the wage rate will equal £15.

7 Answer **B**
Demand for labour (MRP) will increase if marginal physical product increases *or* if marginal revenue increases. A rise in the price of the final product will raise marginal revenue.

   A   will cause a contraction in demand for labour.

   C   will cause a decrease in demand for labour and hence a shift to the left of the demand for labour curve.

   D   will cause a rise in the wage rate and a contraction in demand.

8 Answer **B**
Diminishing marginal productivity sets in when total output rises more slowly as a variable quantity of labour is combined with a fixed quantity of capital.

9 Answer **A**
A monopsonistic employer will employ workers up to the point where the marginal cost of labour equals marginal revenue product. The wage rate paid to this quantity of labour is found from the supply of labour (average cost) curve.

10 Answer **C**
Men in sales occupations earned 55.2 per cent more than women working in the same industry. The gender differential is higher than in any of the other occupations shown. The other occupations which come closest are receptionists, telephonists and related occupations with a 54.5 per cent gender differential.

   A   £289.45 is the average of the earnings of men and women working in the printing and related trades. However, it cannot be concluded that it is the average of the industry as the proportion of male and female workers is not known.

   B   There is no information on what proportion of the earnings was accounted for by the wage rate and what proportion by overtime.

   D   The data show only gross earnings, so it is not possible to conclude that women paid a higher percentage of their earnings in income tax than men. Indeed, it is more likely that women paid a smaller percentage as they earned less and income tax is a progressive tax.

Answers to data response questions

1 a There is no one clear definition of labour flexibility. However, as the extract suggests, it is alternative forms of employment to full-time, permanent employment, e.g. part-time employment and flexitime working.

   b A more flexible labour force may enable a firm to adjust the quantity and quality of output quickly. If demand increases, a firm will want to increase output. This will be easier if existing workers are prepared to work extra hours and more workers can be recruited at little cost.

Similarly, if demand falls, the firm will want to reduce output, reduce workers' hours and shed labour quickly and at little cost. If demand switches from one product to another, firms will want their workers to be prepared, and able, to use different skills. In addition, the more flexible workers are in terms of when, where and how they are prepared to work, the greater is a firm's power to alter its production cheaply and quickly.

c   Some who work part-time choose to do so because the hours fit in with their other commitments. For example, those with young children may seek to work in term time only and between the hours of, say, 9.30 a.m. and 3 p.m. Students fit in their part-time work around their studies, frequently working in the evenings and at weekends.

As well as there being a demand by potential workers for part-time work, there is also a supply of part-time work. In recent years the supply of part-time employment has increased while full-time employment has fallen. From 1981 to 1994 the share of all employees who were part time rose from 21 per cent to 28 per cent.

Some of those working part time are doing so because they are unable to find full-time jobs. In some cases they are undertaking two part-time jobs.

d   Working on a part-time basis means, in most cases, lower earnings. In 1995 the average hourly pay of all part-time employees on adult rates in Great Britain was £5.56 which was 67 per cent of full-time hourly pay. And, of course, by definition, part-timers work fewer hours than full timers. Working on a part-time and particularly on a temporary basis may make it difficult for a worker to get a mortgage on a house from a bank or building society, or to plan ahead.

Part-time and temporary workers may also receive less training than their full-time fellow workers. Employers tend to concentrate their training initiatives on full-time staff. Receiving less training means that part-time and temporary workers' pay, promotion chances and job satisfaction are likely to be less than that of full timers.

e   Two other forms of market flexibility are functional flexibility and flexibility of location. The first refers to workers' ability to switch between different tasks. For example, in 1994 London Zoo retrained its keepers so that they became capable of looking after a variety of species. This was designed to improve the organisation's ability to cover employee absence, to adapt to changing needs and to reduce staffing. Again, if bakers and the shop assistants in a bakery are prepared to switch roles, it becomes easier to cope with fluctuations in the workload.

Flexibility of location refers to the ability and willingness of people to work in locations other than the conventional office or factory. For example, improvements in communications and technology have increased the number of people who work from home, particularly for part of the week. Flexibility of location has the potential to reduce a firm's overheads quite considerably.

In addition to functional flexibility and flexibility of location, there is also numerical flexibility. This refers to a firm's ability to alter the number of workers it employs to match demand.

2 a Two other measures are the number of stoppages and the number of workers involved. The first indicates the number of separate disputes and the second gives an indication of the support that the disputes have.

b Trade union membership fell over the period shown. The overall fall was 1.68 million or 18.75 per cent. The fall per year was:

Year	Fall in trade union membership	
	(millions)	(%)
1990	0.11	1.23
1991	0.22	2.49
1992	0.64	7.42
1993	0.18	2.23
1994	0.26	3.33
1995	0.27	3.58

The largest fall was in 1992 during the recession. There are a number of reasons why trade union membership fell during the period. One is the high level of unemployment. People who lose their jobs do not usually retain membership of a union. Another is the reduction in the power of trade unions. Workers are less likely to belong to a union if they believe the union is unable to provide them with significant benefits. They have also been discouraged by employers from joining trade unions. In some cases employers have given preference to non-union workers in terms of pay and promotion.

c The number of working days lost fell from 1989 to 1992, rose from 1992 to 1993, fell in 1994 and rose in 1995. Unemployment, as a percentage, fell in 1990, rose from then until 1993 and then fell in 1994 and 1995. In three of the six years working days lost moved in the same direction and in three of the years they moved in the opposite direction. However, while the number of working days lost was, on average, very low during the period, unemployment was high.

d The findings in c are that while there is not a clear relationship on a year-to-year basis, over the whole period a low number of working days lost is associated with a high rate of unemployment. The latter relationship is the one which economic theory would lead one to expect. When unemployment is high there are fewer workers to take industrial action. However, perhaps more significantly, when unemployment is high workers may feel insecure in their jobs and so be more reluctant to engage in industrial action. In addition, when unemployment is high, economic activity is likely to be low. So profits will be low and there will not be much surplus over which unions and employers can bargain. On the other hand, when unemployment is low workers will have stronger bargaining power and be less afraid of being replaced by non-union labour if they strike, so an indirect relationship would be expected.

e   There are a number of factors which influence the number of working
days lost in any one year. One is inflation. When inflation is high, unions
have to press for wage rises merely to maintain real wages. This may
bring them into conflict with employers.
Another is the size of the firm and the strength of communications within the firm. Strikes are more likely to occur in large firms with top-heavy
bureaucracy and slow and poor channels of communication. In a smaller
firm workers may have more day-to-day close contact with managers
and problems may be solved more quickly at the shop floor level.
A third factor is the method of payment. Piece rate payment is more likely to give rise to strikes than time rates. This is because of the problems
and disputes which may arise over measuring output and because of the
uncertainty which payment by results schemes create.

Answers to essay questions

1   a   The period of training required to become a worker at McDonald's is
already short. This, combined with the lack of qualifications needed,
means that the number of people able to enter this particular labour
market is high. Indeed the number of people seeking work at
McDonald's exceeds the number of jobs on offer which means that the
wage rate is low. The supply of workers is elastic; an increase in the
wage rate would cause a greater percentage rise in the number of people
seeking employment at McDonald's. The demand is also relatively elastic as retailing is a labour intensive industry with wages forming a relatively large percentage of total costs.
A reduction in the period of training would increase the supply of potential workers. This, in turn, would cause a reduction in the wage rate and
an extension in demand as shown in the diagram below.

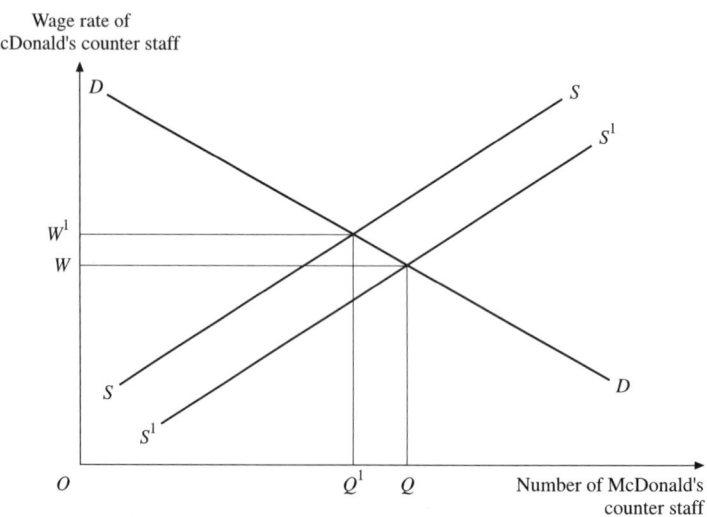

Fig. 7.6

In the longer run the reduction in the period of training may reduce the marginal revenue productivity of workers, which will cause the demand to fall. In turn, this will lower the wage rate.

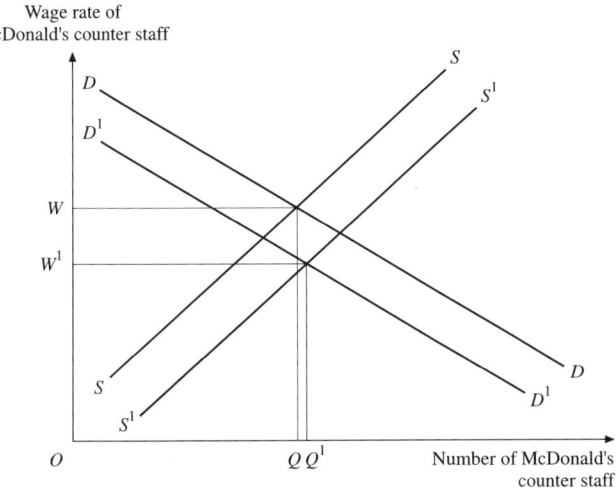

Fig. 7.7

b An increase in vegetarianism will reduce demand for meat products. Demand for counter staff at McDonald's is derived demand. Although McDonald's does sell some vegetarian products, it is associated particularly with beefburgers. If McDonald's loses custom it will employ fewer workers. Demand for counter staff will decrease, the wage rate will fall and supply will contract as shown below.

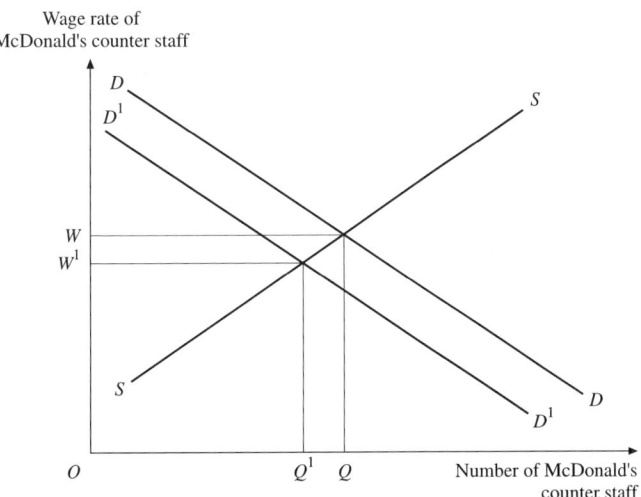

Fig. 7.8

c If Wimpy's raise their wage rate this may encourage some of McDonald's employees to seek jobs at Wimpy's. The extent to which this occurs will depend on the difference between the wages paid by the two companies and also by non-wage features. If Wimpy's originally paid less and, even after the wage rise, still pay less, there may be little movement. Employees may also fail to transfer to Wimpy's if the non-monetary advantages of working at McDonald's outweigh any extra pay that Wimpy's offer. These non-monetary advantages may include shorter working hours, better working conditions and longer holidays. However, if working conditions are similar at the two companies and the increase in the wage rate offered by Wimpy's means that Wimpy's are paying more, the supply of labour to McDonald's will decrease. This will raise the wage rate and cause a contraction in demand.

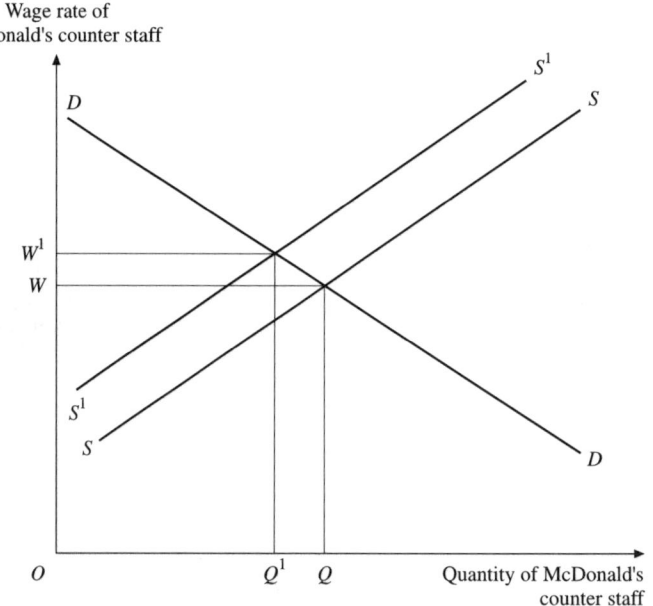

Fig. 7.9

d A decrease in unemployment, if accompanied by a rise in employment, may make it difficult for McDonald's to attract staff. A number of people work at McDonald's because they cannot find alternative employment. The work that McDonald's offer has become associated with low-skilled and low-paid employment. Indeed, the term 'McDonald's jobs' is used to describe employment which requires few skills, is often temporary and/or part-time and is low paid. So if it becomes possible to find better paid employment, the supply of labour to McDonald's will decrease.

Lower unemployment may also result in a rise in incomes and hence an increase in demand for normal goods, including food served at McDonald's. This, in turn, may result in a rise in demand for staff. The decrease in supply and increase in demand for McDonald's counter staff will raise the wage rate.

Fig. 7.10

The effect on the number employed will depend on which effect is greater – the decrease in supply or the increase in demand.

2 a The three main sources of income are earned income, unearned income and transfer payments. Earned income is received by labour in return for work undertaken. It consists of wages paid to employees and the wages the self-employed pay themselves. Unearned income is investment income, i.e. dividends, rent and interest. Transfer payments are welfare payments. They are received from the government not in return for a good or service. Examples include job seekers' allowance and state pensions.

b The main reason why stable grooms receive low pay is because the supply of stable grooms is high relative to demand. Many young people would like a job with horses and a number of people are willing to work as stable grooms in return for the opportunity to train as a jockey. Those who do not make it as jockeys may finish their careers working as stable grooms. Supply is also high and elastic because few qualifications are needed to become a stable groom.

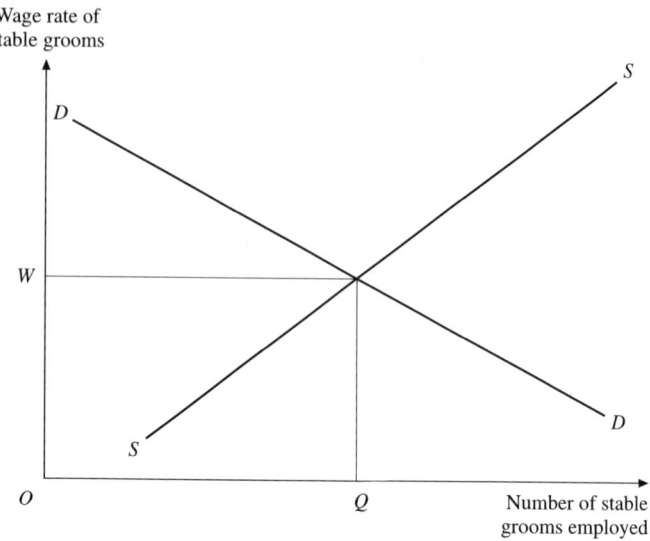

Fig. 7.11

Stable grooms tend to be either relatively young or old. Both age groups tend to receive low pay. The young may have limited experience and training and those nearing retirement may be occupationally and geographically immobile.

Discrimination may be another factor. This may come in the form of age, gender or social background. As mentioned above, stable grooms are often relatively young or old. Some employers have preconceived ideas about the young and old and, on this basis, pay these workers wages below their MRP. For example, some employers believe that the young are unreliable, lack basic social skills and are lazy. In contrast, some employers think that older workers are less adaptable, slow to learn new skills and prone to sickness and illness.

Many stable grooms are female and industries which have a high proportion of female employees tend to be relatively low paid. Some degree of gender discrimination may enter into this. Despite equal pay and opportunities legislation, some employers still base their wage policies on the belief that women are less productive than men. The following diagram shows how labour discrimination reduces the pay and working opportunities of female workers.

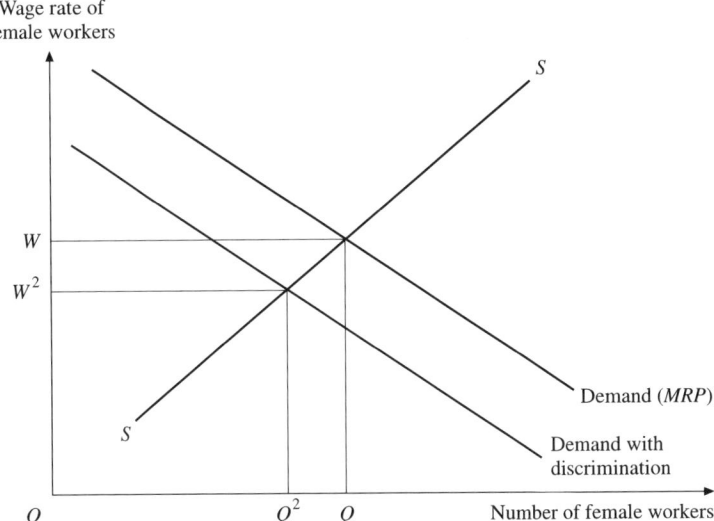

Fig. 7.12

The job of stable groom is not held in particularly high regard by society and this may influence the wage claims made and the wages offered by employers.

Stable grooms also tend to have limited bargaining power. Many are not in a union, they are not concentrated in one area and can be replaced by people outside the industry, including some who would be prepared to work for nothing for free rides.

Stable grooms take into account non-monetary advantages. They may not switch to a better paid job because of their attachment to the horses they look after.

c   The introduction of a national minimum wage, if set above that experienced by the low paid, including stable grooms, may raise the living standards of at least some of the low paid. Indeed one of the main arguments advanced in favour of a national minimum wage is that it will reduce poverty.

A national minimum wage may also offset labour market imperfections, e.g. monopsony and discrimination. In the case of monopsony, a rise in the wage rate may also increase employment. In the following diagram the free market wage is OW (which is below MRP) and the number of workers employed is OQ. The introduction of a minimum wage of W1 raises employment to OQ1.

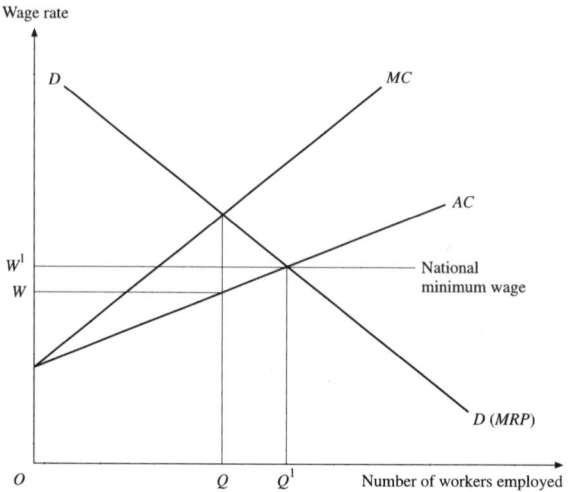

Fig. 7.13

In the case of labour market discrimination the introduction of a minimum wage may mean that an employer has to raise the wages of the discriminated groups to a level closer to their MRP. It may also shift some of the cost of employment from the government to employers. Some employers may pay a wage below MRP in the knowledge that the government will provide benefits to those on low incomes, e.g. family credit. However, some argue that the introduction of a minimum wage will reduce employment. A higher wage will increase firms' costs of production. The diagram below shows that a minimum wage set above the equilibrium level causes an extension in supply but a contraction in demand. Employment falls from OQ to OQD.

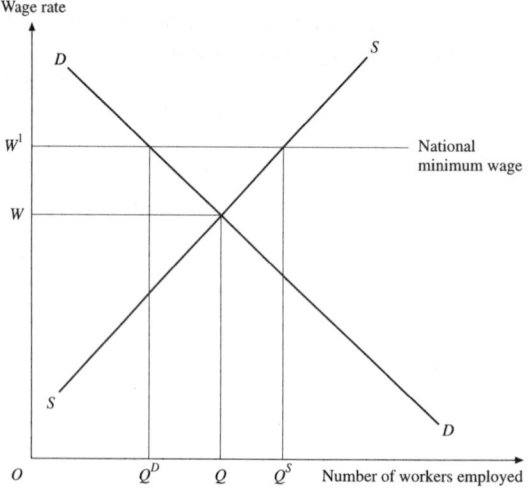

Fig. 7.14

Those who lose their jobs may be the ones most likely to fall into poverty, e.g. the disabled, the less skilled and those from ethnic minorities.

Some Keynesian economists disagree with this analysis. They argue that raising the wage rate, particularly of the poor who have a high marginal propensity to consume, will increase consumption. This, in turn, will increase demand for labour and raise employment as shown in the diagram below.

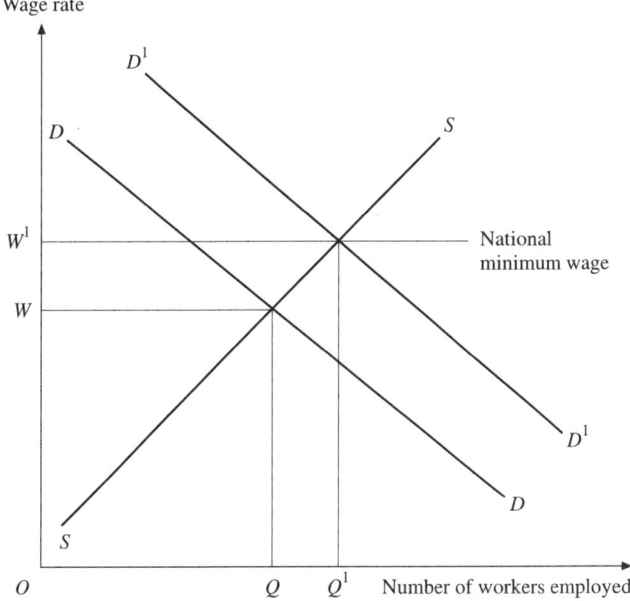

Fig. 7.15

The higher wage rate may also increase the motivation of workers and thereby raise their productivity and reduce absenteeism and labour turnover. All these effects will reduce firms' costs.

However, new classical economists believe that state intervention will reduce the efficiency of the labour market. They argue that, in addition to increasing unemployment, a national minimum wage may reduce labour market flexibility, preventing the wages of the low paid, in different areas with different demand and supply conditions, varying to any great extent.

If, as new classical economists believe, a national minimum wage raises costs of production, it may result in inflation. It may also cause cost push inflation by stimulating those workers who were previously paid an amount equal to, or just above, the minimum wage to press for a pay rise to restore their wage differentials. This will be likely to have a knock on effect through the wage scales.

If inflation does occur and it is above that of other major countries, Britain's international competitiveness may be reduced. This is likely to have an adverse effect on output and employment. However, the introduction of a national minimum wage may put Britain on more equal terms with other countries which already have one, although this will depend on the rates they operate.

A national minimum wage may help to raise the living standards of the previously low paid who remain in employment. However, it will not reduce the poverty experienced by those groups not in employment, e.g. the old, single parents and the unemployed.

Answers to short questions

1 There is no lower limit to ownership of assets but there is a lower limit to income. People can live without owning a house or a car, for example. However, they cannot live without any income. People have to pay for the basic necessities such as food and rent. Their income may be in the form of state benefits and may be low but it cannot be zero. There is also no inherent upper limit to the amount of wealth a person can own. In addition, wealth can be inherited, whereas, to a large extent, earning capacity cannot be.

2 Cash benefits enable the recipients to spend the money on the items they choose. If they are universal, e.g. child benefit, they are an expensive way to reduce poverty. On the other hand, if they are means tested, e.g. income support, people may find it humiliating to apply for the benefits. The provision of services means that a government can ensure that basic necessities and items which may reduce poverty are provided free or at a low price. However, the direct provision of services may be a universal benefit. State education, for example, is available to both rich and poor. In practice the rich are often better informed and in a stronger position to take advantage of state services. A higher proportion of children from well-off families go on to university than children from poor families.

3 Calculating national income by adding up the values of the gross outputs of all the enterprises in the economy would lead to multiple counting. This is because the inputs of some industries are the output of other industries. For example, to add the value of the output of millers to the value of the output of bakers would involve counting the flour content of bread, cakes, etc. twice.

4 New classical economists believe that an increase in savings will cause an increase in investment. They think that a rise in savings increases loanable funds and so results in a fall in the rate of interest. The lower rate of interest reduces the cost of investment and thus encourages firms to purchase new machines, plant, etc. However, Keynesians argue that an increase in savings can reduce investment. This is because an increase in savings will be accompanied by a fall in consumption. With reduced demand for consumer goods, firms will be discouraged from expanding their productive potential.

5 The level of investment is influenced by a number of factors. A key one is changes in the level of income and hence demand. The accelerator theory states that a change in demand for consumer goods will create a greater percentage change in demand for capital goods. The private sector is likely to invest more when income is high and rising, whereas an interventionist government is likely to invest when income is low and falling. Other influences on private sector investment are the rate of interest, the price of capital goods, changes in technology, the rate of corporation tax, government investment subsidies and expectations (animal spirits).

6 The level of national income is determined by aggregate demand and supply. It will be in equilibrium when aggregate demand equals aggregate supply (AD = AS), planned injections equal planned withdrawals (J = W) and when output equals planned expenditure (Y = C + I + G + (X − M). When output equals demand there will be no overall shortages or surpluses and so no reason for producers to increase or reduce output. The equilibrium level of national income can be illustrated by one of three diagrams.

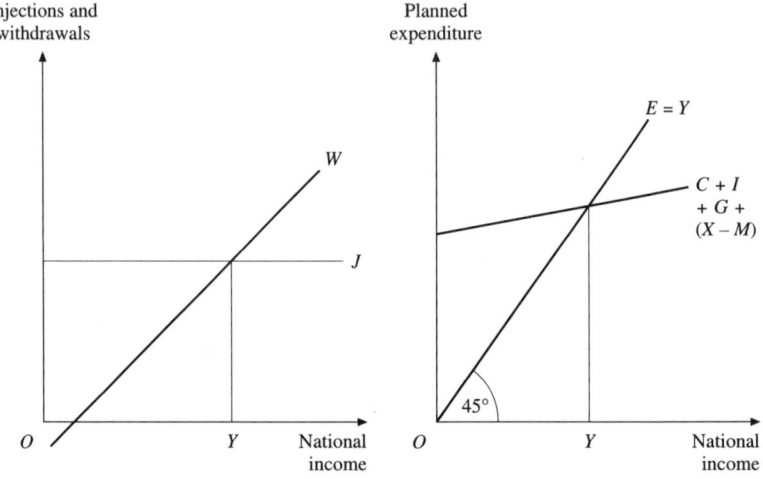

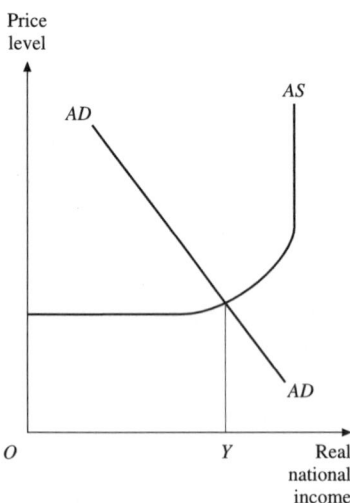

Fig. 8.3

The first diagram shows injections equalling withdrawals (leakages). The amount added to the domestic flow of income equals the amount withdrawn and so the level of national income remains constant. The second diagram shows output equalling planned expenditure and the third shows aggregate demand equalling aggregate supply. Again, in both cases national income (output) will remain constant.

7   A movement along a short-run aggregate supply (SRAS) curve can only be caused by a change in the general price level. The SRAS curve slopes up from left to right. This is because, as output rises, unit costs rise, e.g. because overtime rates have to be paid. So firms will only supply more if they can obtain a higher price. However, unit costs do not rise by significant amounts and so the SRAS curve is elastic.
   The SRAS curve will shift as a result of a change in an influence other than a change in the price level. The SRAS curve will move to the right if costs of production fall or if supply conditions improve for any other reason, e.g. good weather in the case of agricultural goods.

8   If the long-run aggregate supply curve is vertical, output cannot be increased with given resources and technology. So an increase in demand for exports will have no effect on output but will increase the general price level, as illustrated below.

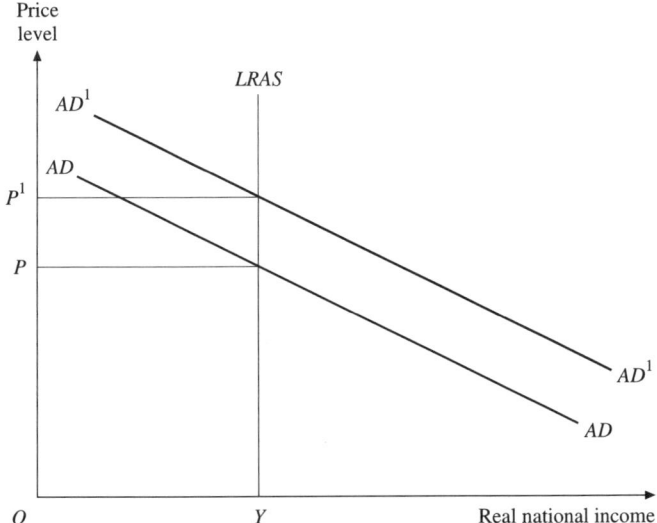

Fig. 8.4

9   Economic growth occurs when the output of goods and services increases. This means that people's material standards of living can rise. It also means that absolute poverty can be reduced without having to redistribute goods from the rich to the poor. This is because extra income, rather than existing income, can be given to the poor. However, economic growth also has disadvantages. It involves an opportunity cost. To grow, an economy has to use some of its resources to produce capital goods. These resources could have been used to produce consumer goods. Economic growth may

also result in the depletion of non-renewable resources and pollution, although it depends on the materials and methods of production used.

10   Economic forecasts might be based on house sales and surveys of entrepreneurs. If house sales are rising, this indicates that people are feeling optimistic and when people buy a new house they are likely to purchase more, e.g. furniture, carpets and paint. So increased activity in the housing market will suggest higher economic growth. Similarly if, for example, a CBI survey of employers finds that they are optimistic and planning to expand output, this points towards increased economic activity.

Answers to multiple choice questions

1   Answer **D**
GDP at factor cost is the output of goods and services produced within a country. GNP is GDP plus net property income from abroad.

2   Answer **C**
To find real GDP, GDP at current prices has to be converted into GDP at constant prices. This is done by multiplying the money (nominal) GDP figure by the price index in the base year and dividing by the price index in the current year, i.e.:

$$£12\,075 \times \frac{100}{105} = £11\,500$$

So, in real terms, GDP has risen by £1500 which is an increase of:

$$\frac{£1500}{£10\,0000} \times 100 = 15\%$$

3   Answer **A**
Average propensity to consume is C/Y. For example an APC of 0.8 means that people spend 80 per cent of their disposable income. Answer **B** is a definition of the marginal propensity to consume.

4   Answer **C**
National income is in equilibrium when injections equal withdrawals (leakages), i.e. when I + G + X = S + T + M. In this case, equilibrium national income is £300m as at this level 50 + 20 + 30 = 50 + 10 + 40.

5   Answer **B**
A transfer payment is money that is given to someone not in return for providing a good or service. There is no corresponding output to match the payment. Job seekers's allowance is paid to the unemployed to meet their living costs and not for providing output. **A**, **C** and **D** are all items for which there is a corresponding good or service.

6   Answer **C**
A paradox is a seemingly contradictory statement. When people decide to save more they may bring about a situation where they are actually able to

save less. This is because if they save more, they spend less, thereby causing output and income to fall. With lower income, people are able to save
less.

7   Answer **A**
The accelerator theory states that a change in the rate of growth of aggregate demand will cause a greater percentage change in demand for capital
goods (investment).

B   The consumption function shows the relationship between consumption and different levels of income.

C   The multiplier is a measure of the extent to which an injection causes a
change in national income, e.g. a multiplier of 2 would mean that a rise
in, say, investment of £10 million would cause national income to rise
by £20 million.

D   The speculative demand for money is the demand to hold wealth in a
money form to take advantage of changes in the price of bonds and the
rate of interest.

8   Answer **C**
The marginal efficiency of a new capital good is its expected yield. This
will increase if anticipated revenue rises or anticipated costs fall. A reduction in the purchase price of new machines will increase the profit margin
of any investment project.
Answers **A**, **B** and **D** all describe events which would reduce the expected
yield.

9   Answer **C**
A reduction in the exchange rate will reduce the price of exports in terms
of foreign currency. This will cause an increase in demand for exports,
shifting the AD curve to the right.

A   would cause an increase in aggregate supply.

B   would cause a decrease in aggregate demand.

D   would cause a movement along the aggregate demand curve – an
extension.

10   Answer **D**
Lorenz curves measure how income is distributed. In Country W income is
completely evenly distributed. The graph also shows that income becomes
more unevenly distributed as the curves move out. Country Z has the most
uneven distribution of income.

A   The graph is concerned with the distribution of income and not levels
of income.

B   Whether an even distribution of income is desirable or not is a value
judgement.

C   There is no direct link between the distribution of income and employment levels.

Answers to data response questions

1 a Personal disposable income is the income of households after direct taxes have been deducted and state benefits have been added. Real personal disposable income is personal disposable income at constant prices, i.e. after the effects of inflation have been deducted. So an increase in real personal disposable income means that households have increased purchasing power. They are able to spend more on such things as mortgage interest payments, food and holidays.

b For most of the period there was a direct relationship between real personal disposable income and consumption, with both moving in the same direction except in 1992 when income rose but consumption fell. However, closer analysis reveals some interesting features of this period.

Year	APC	MPC
1987	0.93	1.41
1988	0.94	1.71
1989	0.93	0.64
1990	0.92	0.36
1991	0.90	16.73
1992	0.88	−0.04
1993	0.89	1.38
1994	0.91	3.41
1995	0.90	0.71

$APC = C/Y$, $MPC = \Delta C/\Delta Y$

APC rises until 1988, then falls to 1992 and then rises again. It is highest in 1988 during the consumer boom and lowest in 1992 during the recession. MPC fluctuates by a considerable amount. It is high in 1987, 1988, 1993 and 1994 and exceptionally high in 1991.

c The findings do not match with what would be predicted by traditional Keynesian economic theory which suggests that while total consumption should rise with income, APC and MPC should fall. At the start and end of the period APC rises as income rises. MPC also fluctuates more than theory would predict, with consumption changing by a greater amount than income in five of the years shown.

These findings suggest that factors other than current income play a role in determining consumption. One is consumer confidence. In 1987 and 1988 consumers were very confident. Unemployment was falling and consumers anticipated that income would rise further in the future. They were optimistic about their future job prospects and income levels and, as a result, increased their spending. Higher levels of consumption were also encouraged and facilitated by the increased availability and lower cost of credit. On the other hand, in 1991 the increase in unemployment, fall in income and increased rate of interest discouraged consumption.

d The savings ratio is the proportion of disposable income which is saved. For example, in 1995 people saved 10.1 per cent of their disposable income. The savings ratio is closely linked to the average propensity to save (APS). A savings ratio of 10.1 per cent is equivalent to an APS of 0.10.

e The main influence on savings is income. However, other influences include the rate of interest, inflation and government policies. An increase in the rate of interest is likely to encourage a number of people to save more as the return is higher. However, those saving with a specific target in mind may also save less.

Rising inflation tends to encourage people to save more. This is because inflation erodes the real value of money wealth. So people save more in an attempt to restore the real value of their financial assets. Government policies may also affect savings. For example, the introduction of saving schemes which do not have tax imposed on them will encourage people to save more.

2 a Aggregate demand is the total of all planned expenditure. In addition to investment (I), the components are consumption (C), government expenditure (G), and net exports (X − M).

b An increase in investment means a rise in aggregate demand. Higher expenditure on capital goods will cause the capital goods industry to increase its output. The effect will not stop there. The increase in incomes enjoyed by those producing capital goods will be spent, which will increase demand for consumer goods. So the rise in investment expenditure will result in a multiple rise in national income. For example, if the multiplier is 3, a rise in investment of £20 million will lead to an increase in national income of £60 million. The diagram below shows how an increase in aggregate demand (resulting from higher investment) causes real national income to rise from OY to OY1.

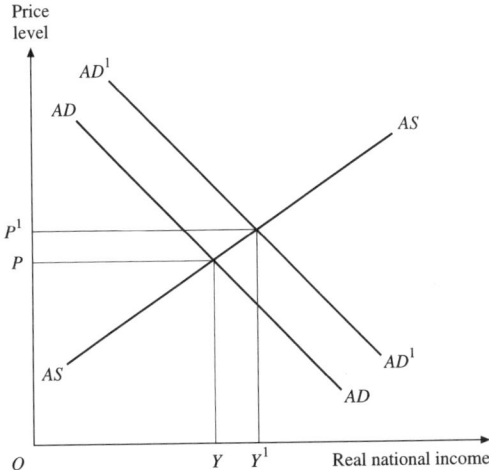

Fig. 8.5

c   The extract distinguishes between growth which occurs as a result of an
    increase in the country's productive capacity and growth arising from
    the greater use of existing resources. An increase in the quality or quan-
    tity of resources will mean that a country is capable of producing a
    higher output. This is illustrated by a move to the right of the production
    possibility curve.

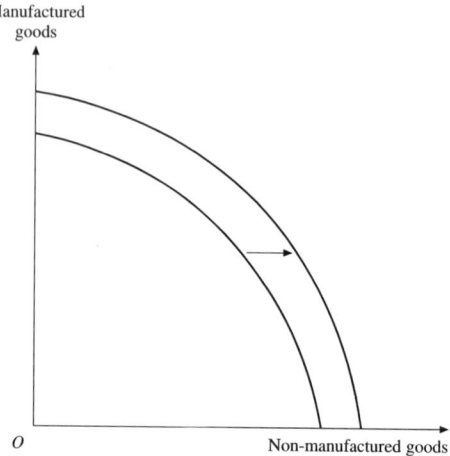

Fig. 8.6

Growth, as it is usually defined, means an increase in output. This can
result not only from an increase in the quantity and quality of resources
but also from better use of existing ones. An improvement in the allocation of resources or the use of previously unemployed resources will
cause a movement from within a production possibility curve towards
the curve.

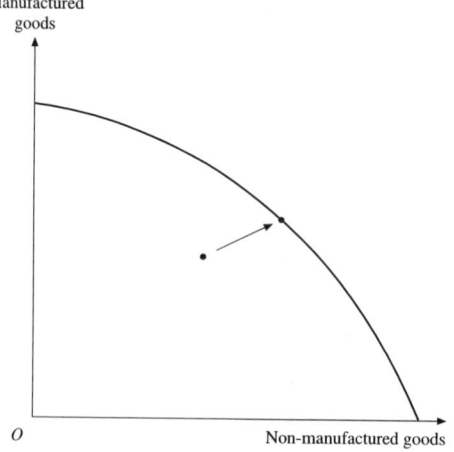

Fig. 8.7

Investment also has a role to play here as an increase in investment will raise aggregate demand which may bring into use previously unemployed resources.

d A country's productive potential may also increase as a result of an increase in the size of the labour force or an improvement in the quality of the labour force. Net immigration of people of working age or an increase in the participation of women in the workforce, for example, would increase the size of the workforce. With more people in the workforce, potential output will increase. If the size of the workforce does not increase but workers' productivity increases due to education and training, the maximum output that the country can produce will increase.

e It is not difficult to establish a direct relationship between growth in investment and growth in output. However, as the extract suggests, it is difficult to establish the line of causation. This is because an increase in investment will cause a greater percentage increase in national income (output) as explained by the multiplier theory, and an increase in income will cause a greater percentage increase in investment as explained by the accelerator theory. If firms spend more on capital goods, e.g. machinery, the capital goods industry will expand output which will, in turn, increase incomes and raise consumption. Similarly, if output (and hence income) increases, firms are likely to buy more capital goods to expand their capacity to meet the resulting higher demand. So if both investment and output are seen to increase, it is difficult to determine which occurred first.

Answers to essay questions

1 a Economists compare living standards over time and between countries for a number of reasons. One is to assess the performance of an economy. If living standards are rising at a faster rate than in previous years and are high in international terms, the country may be considered to be performing well.
Information about living standards also allows economists to make forecasts about such things as consumption, investment and employment. If living standards are rising, consumption, investment and employment levels are likely to be high.
If living standards are falling or rising more slowly than before, economists will make recommendations as to how to reverse the trend. A study of changes in living standards in other countries may provide information and ideas on how to improve the performance of the domestic economy.
A major and related reason for comparing living standards is to assess how the quality of people's lives is changing.

b National income figures, usually GDP at factor cost, are the main figures used to compare living standards. This is because most countries keep and publish detailed national income data.
However, care has to be taken in using national income figures to compare living standards both over time and between countries. It is impor-

tant to use GDP at constant prices (i.e. real national income) so that a misleading impression is not given because of the effects of inflation. It is also important to take into account differences in population size. A country with a large population is likely to produce more than a country with a small population. However, this output has to be shared out among more people so living standards are not necessarily higher. This is why economists divide output by population and compare real GDP per capita. Even when adjustments have been made for inflation and differences in population size, national income figures as a measure of living standards have to be interpreted cautiously.

A rise in real GDP per capita may have resulted from an increase in the output of capital goods. In the longer run this will increase productive capacity and result in more consumer goods being produced. However, in the short run people may not feel any benefit from more capital goods being made. An increase in weapons will also increase GDP but, again, may not necessarily improve living standards. If more police are employed and crime is reduced, the quality of people's lives will be improved. However, if more police are employed to keep pace with rising crime, people will be feeling worse off. So economists have to look not only at the amount of goods and services produced but also at the composition of those goods and why the quantity has changed. In addition, the quality of goods and services produced should be examined. The same quantity could be produced this year as last year or five years ago but if the quality of the output has risen, living standards will have improved.

The distribution of income also has to be taken into account. National income may rise but if it is concentrated in the hands of a few, the living standards of the majority may not rise.

National income figures also fail to take into account some items which affect the quality of people's lives. A certain amount of economic activity is not declared, either to avoid paying taxes or because it is illegal. If there is an increase in, say, people providing home hairdressing services but not declaring them, people's living standards may rise, although this increase will not be reflected in the official figures.

Differences in working hours and working conditions are also not taken into account. If output remains constant but working hours fall, people are likely to have a higher quality of life.

National income figures only take into account economic activities for which a payment is made. They do not take into account externalities and non-marketed activities. So, for example, an increase in pollution will reduce living standards while an increase in people decorating the homes of old people, on a voluntary basis, will improve the quality of life of the elderly. Neither of these will be recorded in national income figures.

All of these factors have to be taken into account in using national income figures to make comparisons both over time and between countries. However, some additional factors have to be considered when making international comparisons. Different statistical methods are employed in some countries and the degree of accuracy can vary. Tastes and needs can be different in different countries. For example, people living in a cold climate have to spend more on heating than those in warm countries, merely to enjoy the same standard of living. There is also the problem of selecting a rate of exchange to make the comparison. Exchange rates fluctuate and do not always reflect relative prices in different countries. For this reason national income figures are often compared using purchasing power parities which compare the cost of a given basket of goods in different countries.

c   A number of indicators can be used to compare living standards. Two which receive a considerable amount of attention are Measurable Economic Welfare (MEW) and the Human Development Index (HDI).

MEW was developed in 1972 by two economists, William Nordhaus and James Tobin. This measure is based on GDP but adjusts this in an attempt to get a more appropriate measure of welfare. Certain items, including leisure and non-marketed goods and services, are added to official national income figures, while things such as negative externalities and expenditure on defence are deducted.

HDI, introduced by the UN in 1990, combines three indicators. One is again GDP and the other two are education and life expectancy. As with MEW, this measure takes into account not merely the quantity of goods and services produced but also other factors which affect the quality of people's lives.

2   a   Aggregate supply is the total planned output of a country at each price level. It is the sum of all the industry supply curves.

In the long run the factors which influence aggregate supply are the quantity and quality of resources. In more detail they are the size of the labour force, the productivity of the labour force, the capital stock, technological progress and the quality and discovery of natural resources.

A number of factors can cause an increase in aggregate supply. For example, improvements in education and training should improve the productivity of the labour force and thereby aggregate supply. Similarly, a more efficient financial sector may make it easier for existing firms to expand and for new ventures to become established. This will increase the capital stock and aggregate supply.

b   The long-run aggregate supply (LRAS) curve shows the relationship between planned output and the general price level. The Keynesian view is that the shape of the LRAS curve will vary according to the level of output and employment. At low levels of output and employment the LRAS curve will be horizontal. This is because output can be increased without a rise in costs. New workers can be taken on at the going wage rate and existing workers will be too afraid of losing their jobs to press for a pay rise. At low levels of unemployment higher wages will have to be paid to attract new workers, especially skilled workers. Existing workers will also be in a stronger position to press for pay rises and more money may have to be paid to obtain raw materials. The resulting rise in costs of production will mean that the LRAS slopes upwards. When the economy reaches the full employment level it will not be possible to increase output any more and the LRAS curve becomes vertical.

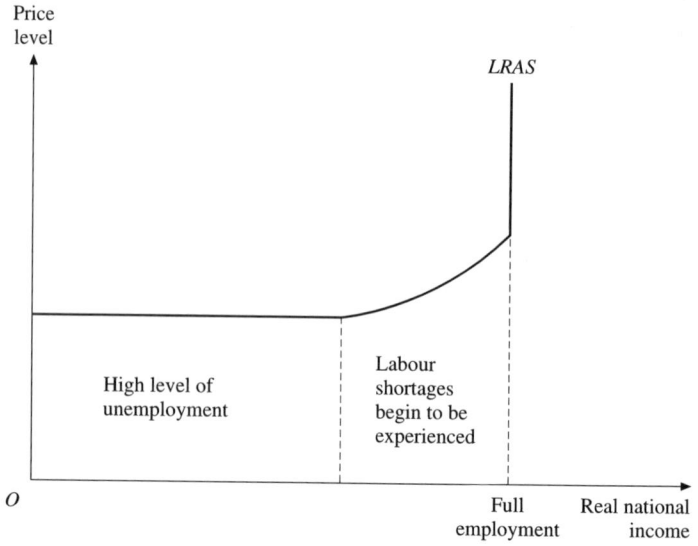

Fig. 8.8

In contrast new classical economists believe that, in the long run, markets, including the labour market, clear, and the economy will operate at the maximum potential output with given resources. So they argue that the LRAS curve will be vertical.

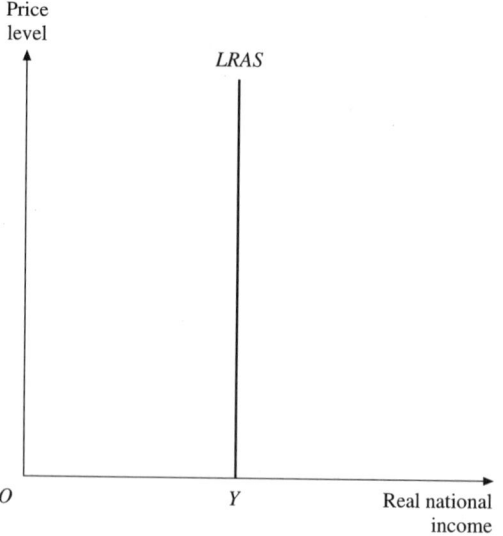

Fig. 8.9

c   Because of their different views on the shape of the LRAS curve, Keynesians and new classical economists have different views on the effects of an increase in government expenditure on output, employment and the general price level.

Keynesians believe that an increase in government spending at a time of low economic activity is likely to increase output and employment and have no effect on the general price level. The diagram below shows how the increase in aggregate demand resulting from a rise in government spending causes national income to rise from OY to OY1. The higher output is likely to result in a rise in employment. The price level remains at OP.

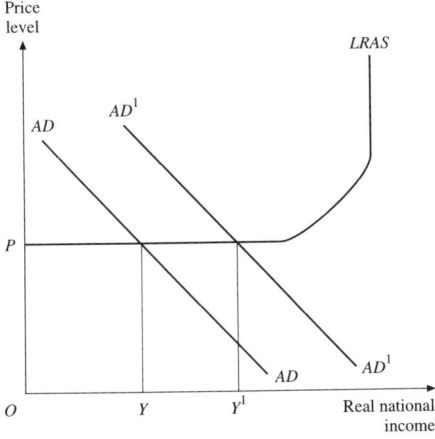

Fig. 8.10

When the economy is approaching full employment, an increase in government spending or any of the other components of aggregate demand will increase output (and hence employment) and the price level as shown below.

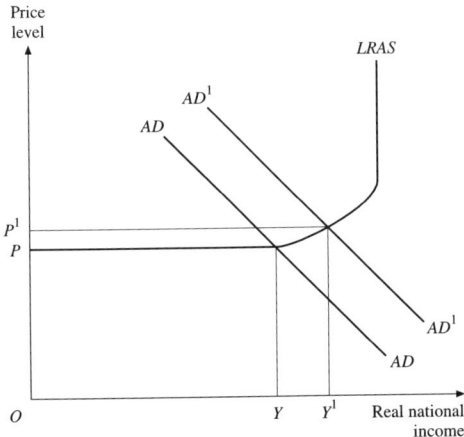

Fig. 8.11

A government may consider that it is worth risking a rise in the price level to reduce unemployment further. This trade-off relationship can also be illustrated by the traditional Phillips curve.

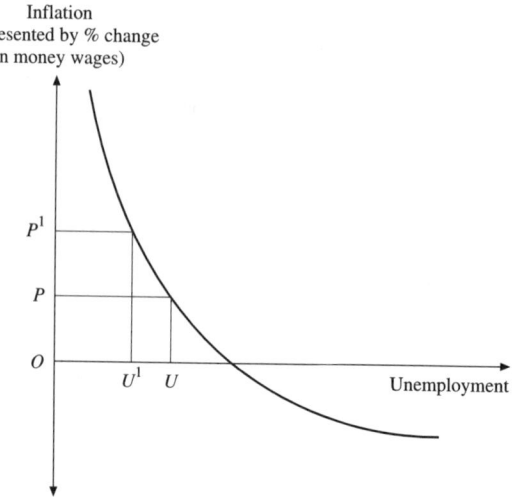

Fig. 8.12

Here an increase in government spending causes aggregate demand to rise which, in turn, reduces unemployment from U to U1. The fall in unemployment results in a rise in money wages from OP to OP1 and thereby raises the price level.

At the full employment level an increase in government spending will have no effect on output and employment but will raise the price level.

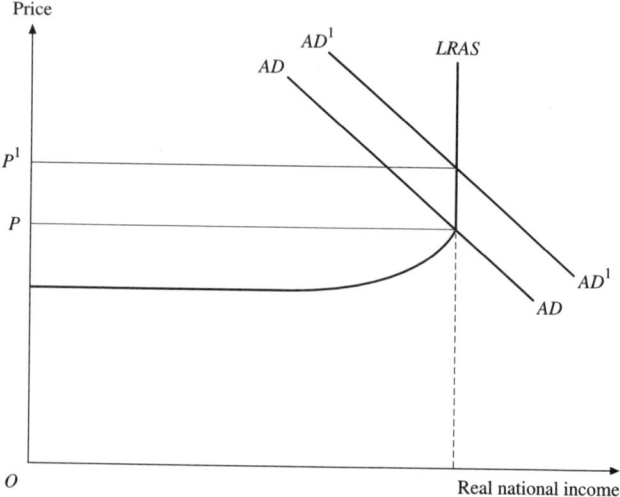

Fig. 8.13

As new classical economists believe that the LRAS curve is vertical, they think that an increase in government spending cannot raise output and employment in the long run, but will cause inflation.

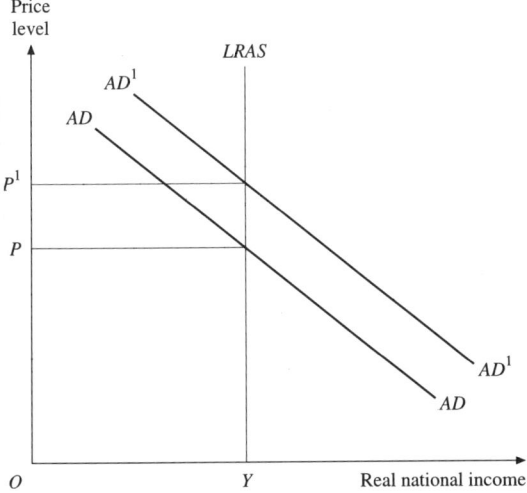

Fig. 8.14

New classical economists also use the expectations-augmented Phillips curve to illustrate this point.

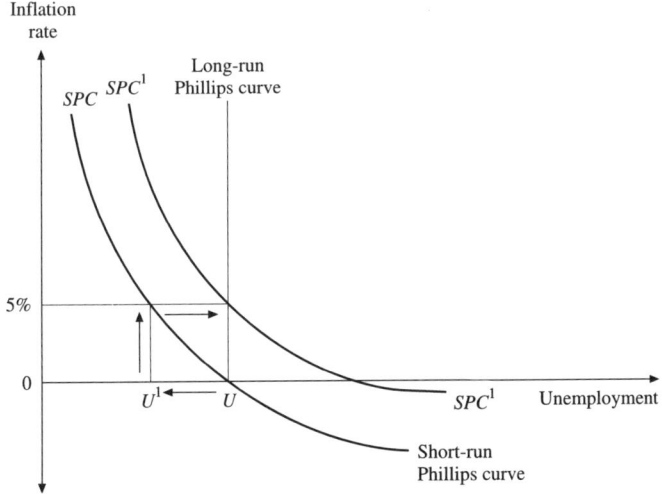

Fig. 8.15

An increase in government spending reduces unemployment in the short run but, in the long run, unemployment returns to the natural rate but with an inflation rate of 5 per cent.

Answers to short questions

1 The real rate of interest is the nominal (money) rate of interest minus the inflation rate. It is possible for the real rate of interest to be negative. This occurs when the rate of inflation exceeds the nominal rate of interest. For example, if the nominal rate of interest is 6 per cent and inflation is 8 per cent, the real rate of interest would be minus 2 per cent. Savers would experience a fall in their purchasing power.

2 Transactions, precautionary and speculative motives are all reasons why people may choose to hold their wealth in a money form. The transactions motive covers money held in order to buy goods and services. The precautionary motive covers money held in order to meet unexpected expenses and to take advantage of unexpected bargains. Both the transactions and precautionary motives are relatively stable and interest inelastic. The speculative motive is more volatile and interest elastic. People hold money for speculative reasons in order to take advantage of changes in the price of bonds and hence the rate of interest.

3 A fall in the price of bonds will be associated with a rise in the rate of interest expressed in percentage terms. A bond issued for, say, £100 may pay £5 interest, i.e. 5 per cent. If the price of the bond falls to £50, the actual interest paid will still be £5. However, in percentage terms it has risen to 10 per cent. So the price of bonds and the rate of interest are inversely related.

4 Money is any item which carries out the functions of money. To carry out these functions an item does not have to be legal tender. However, it must be generally acceptable. In the UK the main forms of money are notes, coins, and bank and building society deposits.

5 There are four functions of money. One is that money acts as a medium of exchange. This means it is used to buy goods and services and overcomes the need for barter. Another function is that it is a store of value – money can be saved. It also acts as a unit of account. This function may also be referred to as a measure of value and refers to money's role in expressing the financial value of goods and services. Finally, money acts as a standard for deferred payments. It enables people to borrow and lend because it allows people to agree on an amount to be repaid.

6 The functions of money are adversely affected by inflation. The first function likely to be affected is that of a store of value. People may become reluctant to hold their savings in a money form if the real rate of interest is falling – possibly even becoming negative. Then the functions of unit of account and standard for deferred payments are likely to be affected. Firms will have to adjust their accounting figures to real values and interest rates will have to rise in line with inflation to ensure they retain their real value.

7 MO is a narrow measure of the money supply covering money used principally as a medium of exchange. On the other hand, M4 is a broad measure of the money supply and covers money used both as a medium of exchange and store of value. MO includes notes, coins and commercial banks' operational balances with the Bank of England. M4 covers the items in MO plus bank and building societies' deposits.

8 Banks have obligations to their shareholders to make adequate profits, and obligations to their depositors to maintain an adequate supply of liquid assets. The most liquid assets, however, are the least profitable, while the illiquid assets are the most profitable.

9 One of the main limitations of using the RPI as a measure of changes in the cost of living is that the pattern of consumer spending is regularly changing. Also, new products come on to the market and the quality and nature of products change. The RPI measures changes in retail prices as they affect the average family but not all households. To overcome the problem of products changing, the weights in the RPI are changed regularly but, even so, they may not truly reflect the pattern of consumer expenditure. A separate index is calculated for pensioners, taking into account their differential expenditure patterns.

10 The formula for the quantity theory is $MV = PT$, where M is the money supply, V is the velocity of circulation, P is the price level and T is output (transactions). An increase in the money supply will result in an increase in output if V and P are constant. Similarly, an increase in M will cause an increase in P if V and T are constant. For example, if initially $4 \times 10 = 2 \times 20$ and then M rises to 6 and V and T stay constant, P will rise to 3. This is the view of the monetarists. However, Keynesians believe that the quantity theory is not useful for making predictions as it cannot be assumed that any of the variables will remain constant. An increase in the money supply could increase both P and T. For example, M may rise to 9, V stay at 10, P rise to 3 and T rise to 30.

Answers to multiple choice questions

1 Answer **D**
An item must be generally acceptable for it to act as money. If it is not, people will not use it and it will go out of circulation.

B If money is issued by the state it increases its chances of being generally acceptable but it does not guarantee it.

A and **C** are desirable but not sufficient qualities of money.

2 Answer **C**
The credit creation (or bank multiplier) is 1/cash ratio. In this case it is (1/0.1)/10, i.e. 10. So the £10 million cash deposit will support bank deposits of £100 million. The payment of the cash into the bank will create a deposit of £10 million. This will enable the banking system to create a further £90 million of deposits by making loans.

3   Answer **B**
The quantity theory identity is MV = PT. In year 4:

$$140 \times 100 = ? \times 110$$
$$\frac{14\,000}{110} = 127 \text{ approximately}$$

4   Answer **A**
Banks' most profitable, and also least liquid, asset is advances.
C is a liability of a bank and not an asset.

5   Answer **A**
When the Bank of England buys securities (government bonds) it gives
people money in exchange. This money is transferred from the Bank of
England into the sellers' bank deposits by means of a cheque.
Commercial banks' liquid assets will rise which will enable them to lend
more. The money supply will increase.
B When the Bank of England purchases securities, it increases demand for
them. This raises their price and lowers the rate of interest.

6   Answer **C**
The income velocity of circulation is a measure of how many times money
changes hands. If national income is £30 000 million, national expenditure
is also £30 000 million. If £30 000 million has been spent and the money
supply is £5000 million, on average each £1 must have changed hands
£30 000 million/£5000 million = 6 times.

7   Answer **B**
The weights in the Retail Price Index reflect the proportion of total expenditure spent on a particular category of good. For example, if £20 out of
£100 were spent on a particular good, it would be given a weight of 1/5.
Using a weighted price index to measure price changes ensures that
changes in the prices of items people spend a large proportion on are given
more importance than items on which they spend only a small percentage.

8   Answer **B**
Here it is necessary to construct a weighted price index:

Commodity	Weight		Price change		Weighted price change
Tobacco	1/10	×	0	=	0
Housing	3/10	×	−10	=	−3
Food	2/10	×	5	=	1
Other goods	4/10	×	20	=	8
					6

9 Answer **C**

The speculative demand for money is the demand to hold wealth in a liquid form in order to take advantage of changes in the price of bonds and hence the rate of interest. The speculative demand for money will be high when the price of bonds is high and the rate of interest is low. This is because people will be expecting the price of bonds to fall and so will not want to buy bonds now for fear of making a capital loss. With a low rate of interest the opportunity cost of holding money will also be low.

A and **D** influence the transactions demand for money.

B influences expenditure on capital goods.

10 Answer **A**

Liquidity preference is a wish to hold wealth in a liquid form and the most liquid form is money. So liquidity preference is demand for money.

Answers to data response questions

1 a The first sentence mentions that textbooks state that the rate of interest is determined by the demand for, and supply of, money. This describes the Keynesian liquidity preference theory of interest rate determination. Keynes identified three motives for holding money – the transactions, precautionary and speculative motives.

b An alternative theory of interest rate determination is the loanable funds theory. This states that the rate of interest is determined by the demand for loanable funds (investment) and the supply of loanable funds (savings).

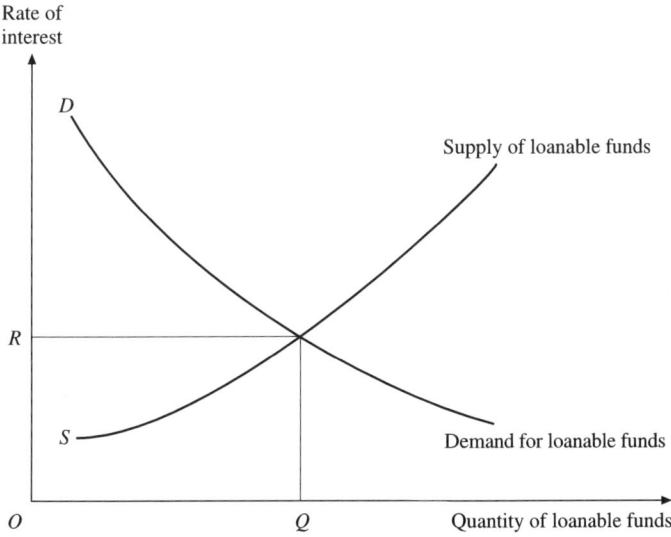

Fig. 9.1

This theory suggests that an increase in demand for loanable funds and/or a decrease in the supply of loanable funds will cause a rise in the rate of interest.

c Open market operations refer to the purchase and sale of government securities by the Bank of England in order to influence the money supply. If the Bank of England wishes to reduce the money supply, it will sell government bonds. Those purchasing the government bonds will draw out money from their bank deposits. These withdrawals will reduce the banks' liquid assets and thereby their ability to lend. A reduction in advances reduces the money supply.

d One advantage claimed for giving the Bank of England more independence, which is discussed in the extract, is that inflation is likely to be lower. This is because a central bank, charged with maintaining price stability, will not, unlike a government, ease monetary policy in an attempt to achieve another economic objective or to gain political popularity.

However, enabling the central bank to conduct monetary policy free from government policy will reduce a government's policy options. The economy is subject to fluctuations in economic activity caused by, for example, recessions abroad and an increase in consumer pessimism and a government may wish, for example, to reduce the rate of interest in order to increase the rate of growth and employment.

e There are a number of limitations on the authorities' ability to set interest rates. One is the effect that changes in interest rates have on government objectives. For example, a low rate of interest may reduce unemployment but may also contribute to inflationary pressure. In addition, UK interest rates cannot vary significantly from those prevailing in other major economies without causing changes in capital flows and the exchange rate. Linked to this is that the government cannot set interest rates which are out of line with what the financial markets judge is appropriate. For example, if UK interest rates are set below what is considered to be an appropriate rate, funds will be withdrawn from the UK.

2 a Base rate is the rate of interest used by the banking sector as the basis on which to calculate the rates of interest they charge to borrowers. Banks add percentage points to base rate according to the creditworthiness of their customers. For example, a 'blue chip' firm such as Marks and Spencer might be charged one percentage point above base rate, whereas an individual with no record of regular saving or repayments of previous loans might be charged six percentage points above.

b The data suggest a high level of economic activity at the start of the period, a decline in activity from 1990 to approximately 1992 and then a rise in activity. New car registrations and housing starts are likely to be high and increasing when income levels are rising. Both cars and housing have positive income elasticity of demand and are very sensitive to changes in income and expected changes in income. New car registrations and housing starts were relatively high in 1988. New car registrations rose in 1989 but then fell to 1991, with the largest fall being in 1991. Housing starts fell after 1988 to 1992, with the largest falls being in 1989 and 1990. When the economy came out of recession, at the end of 1992, both began to pick up, although house starts fell in 1995.

c i For four of the six years from 1989 to 1995 new car registrations and the base rate moved in opposite directions. The largest fall in car registrations occurred in 1991, a year after the base rate reached the very high level of 14.8 per cent. Car registrations were relatively high in 1993 to 1995 when the base rate was relatively low.

Many people borrow to buy a car. So a rise in the rate of interest raises the cost of buying a car and is likely to reduce demand for cars.

ii The real base rate is the nominal base rate minus the inflation rate. An increase in the nominal base rate, which is less than the increase in the rate of inflation, will actually mean a decrease in the real rate of interest.

Whether the real base rate would provide a better understanding of the relationship between changes in the rate of interest and car registrations would depend on whether people in the car market base their decisions on nominal or real values. As people have become more aware of the effects of inflation there is evidence of some people recognising that a high nominal interest rate may actually mean a low real payment (or even a negative real payment) if inflation is high. However, possibly still more people suffer from 'money illusion' and fail to recognise the effects changes in inflation can have on the real burden of interest repayments. So if people do base their decisions as to whether to borrow to buy a car on the nominal rate, this will provide a better understanding of the relationship.

d A change in the base rate will affect other interest rates and thereby the housing market. A rise in base rate will raise the mortgage interest rate. Most people buy a house with the use of a mortgage loan. A higher rate of mortgage interest repayments will discourage new buyers from entering the housing market. It will also reduce the discretionary income of existing home owners and make them less willing and able to 'trade up' by selling their home and purchasing a more expensive one. Higher mortgage interest rates may make people more worried about the negative equity trap. This occurs when the price a person can receive from selling their home is less than the mortgage loan they have to pay. As well as the mortgage interest rate rising, the interest rate on personal loans will also rise. Those who have previously taken out loans on variable interest rate terms will have reduced discretionary income and those who had been planning to borrow to buy complements, in particular furniture, for a new home may be further discouraged from buying a new home.

A rise in the base rate will also increase the interest rate on loans to firms, including construction firms. This will increase firms' costs of production and will probably reduce supply.

e A change in the rate of interest will affect a number of economic variables including the exchange rate and the money supply. A rise in the UK rate of interest, for example, is likely to encourage people to place money in UK financial institutions. This will increase demand for sterling and thereby raise its value.

On the other hand, an increase in the rate of interest is likely to reduce the money supply, or at least the growth in the money supply. This is because a higher interest rate will reduce demand for bank loans and hence the ability of commercial banks to create credit.

Answers to essay questions

1 a Commercial banks create credit (money) when they lend. Bank deposits (including those which are loan deposits) are the largest component of the money supply in industrialised countries.

Commercial banks have learned from experience that most deposits are not cashed. In practice most large payments are not made by cash but by transferring money from one bank deposit to another, e.g. by cheque or direct debit. So when banks receive new deposits they can use these as the basis for advances (loans) of a greater amount.

If a bank has estimated that, at most, say 5 per cent of its deposits are cashed, it may decide to keep a liquidity ratio of, say, 10 per cent. Liquid assets are assets which can be converted into money quickly and without loss of value. The liquidity ratio is the percentage of a bank's total assets which are in a liquid form.

A liquidity ratio of 10 per cent would give a credit creation (bank) multiplier of 10 (1/0.1). In this case if, say, £6 million is deposited in a bank, the bank can use it to support total deposits (liabilities) of £60 million. These deposits will include the £6 million original deposit, so £54 million deposits (advances) can be created.

The smaller the liquidity ratio the banking system keeps the greater the power of banks to add to the money supply. For instance, a liquidity ratio of 20 per cent would give a credit creation multiplier of 5, whereas a liquidity ratio of 2 per cent would give a credit creation multiplier of 50. Commercial banks are keen to lend as lending is their most profitable activity.

b The liquidity ratio which banks decide to keep puts a limit on their ability to lend. A bank multiplier of 8 would mean that a bank with deposits of £2000 million could lend up to £14 000 million but no more.

The credit creation multiplier shows the maximum amount of advances the banking system can supply. However, there is no guarantee that there will be enough demand for advances for banks to lend this amount. The amount that people want to borrow puts a limit on the amount banks can lend. There may be occasions, especially when firms and individuals are pessimistic about the future, when the private sector will not wish to borrow as much as banks would like to lend.

When banks lend they have to be reasonably sure of repayment. So another limitation may be not a shortage of potential borrowers in total, but a shortage of potential creditworthy borrowers.

Banks also have to follow similar lending policies. If one bank lends more than the other banks, its customers will transfer some of the deposits advanced to people with deposits at other banks. To settle these transfers the lending bank will have to reduce its operational balances at the Bank of England, one of its key liquid assets. This reduction will force it to reduce its advances.

The government, through the Bank of England, can limit commercial banks' ability to lend in a number of ways. The Bank of England can set a formal liquidity ratio or make recommendations to banks, on an individual basis, as to what would be a prudent liquidity ratio, given the types of customers they have.

The Bank of England can also reduce banks' ability to lend by engaging in restrictive open market operations. The sale of government securities will result in the withdrawal of funds from the commercial banks. This will reduce their liquid assets and hence reduce their ability to lend if they are operating with the minimum level of liquid assets.

Open market operations will also influence the rate of interest. If the government wants to reduce bank lending, perhaps to reduce inflation, it will raise the rate of interest. A higher rate of interest will increase the cost of borrowing and so be likely to reduce demand for loans.

To reduce the supply of liquid assets the Bank of England may issue more long-term securities (which are not liquid assets) and fewer Treasury bills (which are liquid assets). This is referred to as funding.

Among the more formal measures the Bank of England might employ to limit the banking sector's ability to create credit are a call for special deposits and the imposition of quantitative and/or qualitative controls. The Bank of England can require commercial banks to place a given percentage of their liquid assets with it. These remain the property of the commercial banks but cannot be counted in their liquidity ratios, so this is a method of reducing banks' liquidity bases for lending. The Bank of England can also place a formal limit on the amount banks can lend or instruct banks on to whom to lend to.

The extent to which the government places limitations on banks' ability to lend will depend mainly on the state of the economy and the extent to which the government believes that intervention in the commercial banking market is useful and effective.

2 a A fall in the rate of interest can arise as a result of changes in free market forces or as a result of government intervention.

According to the liquidity preference theory, a fall in the rate of interest can occur due to a fall in demand for money or an increase in the supply of money. A decrease in demand for money can be as a result of a fall in demand for money held for transactions, precautionary or speculative motives. The speculative motive is the most volatile. If, for example, people become convinced that the price of bonds will rise, they will be likely to choose to hold less money and buy bonds. This decrease in demand for money will cause the rate of interest to fall as shown in the following diagram.

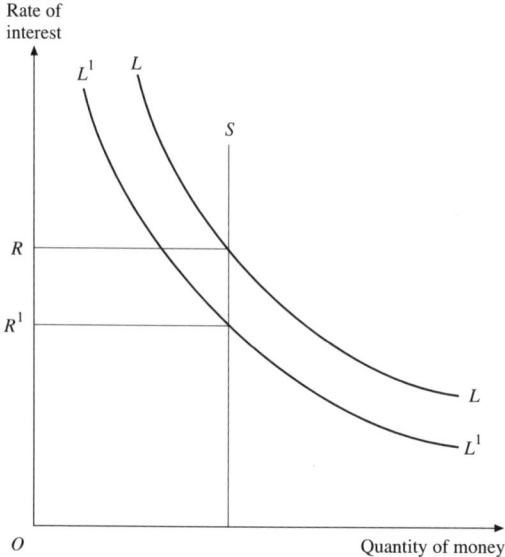

Fig. 9.2

The loanable funds theory suggests that the rate of interest will fall if the supply of loanable funds increases or the demand for loanable funds falls. If financial institutions have more to lend or people and firms are more reluctant to borrow, the rate of interest may be lowered. The diagram below shows the rate of interest falling as a result of an increase in the supply of loanable funds.

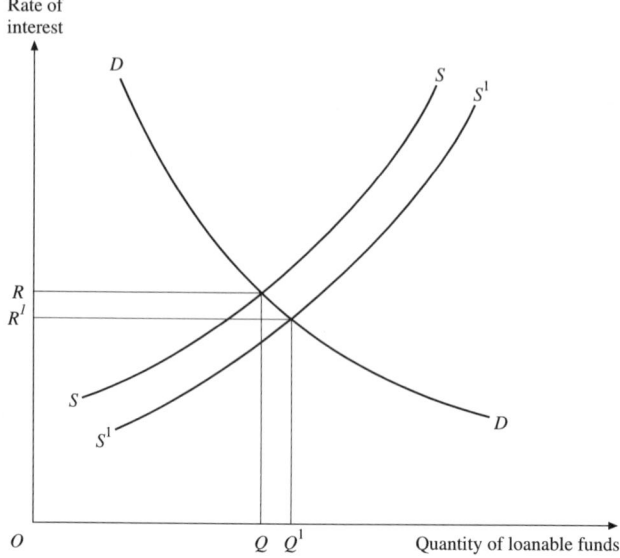

Fig. 9.3

A fall in relative interest rates in Germany, the USA or any of the other major industrialised countries may cause the UK government to lower the UK rate of interest in order to maintain the sterling effective exchange rate. The government may also wish to lower the rate of interest in order to stimulate economic activity.

The Bank of England, acting on behalf of the government, operates in the money market and can change interest rates by engaging in open market operations. To reduce short-term interest rates it will buy, say, Treasury bills at a higher price. This will lower the rate of interest on short-term securities. This lower rate will work through the banking sector with, for example, commercial banks lowering their base rates.

The government can also resort to the use of MLR (Minimum Lending Rate) which is the formal, publicly announced, rate at which the Bank of England will lend to the discount houses. Its use was suspended in 1981 but since then it has been used on more than six occasions, with the Bank of England announcing MLR for one day in order to change interest rates.

b A fall in the rate of interest would be likely to increase consumption and investment. However, there are some circumstances when this might not occur. For example, consumers and entrepreneurs may be feeling pessimistic about the future, the lower rate of interest might not be expected to last or the rate of interest may be falling by a greater amount, thereby leaving the real rate of interest higher, and people may not suffer from money illusion.

Nevertheless, in most cases a fall in the rate of interest, especially a fall in the real rate of interest, leads to a rise in consumption. A lower interest rate reduces the return on saving and thereby reduces the incentive to save. It also reduces the cost of borrowing. This encourages consumers to buy more of those items which are purchased with the use of loans. In particular, demand for consumer durables, cars, foreign holidays and housing will rise. The housing market is especially sensitive to interest rate changes as mortgage interest payments take up a significant proportion of many people's incomes.

A lower interest rate will also stimulate consumption by raising the discretionary income of those people who have a mortgage and/or other personal loans borrowed on variable interest rates. Paying less in interest means that people have more money to spend on, say, entertainment.

This rise in consumption resulting from a lower interest rate is only one of the three main reasons why this reduction may raise investment. The main influence on capital expenditure which firms undertake is probably the expected future level of demand for the products the firms produce. If people are buying more goods because of a lower interest rate, it will lead firms to expect higher sales and hence a higher return from the purchase of, for example, machinery and the expansion of plant.

A lower interest rate will also reduce the cost of investment. Those firms which borrow to buy capital goods will experience a direct fall in the cost of investment. However, in practice most private sector capital expenditure is financed by retained profits. Even here the rate of interest is significant. A fall in the rate of interest will reduce the opportunity cost of using retained profits. Spending on capital projects, which previously would have resulted in a lower return than placing money in bank time deposits, may now be viable. The diagram below illustrates the relationship between investment and the rate of interest, with a fall in the rate of interest resulting in a rise in investment.

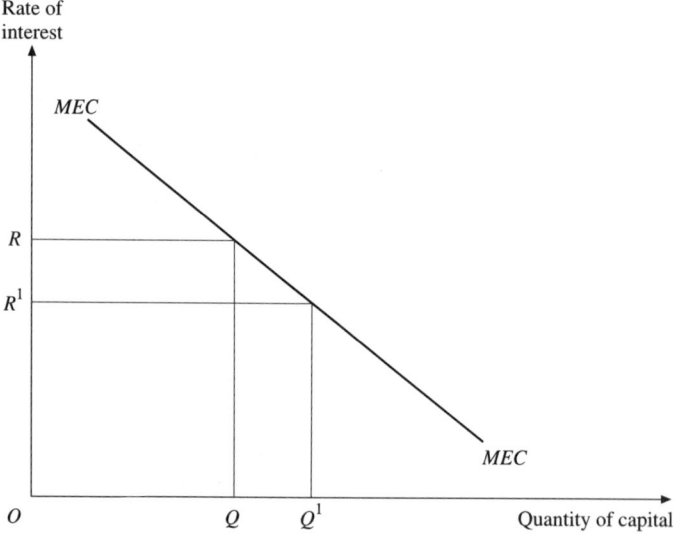

Fig. 9.4

A lower interest rate may also enable firms to undertake more investment because of the reduction in the cost of paying the interest on any previous loans.

Changes in interest rates can have a significant short-term effect on the exchange rate. If the rate of interest falls in the UK relative to interest rates in other countries, it will tend to lead to a capital outflow. People with money invested in UK financial institutions will be encouraged to switch their funds to overseas banks and to buy, say, overseas government securities in search of a higher rate of return. These people will sell sterling in return for foreign currency. This will increase the supply of sterling on the foreign exchange market. In the case of a floating exchange rate system, this will reduce the exchange rate as illustrated below.

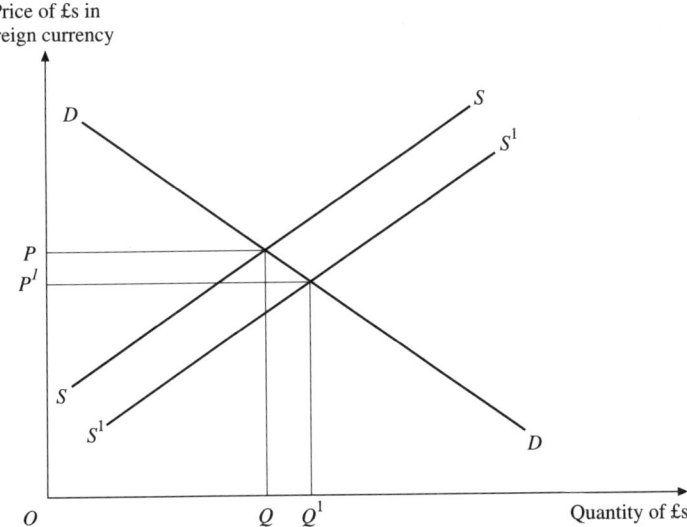

Fig. 9.5

In the case of a fixed exchange rate, it will place downward pressure on the exchange rate, which the government may attempt to resist by purchasing the domestic currency.

Answers to short questions

1 Stagflation is a situation of both high unemployment and inflation. The other main feature is zero or a very low rate of economic growth.

2 The headline rate of inflation is the one which often appears in the news media. It is the Retail Price Index (RPI). The underlying rate of inflation is RPI minus mortgage interest payments, indirect and local authority taxes. It is known as RPIY.

3 There are a number of potential costs of zero inflation. One is the possibility of reduced efficiency. Firms wishing to reduce real wages to respond to falling demand will have to cut nominal wages, which may result in industrial unrest, or reduce their labour force and thereby create unemployment. With zero inflation real interest rates have to be positive and this may discourage spending on consumer durables and capital goods. Costs may also be incurred in reducing inflation to zero. Deflationary fiscal and monetary policy may reduce growth and employment.

4 Government borrowing may be inflationary but it need not be. It will depend principally on the state of the economy and how economic agents react. The government may borrow from the banking or non-banking sector. The former adds to the money supply, while the latter does not. However, in both cases government borrowing to finance increased government expenditure will add to aggregate demand. Keynesians believe that increased aggregate demand, with unused capacity, will result in a rise in output and employment. However, new classical economists believe that government borrowing, especially if it is financed by borrowing from the banking sector, will lead to inflation as producers respond to the extra demand by raising their prices.

5 Inflation, if it is higher than in rival countries, is likely to have a detrimental effect on a country's balance of trade, at least in the short run. Higher rises in domestic prices will reduce the price competitiveness of the country's goods at home and abroad. Fewer exports will be sold and more imports will be purchased. If the country is operating a floating exchange rate, it will depreciate to restore the country's international competitiveness.

6 Full employment does not mean zero unemployment. This is because even at times of high economic activity some people will be changing their jobs. It can be defined as the level of unemployment which exists when everyone who wants a job at the current wage rate is able to obtain one.

7 The official unemployment figure is based on the claimant count so it may underestimate the true unemployment figure because it does not include a number of groups who are looking for employment but who are not entitled to receive job seekers' allowance. These groups include those over 60, those who choose not to register, those who enter education but would prefer to work and those on government special employment schemes.

8 There are some possible benefits from unemployment. Employers may find that it is easier to recruit new staff, may find workers reluctant to take industrial action and may be more flexible in their working practices. Individuals and the economy will benefit if a period of unemployment enables people to spend time searching for the job they are most suited to. The existence of unemployment may also reduce cost push inflation as unions will be weaker and workers more wary of pressing for wage rises.

9 Equilibrium unemployment is the same as NAIRU (i.e. the non-accelerating inflation rate of unemployment). It is the number of people out of work when the labour market is in equilibrium, with the aggregate demand for labour equalling the aggregate supply of labour. These people will be those who are unwilling or unable to obtain a job at the current wage rate. In contrast, disequilibrium or cyclical unemployment occurs when the aggregate supply of labour exceeds the aggregate demand for labour at the current wage rate. Wages are above the equilibrium level. So those unemployed are unable to obtain employment because of the shortage of jobs.

10 Both new classical and Keynesian economists believe that reducing income tax can lower unemployment. New classical economists argue that it will increase the incentive for people to work and thereby reduce equilibrium unemployment. Keynesians believe it will reduce unemployment by increasing aggregate demand. However, they argue that other methods, such as increasing state benefits, are likely to be more effective as the poor will have a higher marginal propensity to consume than the main beneficiaries of tax cuts, i.e. the rich.

New classical economists support both cuts in income tax and job seekers' allowance as methods of reducing unemployment. They argue that a cut in job seekers' allowance will cause the unemployed to look more actively for employment and to be more willing to accept a job when one is offered. However, Keynesians believe that this method would actually increase unemployment. They argue that those unemployed are unable to find work because there are insufficient jobs on offer and that reducing welfare payments to the poor will lower aggregate demand and reduce the jobs on offer even further.

Answers to multiple choice questions

1 Answer **D**
Cost push inflation occurs when there is a sustained rise in the general price level caused by an increase in the costs of production. A rise in the price of imported raw materials' costs will increase firms' costs of production which they may pass on to customers in the form of higher prices.
A, **B** and **C** will all increase aggregate demand and so may result in demand pull inflation.

2   Answer B
The economy is operating at full employment so a rise in consumer expenditure will raise prices but leave real national income (and aggregate supply and unemployment) unaffected.

3   Answer A
The non-accelerating inflation rate of unemployment may also be called the natural rate. It is the rate at which demand for, and supply of, labour are equal at the current real wage rate, and hence the aggregate labour market is in equilibrium. It is the rate of unemployment which is consistent with a stable rate of inflation.

4   Answer B
The main cost to society of unemployment is the forgone output. This output is lost for all time.
A and **D** are financial costs to the government. **C** is a cost to workers.

5   Answer B
In a situation of full employment an increase in aggregate demand will cause inflation as, *ceteris paribus*, it will not be possible to increase output. A fall in taxation, with unchanged government expenditure, will increase overall demand. Private sector spending will fall while public sector spending remains unchanged. **A** and **C** will reduce aggregate demand and thereby reduce inflationary pressure. **D** will increase aggregate supply and again reduce inflationary pressure.

6   Answer C
The natural rate of unemployment (or NAIRU) will be reduced by an increase in aggregate supply. New training initiatives are likely to increase labour productivity and thereby raise supply.
A and **B** will increase aggregate demand which, according to new classical economists, will not reduce the natural rate of unemployment.
D   The introduction of a statutory incomes policy is a Keynesian measure designed to reduce cost push inflation without causing unemployment. However, new classical economists are opposed to incomes policies on the grounds that they interfere with the workings of free market forces, which may increase inefficiency and raise unemployment.

7   Answer C
The diagram shows that, at the going wage rate, the aggregate supply of labour exceeds the aggregate demand for labour. Unemployment results from the disequilibrium which exists in the labour market.
D   The natural rate of unemployment is the rate which exists when the labour market is in equilibrium.

8   Answer C
At an inflation rate of 5 per cent the economy is operating on the short-run Phillips curve labelled SPC1. Attempting to reduce unemployment to OZ will raise the economy on to SPC2 and inflation will rise to 7 per cent. In the long run, unemployment will return to OX.

9   Answer **A**
A revaluation of the exchange rate will lower the price of imported raw materials, which will reduce the costs of production.

B   A reduction in government spending may reduce demand pull inflation.

C   may reduce demand pull inflation but may increase cost push inflation.

D   again may reduce demand pull inflation but may increase cost push inflation if corporation tax is raised or if workers respond to increases in income tax by pressing successfully for wage rises.

10   Answer **C**
Unemployment rose by 23.4 per cent in Germany, 19 per cent in Japan, 4 per cent in the UK and fell by 6.8 per cent in the USA.

A   Unemployment rose in Japan from 1993 to 1995. This may have resulted in a fall in output. However, it is possible that output rose if, for example, labour productivity increased. No figures are given for output so a definite conclusion cannot be reached.

B   From 1993 to 1995 unemployment fell in both the USA and UK. However, it is possible for the unemployment percentage to fall without the numbers employed increasing. This could occur if people leave the official count because, for example, they retire or enter higher education.

D   Japan's unemployment rate was below the OECD average throughout the period shown. However, while Germany's unemployment rate was also below the OECD average from 1989 to 1994, it was above it in 1995.

Answers to data response questions

1   **a**   Throughout the period shown, the unemployment percentage and the inflation rate (which is the annual percentage change in retail prices) move in opposite directions. From 1986 to 1990 unemployment falls while the rate of inflation rises. Then, from 1990 to 1993, unemployment rises while the rate of inflation falls. In the final two years this inverse relationship is exhibited again, with unemployment falling and inflation rising.

Inflation reaches its peak in 1990 when unemployment was at its lowest level. In 1993 when inflation was at its lowest level for many years, unemployment was at the high level of 10.4 per cent.

The relationship between unemployment and inflation can be shown using either a time series graph or a Phillips curve graph.

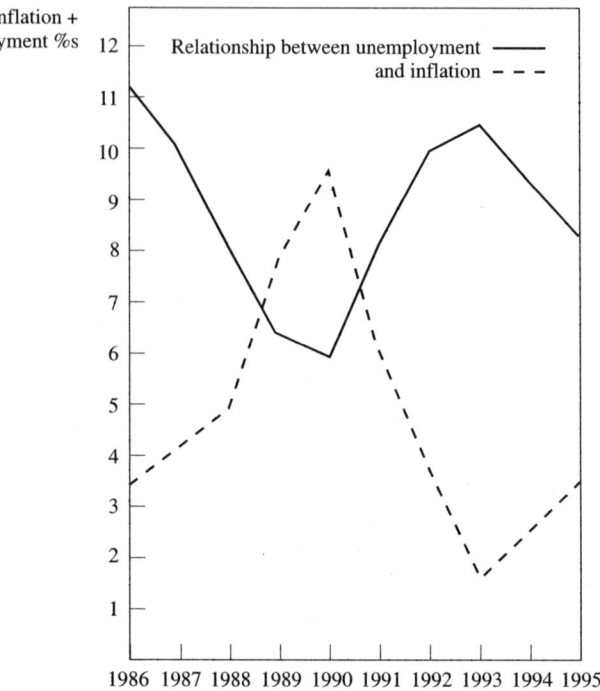

Fig. 10.4

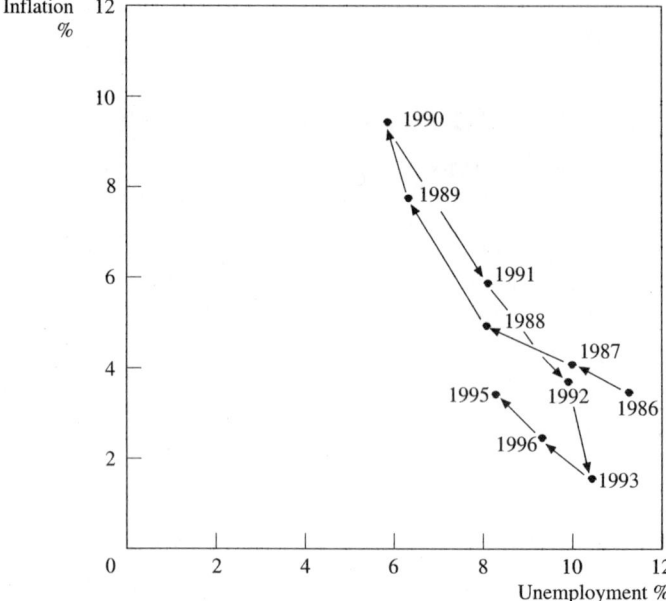

Fig. 10.5

b Keynesian economic analysis would suggest an inverse relationship between unemployment and inflation as the data show. This can be illustrated by the traditional Phillips curve.

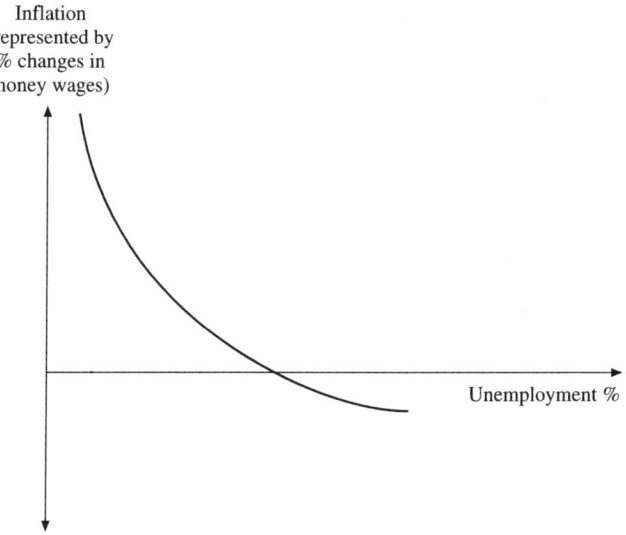

Fig. 10.6

When aggregate demand is high, unemployment is likely to be low and inflation high. On the other hand, a fall in aggregate demand will tend to increase unemployment and reduce inflation.

However, closer analysis of the second graph (Phillips curve graph) shows that while there was an inverse relationship between unemployment and inflation for the period shown, it was not as stable as the traditional curve analysis would suggest. The Phillips curve appears to have shifted slightly to the right in 1990 and 1991 and slightly to the left in 1994 and 1995. This may be explained by changes in external inflationary pressures, such as the price of imported goods, or a change in the relationship between unemployment and wage rates.

c A totally clear pattern does not emerge but on six out of the nine occasions the exchange rate and the inflation rate move in opposite directions. It is in 1987–88, 1991–92 and 1992–93 that they move in the same direction.

As the following graph illustrates, the exchange rate showed a downward trend. At the start of the period one pound sterling was exchanged for 3.14DM, whereas by the end of the period its value had fallen to 2.24DM. In contrast, inflation rose at the start, then fell to a low level and started to rise again at the end of the period.

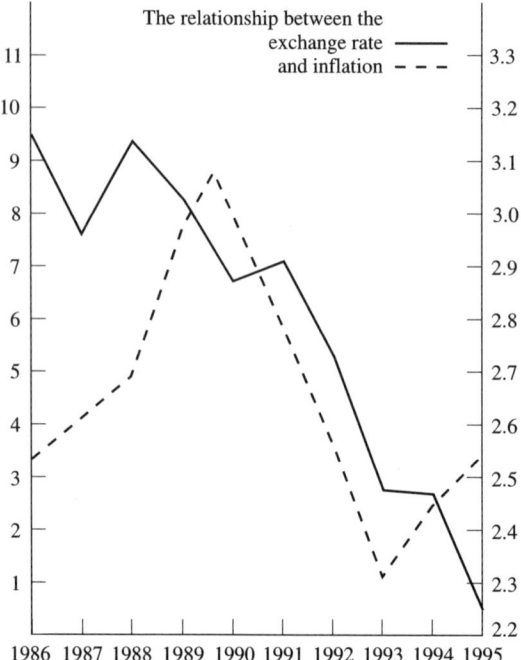

Fig. 10.7

d Economic theory predicts an inverse relationship between the effective exchange rate and the rate of inflation. The data, however, show only the value of sterling in terms of one currency, the DM. It is possible that the value of sterling may fall against the DM but rise against, say, the US dollar, French franc and Dutch guilder. However, if the sterling effective exchange rate falls, as well as the sterling–DM exchange rate, the rate of inflation may be expected to increase. This is because a fall in the value of sterling will mean that the price of UK imports will rise while the price of UK exports, denominated in foreign currency, will fall. A rise in the price of finished imported goods and imported raw materials and a reduction in the pressure on UK firms to keep their prices low will be likely to raise the Retail Price Index. Similarly, a rise in the rate of inflation will probably put downward pressure on the exchange rate. Domestic products will become less price competitive, with the likely consequences that demand for UK exports will fall and the UK demand for imports will rise. This will decrease demand for, and increase the supply of, sterling on the foreign exchange market.

e The rate of inflation may also be influenced by changes in the money supply and by firms raising prices to ensure larger profits.
Monetarists argue that the cause of inflation is the money supply growing faster than the rate of output. Using the quantity theory, they argue that people will react to increases in the money supply by increasing demand. In turn, producers will respond by raising prices. Cost push inflation can arise from an increase in any one of the costs of production

which occur over a period of time. If entrepreneurs push up prices, independently of increases in demand, to increase profit margins, cost push inflation will occur.

2 a The extract mentions that unemployment may fall in the future as increasing job insecurity and the growth in part-time employment have resulted in workers accepting lower wage increases.

The introduction of temporary contracts, the shedding of labour in a number of sectors and reduced trade union power have reduced the willingness and ability of workers to press for wage increase. The growth of part-time employment at the expense of full-time employment has also reduced trade union power as fewer part-timers belong to unions. Part-time hourly wage rates are also lower than full-time rates as the supply of people seeking part-time employment is high relative to the demand. Lower wage increases in the future may make labour more attractive to employers. Firms' profits may increase, encouraging them to expand and employ more workers.

b The official unemployment total is a measure of those on the claimant count, i.e. those who are claiming job seekers' allowance. The natural rate of unemployment is the rate of unemployment which is consistent with a stable rate of inflation and which exists when the labour market is in equilibrium with aggregate demand for labour equalling the aggregate supply of labour. It may also be referred to as the non-accelerating inflation rate of unemployment (NAIRU) or equilibrium unemployment and includes structional and frictional unemployment.

Actual unemployment may exceed the natural rate if there is both equilibrium and disequilibrium unemployment, i.e. if people are out of work because of an unwillingness or inability to work or they lack the necessary information to take up existing vacancies, and people are unemployed because of a lack of aggregate demand and hence of vacancies.

c A fall in unemployment may increase workers' feelings of job security. It will not then be so easy for firms to replace them by taking on unemployed workers. A rise in employment may also result in an increase in trade union membership and thereby trade union power. Both of these effects may encourage workers to press for pay rises. If they are successful and wage rates continue to rise independently of the demand for labour, wage push, a form of cost push, inflation will occur. In addition, a fall in unemployment to a low level is likely to raise wage rates as a result of an accompanying shortage of workers, particularly skilled workers. Firms competing to attract workers will bid up wage rates.

d A fall in earnings growth may mean that the natural rate of unemployment is lower than it was a decade ago because the aggregate demand for labour may be higher. Firms will be less worried about their profits being squeezed by large increases in labour costs. It is also possible that wages are rising by less than labour productivity so unit labour costs may be falling and a higher return may be being gained from employing labour.

It is also possible that the fall in earnings growth may reduce search unemployment. Some of the unemployed, who were previously turning down jobs in the hope of a better paid job, may lower their expectations and accept the jobs on offer.

e   The natural rate of unemployment will fall if the aggregate demand for labour (ADL) increases and/or the aggregate supply of labour (ASL) increases. The latter will reduce the gap between the aggregate supply of labour and the aggregate labour force.

New classical economists argue that reducing job seekers' allowance will make unemployment less attractive and increase the incentive to work. More of the aggregate labour force will actively seek employment and reduce the time they spend between jobs. The ASL curve will shift to the right. The diagram below shows that this reduces the natural rate of unemployment from WX to YZ and lowers the wage rate.

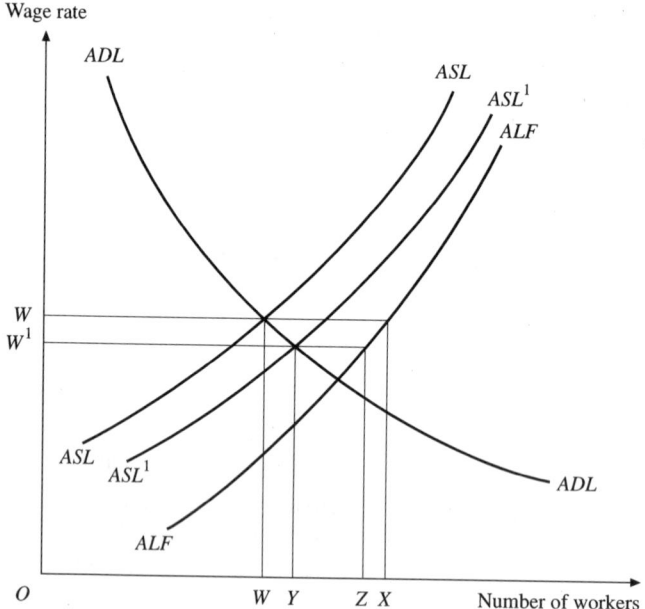

Fig. 10.8

Another possible cause of a fall in the natural rate is improved training. This will increase the marginal productivity of labour which, in turn, will encourage firms to employ more workers. The resulting shift to the right of the ADL curve reduces the natural rate of unemployment from WX to YZ, but this time it raises the wage rate.

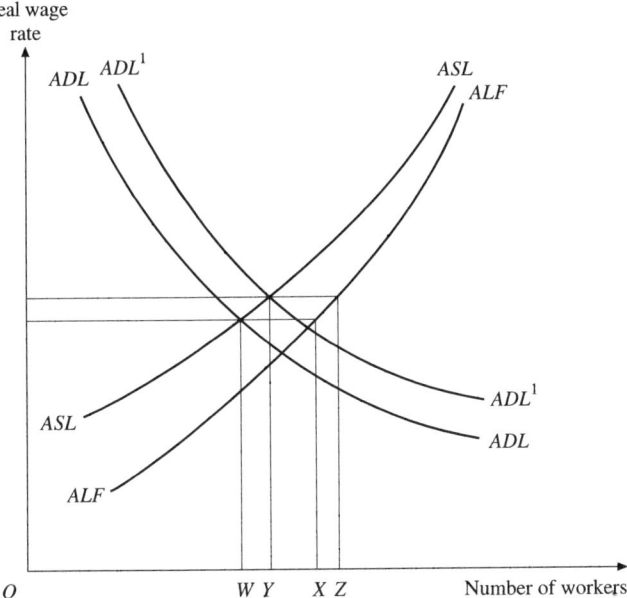

Fig. 10.9

Answers to essay questions

1 a Inflation is a sustained rise in the general price level. It is synonymous with a fall in the value of money. Unemployment is the non-use of labour resources. The inflation rate is the percentage rise in the general price level and the unemployment rate is the percentage of the workforce without a job.

In both cases a number of different measures are used. The rate of inflation is measured by the headline rate (the Retail Price Index: RPI), the target rate (RPIX), the underlying rate (RPIY), the Tax and Price Index (TPI) and the GDP deflator. The most common measure is the RPI which is a measure of the changes in the prices of the goods and services bought by the average household.

The two main measures of unemployment are the official claimant count and the Labour Force Survey. The first counts those receiving unemployment-related benefits, for example, job seekers' allowance, while the second includes all those actively seeking, and available to start, work.

b Both inflation and unemployment inflict costs on consumers, producers and the economy as a whole. Whether the costs of inflation or unemployment are higher will be influenced by their relative rates and duration. A high rate of inflation which lasts, say, ten years is likely to have more damaging effects than a low rate of unemployment lasting, say, six months.

However, given similar rates of inflation and unemployment it could be argued that unemployment may impose the more serious costs.

The costs of inflation can be divided into the costs of anticipated and unanticipated inflation. If inflation is at a relatively stable and predictable rate, measures can be taken to offset the effects. Wages, pensions and the rate of interest can be index-linked so that they rise in line with inflation. Fiscal drag can be avoided by raising tax thresholds so that tax payers do not pay more tax when their money incomes rise but their real incomes remain unchanged.

The effects of unanticipated inflation are more serious. If firms are uncertain what the future rate of inflation will be, they will have to spend time and money estimating future raw material costs, what prices to charge and what value to place on their assets. Shoe leather and menu costs will be experienced, with firms keeping their cash balances as low as possible and changing their prices frequently. The uncertainty surrounding the future price level may also discourage investment. People may suffer from money illusion and make their decisions on the basis of nominal rather than real values.

There may be an arbitrary redistribution of income. For example, if the nominal rate of interest is rising more slowly than the inflation rate, the real rate of interest will fall and borrowers will gain at the expense of lenders.

Trade unions may come into conflict with employers because they will have to press for wage rises to maintain their members' real incomes. If there is uncertainty about the future rate of inflation, even employers who are willing to raise wages in line with inflation may disagree with unions' estimates.

A major cost may be a reduction in the country's international competitiveness. If the country's inflation rate exceeds that of other countries, export revenue may fall and import expenditure rise. This may result in a balance of trade deficit and a fall in domestic output which can, in turn, cause unemployment. Under a floating exchange rate system, however, the value of the domestic currency is likely to fall until a balance of trade equilibrium is restored. The danger with this is that a falling exchange rate often results in an even higher rate of inflation. In the case of unanticipated inflation, measures can be taken retrospectively to offset the effects. For example, the government can promote arbitration in the case of industrial disputes, provide economic forecasts about expected future inflation rates, reduce taxation on savings and introduce measures to raise the quality and price competitiveness of UK goods, e.g. improved training.

A low level of demand pull inflation may even be beneficial. It will encourage production. Investment and employment may also be stimulated if the real rate of interest and the real wage rate are falling and if domestic inflation is below that prevailing in other countries. Consumers will feel better off if the value of their houses is rising faster than inflation. Of course, if inflation is higher, measures should be taken to reduce it and thereby reduce the distortionary effects it has. However, it is possible to live with inflation.

In contrast, some people find it very difficult to live with unemployment. The costs of unemployment are unevenly spread and may be very high.

The main cost to society is the lost output which the unemployed could have produced. This output is lost for all time and it results in living standards being below their potential level. The economy will operate inside its production possibility curve.

The government loses potential direct and indirect tax revenue and has to pay out more in unemployment-related benefits. This reduces its ability to, say, raise educational standards or reduce poverty. The costs to those unemployed include reduced income and loss of status. The longer people are unemployed, the more they miss out on training and promotion opportunities and the more difficulty they experience in gaining employment.

The physical and mental health of the unemployed may also suffer. People on low incomes are more subject to certain illnesses, e.g. tuberculosis. Some of these effects may be offset by raising job seekers' allowance. However, even with higher benefits, the mental stress which many unemployed people experience is still likely to occur. The loss of status and sense of failure may lead to divorce, mental illness and, in some cases, suicide.

Certain groups are particularly vulnerable to unemployment. These include the old, the young, the disabled and those from ethnic minorities. These groups can become disengaged from society. Unemployment is also unevenly spread through the country and within regions. There are some estates where more than 60 per cent of adults are unemployed. This can result in a sense of hopelessness and can contribute to crime which imposes costs on the whole society.

2 a Keynesians believe it is possible to reduce unemployment by increasing demand. They believe that this will not increase the rate of inflation if either the economy is initially operating at a low level of economic activity or if the increase in aggregate demand is accompanied by anti-inflationary measures.

When unemployment is high and real national income is low, Keynesians argue that the long-run aggregate supply (LRAS) curve is horizontal. An increase in aggregate demand, resulting from an increase in government expenditure, will raise output but leave the price level as unchanged as shown below.

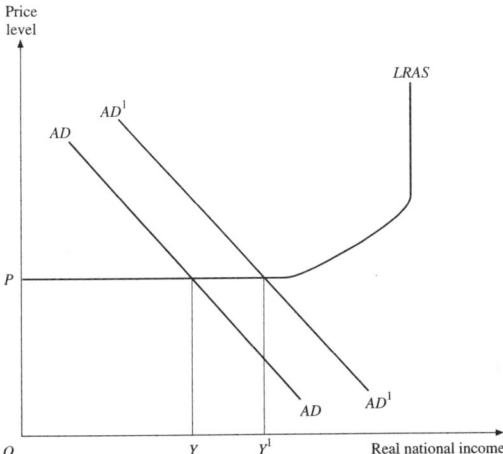

Fig. 10.10

When output and employment levels are low, firms may be able to expand production by offering the current wage to attract more workers and by paying the same price to purchase capital equipment. So unit costs will not rise and the price level will not be affected.

When the economy approaches full employment, there is a risk that an increase in aggregate demand will raise both employment and the price level. A government that is keen to raise output and employment may decide to increase aggregate demand but to accompany reflationary fiscal or monetary policy by the introduction of a prices and incomes policy. Such a policy will restrict or freeze price and wage rises and, if successful, may avoid inflation. Of course, in practice, a number of difficulties occur with prices and incomes policies. For example, it has to be decided whether exceptions should be made to allow wages to rise by more than limits in the cases of increased productivity, labour shortages and low pay.

Producers may get round price limits by redesigning their products. For example, chocolate manufacturers may reduce the weight of their bars. There is also the risk that, when the limits are removed, pent-up pressures are released and wages and prices increase significantly. New classical economists oppose prices and incomes policies on the grounds that they interfere with free market forces and do not tackle the real causes of inflation. They also believe that increasing government expenditure to reduce unemployment will, in the long run, fail to lower unemployment below the non-accelerating inflation rate of unemployment (NAIRU). They argue that, initially, an increase in aggregate demand, resulting from higher government spending, will encourage firms to expand and take on more workers. They will offer higher wages which will attract more workers. However, the rise in wages, combined with higher prices of raw materials and capital equipment, will raise firms' costs of production. Inflation will occur. Firms' real profits will fall and they will reduce production and employment. Workers' real wages will return to the previous level and those attracted into employment by higher real wages will withdraw from employment. Unemployment will return to NAIRU but with inflation and the expectation of inflation. Wage settlements and price rises will be set on the basis of this rate. Inflation will remain stable in the absence of changes in aggregate demand and supply conditions. However, should the government seek to reduce unemployment again, inflation will accelerate further.

This view of the effect that an increase in aggregate demand has on unemployment can be illustrated by the expectations-augmented Phillips curve.

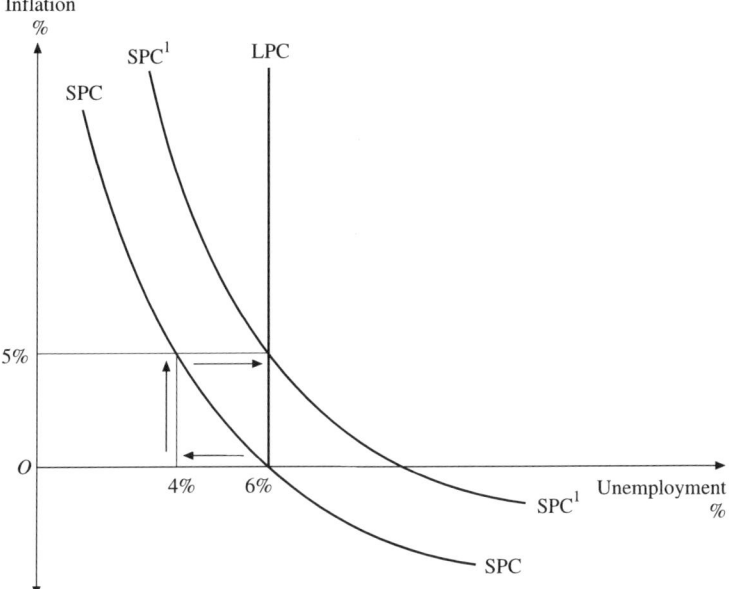

Fig. 10.11

Initially, the economy operates at a NAIRU of 6 per cent and there is price stability. An increase in government spending reduces unemployment to 4 per cent in the short run. However, the higher demand leads to inflation of 5 per cent. In the longer run, as firms cut back on output in response to higher costs and some workers are made redundant and some choose to leave employment, unemployment returns to 6 per cent. However, the economy is now operating on a higher short-run Phillips curve with inflation remaining at 5 per cent. So new classical economists do not believe that it is possible to obtain a sustained reduction in unemployment by increasing aggregate demand. However, they do believe that it is possible to reduce unemployment without increasing inflation by using supply side policies. For example, they argue that reducing job seekers' allowance and cutting income tax will encourage the unemployed to seek work more actively. Other policies they advocate include improved training to raise the productivity of workers and to encourage firms to employ more workers, and privatisation to increase the efficiency of markets.

Shifting the long-run aggregate supply curve to the right may increase output and lower NAIRU and the price level.

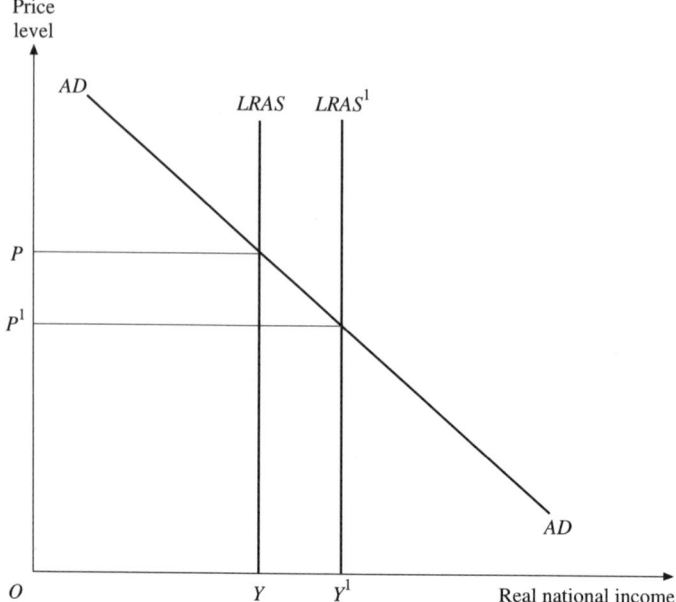

Fig. 10.12

Some supply side measures will also affect aggregate demand. For example, improved training may result from increased government spending, and reductions in income tax and corporation tax will raise aggregate demand. Keynesians also suggest some supply side measures, such as increased government spending on training schemes, but argue that increasing aggregate supply and potential output will not be effective in lowering unemployment unless there is sufficient demand. An equal increase in aggregate demand and aggregate supply should raise output and employment and leave the price level unaffected. In practice, many economists recommend measures which would increase both aggregate demand and supply.

b   As indicated above, new classical economists believe that reflationary fiscal and monetary policies, designed to reduce unemployment, may result in inflation. A government may also seek to reduce unemployment by lowering the exchange rate. By raising the price of imports, this may also have inflationary effects.

A number of other possible disadvantages may arise as a result of policies implemented to reduce unemployment. Increased government expenditure, for example, will raise aggregate demand. This, in turn, may result in a rise in imports. UK firms facing higher demand at home may also divert goods from overseas to the domestic market and so exports may fall. The rise in import expenditure and fall in export revenue may result in a deficit on the current account of the balance of payments.

Cutting interest rates to stimulate the economy and thereby reduce unemployment may result in households and firms borrowing more than they can afford to repay, or more than they could repay if interest rates were to rise in the future. Lower interest rates may also result in new, inefficient ventures being established, which will go out of business quickly. If personal and corporate debt develop, then future consumption and output are likely to be lower.

Prices and incomes policies may reduce the flexibility in markets and may make it difficult for firms to respond to changing market conditions. For example, a firm wishing to expand output to meet increasing demand may be unable to do so because it is prevented from raising the wage rate high enough to attract more workers.

Some supply side measures, e.g. reducing trade union power, may or may not raise employment but may also reduce working conditions and workers' sense of job security. Cutting job seekers' allowance will lower the living standard of those who remain unemployed and may cause a downward multiplier effect which would lead to higher unemployment.

Answers to short questions

1 International trade is usually, but not always, conducted over longer distances than trade within a country. Trade restrictions may exist between countries; there may also be differences in languages and technical and legal requirements which will add to costs. Firms engaged in international trade may also be affected by the policies, not only of their own government but also of the governments of the countries they trade with. When importing and exporting, firms may also have to change currencies. This, again, involves a cost and there is the risk that the value of currencies may change.

2 Countries may not benefit from specialisation and trade for a number of reasons. Comparative advantage will not exist if the opportunity cost ratios of the countries are the same. However, in most cases there are differences in the relative efficiency of countries in different products. Transport costs may, nevertheless, offset the benefits of specialisation and trade. A product may be produced abroad at a lower opportunity cost but, when transport costs are added, it may be possible to produce it more efficiently at home. A common reason why some countries may not benefit from specialisation and trade is market imperfections. For example, the imposition of tariffs will reduce the benefits of trade. The exchange rate may also lie outside the opportunity cost ratios and so not all countries will benefit. There is also a risk of specialisation. A country may be very efficient in producing a product but if it devotes a large proportion of its resources to it and demand falls, or there are supply problems, it will run into difficulties. For this reason, a number of countries seek to encourage a diversified industrial structure.

3 An adverse movement in the terms of trade occurs when export prices fall relative to import prices. In the short run, before there is time for demand to adjust fully, this is likely to have an adverse effect on the balance of trade. A similar amount will be exported at relatively lower prices and a similar amount will be imported at relatively higher prices. However, in the longer run, when demand has had time to change, the balance of trade will improve if demand for exports and imports is elastic. This is because demand for exports will increase by a greater percentage than the fall in price and so export revenue will rise. Demand for imports will fall by a greater percentage than the rise in price and so expenditure on imports will fall.

4 Whether a deficit on the current account of the balance of payments matters or not depends on its size, duration and cause. A small deficit which will last a short time is obviously less significant than a large deficit which has already existed for some time. A deficit which arises because, for example, the country is importing raw materials which will be turned into finished goods, some of which will be exported, may be self-correcting. On the other hand, a deficit which arises because of an underlying

problem, such as a lack of price competitiveness, poor quality or the production of goods which are not in world demand, will not be self-correcting.

5   The effective exchange rate is the value of a currency measured in terms of a group or basket of currencies. It is calculated as a weighted average of the exchange rate and is expressed as an index number relative to the base year. The weights reflect the importance of the currencies in trade with the country concerned.

6   A rise in a country's effective exchange rate is likely to reduce the country's rate of inflation. A rise in the effective exchange rate will reduce the price of imports in terms of the domestic currency and will raise the price of exports in terms of overseas currencies. Lower import prices will reduce the price of imported finished products which count in the Retail Price Index, and will also reduce the price of imported raw materials, which will cut firms' costs of production and, thereby, possibly also cut the prices they charge. Lower import prices and higher export prices will also put pressure on domestic firms to keep their costs and prices low in order to remain competitive at home and abroad.

7   Hot money is short-term flows of money into and out of countries. The owners of this money move it around the world to take advantage of expected changes in the value of currencies and differences in interest rates. These speculative capital movements are volatile and potentially disruptive as they can cause unexpected movements in the exchange rate and problems for the financial sector.

8   A number of factors influence the growth of a country's exports. One is price competitiveness. The lower the price of a country's exports relative to other countries' products, the more are likely to be sold. A fall in the effective exchange rate will reduce the price of exports in terms of other currencies and improve the exports' price competitiveness.
Growth of exports is also likely to be high if the quality of the exports is good, if the products produced are in high demand internationally, if the exporting firms engage in effective marketing and if there is an absence of trade restrictions. More exports are likely to be sold if real incomes are rising abroad as this will increase foreigners' demand for raw materials and finished products. In contrast, low incomes at home may favour the growth of exports. This is because firms that are unable to sell much at home may be forced to sell more abroad.

9   The main aims of the IMF include assisting the growth of world trade, helping countries with balance of payments difficulties and promoting exchange rate stability. The World Trade Organisation, which replaced the General Agreement on Tariffs and Trade, seeks to regulate international trade. In particular, it aims to liberalise international trade by discouraging the imposition of new trade restrictions and dismantling existing trade restrictions.

10 Among the strategies a country can take to increase its economic performance is improving the quality of education and training. A better educated and trained workforce will lower unit costs of production and

improve the quality of output, both of which will increase demand for the country's products. This is one of the main strategies being used by the so-called Asian Tigers, including South Korea and China. A country may also seek to promote its economic performance by developing new industries making products which are in high world demand. These infant industries may initially be protected against foreign competition by tariffs but, once established and able to take advantage of economies of scale, protectionism may be removed from them.

Answers to multiple choice questions

1   Answer **D**
International trade occurs because different types of goods need different kinds of resources in different proportions to produce them. Different types of economic resources are unevenly distributed throughout the world and these have limited geographical mobility. So, as it is difficult to move resources between countries, goods move.

2   Answer **C**
An exchange rate which will be acceptable to both countries will lie between the two countries' opportunity cost ratios. In Country X it takes the same resources to produce 10 cars as to produce 50 TVs so the opportunity cost of one car is 5 TVs. In Country Y 4 cars take the same resources to produce as 32 TVs so in this country the opportunity cost of one car is 8 TVs. So the exchange rate must be one car for more than 5 and less than 8 TVs.

3   Answer **A**
The comparative advantage in the production of agricultural goods lies with Country Z. The opportunity cost it experiences in producing agricultural goods is lower – one manufactured good as opposed to two manufactured goods in Country Y. It can produce two-thirds as many agricultural goods as Country Y but only half as many manufactured goods. Comparatively, it is better at producing agricultural goods.

   B   Country Y has the comparative advantage in producing manufactured goods. It can produce twice as many manufactured goods as Country Z and its opportunity cost is lower – three-fifths of an agricultural product as opposed to one in Country Z. So Country Y will export manufactured goods and import agricultural goods.

   C   Country Y is able to produce more agricultural and manufactured goods than Country Z, so it has the absolute advantage in producing both.

   D   Although Country Y can produce more of both goods than Country Z, it will pay Country Y to trade with Country Z as their opportunity cost ratios differ. Trade with Country Z will enable Country Y to concentrate on producing the product it is even better at making.

4   Answer **D**
The terms of trade are the index of export prices divided by the index of

import prices multiplied by 100. An adverse movement occurs when the number gets smaller. It is caused by export prices falling relative to import prices.

5 Answer **D**
A change in price causes a change in the quantity demanded (volume) of a good. A depreciation of the pound sterling will cause the price of exports to fall in terms of overseas currency. If price elasticity of demand for UK exports is 2.5, a fall in price of 5 per cent will cause the volume of exports to rise by:

$$PED = \frac{\%\Delta QD}{\%\Delta P}$$
$$2.5 = \frac{?}{5\%}$$
$$2.5 \times 5\% = ?$$
$$12.5\% = \%\Delta QD$$

6 Answer **B**
The transaction in liabilities section covers portfolio and direct investment coming into the UK from abroad. The transactions are credit items. A South Korean firm building a motor assembly plant in the UK will bring money into the UK in the form of direct investment.

A would appear in the transactions in assets section.

C and **D** would appear as debit items in the invisible section of the current account.

7 Answer **B**
With free trade, domestic consumption is OZ. Of this, OV is supplied by domestic producers and VZ is imported. When the tariff is imposed, domestic consumption falls to OY, domestic output rises to OW and imports fall to WY.

8 Answer **D**
The diagram shows that an increase in demand for pounds sterling has raised the value of the pound. If UK interest rates rise relative to German interest rates, more people, including some who are holding foreign currency, will wish to place money in financial assets denominated in pounds. So they will buy pounds using foreign currency, thereby raising the value of the pound.

A would increase the supply of pounds as UK citizens seek to buy German goods and lower the price of the pound.

B would again increase the supply of pounds on the foreign exchange market as some of the extra spending will go on imports.

C would reduce demand for pounds and increase supply as the competitiveness of UK goods falls.

9   Answer **D**

A change in the value of the pound from 1490 to 1692 lire means that the value of the pound is rising relative to the lira. To obtain a given quantity of lire now, a smaller amount of pounds would have to be given. For example, initially £25 would have had to be exchanged to obtain 37 250 lire. After the change in value, the same amount of lire could be bought with £22.87.

A   This cannot be concluded without further information, e.g. about the long-run equilibrium value.

C   A rise in the value of the pound will mean that UK exports will rise in price in terms of overseas currency.

D   Italian exports to the UK are imports into the UK and these become cheaper as the value of the pound rises relative to the lira.

10   Answer **A**

The balance of trade (also called the visible balance) is:
£152 671m − £164 221 = − £11 550m.
The invisible balance is £5713m + £6638m − £7471m = £4880m.
The current balance is − £11 550m + £4880m = − £6670m.
Net transactions are − £116 889m + £121 687m = £4798m.
So the balancing item is the reverse sign of:
− £6670m + £4798m = − £1872m, i.e. £1872m.

Answers to data response questions

1   **a**   An American exporter selling computers in Japan needs to be concerned about exchange rates as changes in these will affect its profits. For example, a fall in the value of the dollar against the Japanese yen gives the exporter the opportunity of increasing its profits. This may be achieved in one of two ways. It can follow the depreciation and thereby make its computers cheaper in terms of Japanese yen or keep the price the same in terms of Japanese yen and thereby raise its profit margins. For example, if, initially, 1 dollar = 90 yen, an American good priced at $3 will sell in Japan for 270 yen. If the value of the dollar then falls to 80 yen the price can be allowed to fall in Japan to 240 yen which will increase demand. Alternatively, the price can be maintained at 270 yen. If, say, 100 goods are sold per day, initially daily revenue in dollars would have been $100 \times 270 \div 90 = \$300$. Then, after devaluation, total revenue will be $100 \times 270 \div 80 = \$337.50$.

An American exporter has to be concerned not just with changes in the dollar–yen exchange rate but also with changes in other exchange rates. For example, if the sterling effective exchange falls, UK firms may capture some of the American exporter's market in Japan.

A Briton planning a skiing holiday should also be concerned with exchange rates as they influence the cost of the holiday. If the value of sterling rises relative to the French franc, holidays in France will become cheaper.

b   Devaluation is a government-administered reduction in the exchange rate from one fixed parity to a lower fixed parity. For example, in the summer of 1992 the Spanish government lowered the peseta by 5 per cent.

c One possible advantage of devaluation is an improvement in the country's balance of payments on current account position. This is a common reason why a government devalues its currency. Exports fall in price in terms of overseas currencies and imports rise in terms of domestic currency. Lower export prices should result in an increase in the quantity of exports sold and higher prices should reduce the volume of imports bought. If the combined elasticities of demand for exports and imports are greater than one, devaluation will result in an improvement on the current account.
The major drawback of devaluation is that it can result in inflation. A rise in import prices increases the price of imported finished products. It can also increase domestic costs of production by raising the price of imported raw materials and by stimulating workers to press for wage rises to restore their real wages. In addition, it reduces the competitive pressure on domestic firms to keep their prices low. This is because rival overseas products are now relatively more expensive both at home and abroad.

d Devaluation can be a useful tool in improving the current account position and raising output, employment and growth if certain conditions are met. As mentioned in **c**, it is important that the elasticity of demand for exports and imports must be greater than one. This is known as the Marshall-Lerner condition.
To have any effect, the currency must actually fall in value. So it is necessary that other countries do not devalue or at least do not devalue by equal or greater amounts.
There must also be spare capacity and flexibility in the economy. By lowering export prices and raising import prices, increased demand for domestic goods is created but if this higher demand cannot be met by domestic producers, devaluation will not be successful.
For devaluation to be a useful tool it is also beneficial that other countries do not impose further trade restrictions. A low domestic marginal propensity to import is useful so that the rise in incomes which follows an increase in export revenue does not result in a significant rise in import expenditure.
It is also important that workers do not press for wage rises immediately after a devaluation in order to compensate for higher import prices. If they do so, the competitive advantage gained from devaluation will be lost. So flexibility of real wages increases the effectiveness of devaluation.

e The exchange rate can be either an instrument of government policy or a goal of policy. When a government operates a fixed exchange rate or an adjustable peg system, such as the ERM, it seeks to ensure that the parity remains stable. To achieve this aim it will, for example, purchase its own currency or raise interest rates when there are market pressures for them to fall.
A government may operate the policy of a high exchange rate in the belief that it is a sign of economic strength. However, it is more common for a government to maintain the exchange rate at a set level because it

believes this will provide stability and thereby promote international trade. It may also consider that this policy will lower inflationary pressures. If firms know that the government will not allow the value of the domestic currency to fall in order to regain international competitiveness lost through inflation, they will be more concerned to prevent costs and prices rising.

In these latter two cases, while a certain parity is a target and the government will use policy instruments to achieve it, the target is, itself, set to achieve other aims.

A government may also use the exchange rate more directly as a policy tool. To improve the balance of payments on current account position and/or to increase employment and growth, a government may lower the exchange rate, whereas it may raise the exchange rate to reduce inflation.

2 a   The visible balance plus the invisible balance equals the current account balance. So the current account balance minus the visible balance equals the invisible balance. For example, in 1986 the invisible balance was $-£871m - -£9\,559m = £8\,688m$. The invisible balance for the period shown is:

Year	Invisible balance (£ million)	Year	Invisible balance (£ million)
1986	8688	1991	2108
1987	6599	1992	3273
1988	4863	1993	2336
1989	2171	1994	8751
1990	−266	1995	4880

Note that at the end of 1996 the format of the current account was changed. The visible balance is now known as trade in goods. The term invisibles has also been dropped in favour of trade in services, investment income and transfers.

b   The visible balance was in deficit throughout the period shown whereas for all but one year, 1990, the invisible balance was in surplus. In none of the years was the surplus on the invisible balance large enough to offset the deficit on the visible balance.

Both the visible balance and the invisible balance fluctuated quite considerably over the period. There was a clearer trend at the start of the period when the position on both the visible and invisible balance deteriorated.

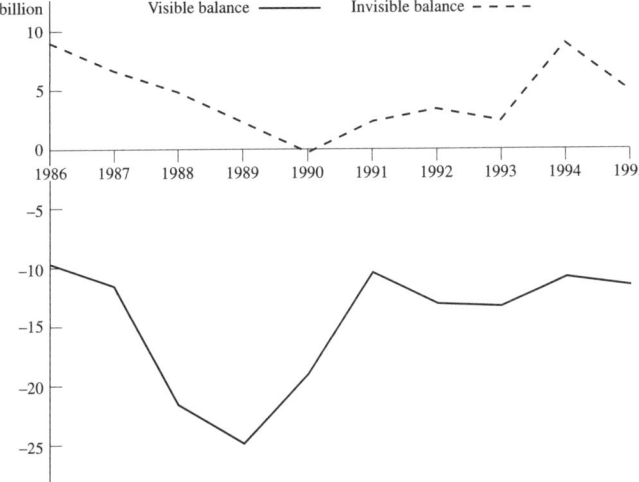

Fig. 11.4

The surplus on invisible trade was lower at the end of the period and the deficit on visible trade (the visible trade gap) was slightly higher.

c

Year	Growth (%ΔGDP)	Year	Growth (%ΔGDP)
1987	4.16	1992	− 0.52
1988	4.94	1993	2.25
1989	2.25	1994	4.08
1990	0.56	1995	2.39
1991	− 2.08		

The current balance deficit increased at the start of the period when GDP was increasing at a rapid rate. The deficit continued to increase in 1989 even though the rate of growth decreased. When the economy entered recession, with negative growth in 1991 and 1992, the deficit was smaller. As growth increased in 1993 the deficit got larger. However, it got smaller in 1994 when growth accelerated, and then rose in 1995 when the rate of growth fell.

d   The relationship at the start of the period is the one which economic theory would predict may occur in certain circumstances. When growth is high, particularly when it is driven by increased consumption as it was in the late 1980s, it is likely to be associated with an increased expenditure on imports. Increasing incomes may also result in goods being switched from the export to the home market, which will also contribute to a growing deficit on the current account balance.

When an economy is in recession, as it was in 1991 and 1992, an improvement in the current account position might be expected. Falling incomes reduce the ability of the home population to buy imports. Lower domestic demand will also reduce firms' demand for imported raw materials and, being unable to sell as many goods at home, will encourage them to export more.

In the latter part of the period a different relationship appeared. In 1994, for example, an increase in the growth rate was accompanied by a fall in the current account deficit. This, again, can be explained by economic theory. In 1994 the main driving force behind the increase in output was a rise in exports.

e   A deficit on the current balance can be caused by a number of factors. A fall in incomes abroad will reduce the purchasing power of overseas residents. This is likely to result in a fall in demand for UK goods and an increased incentive for overseas firms to export to the UK. A reduction in the quality of UK goods relative to overseas goods may also result in a deficit on the current account as exports will fall and imports will rise. A third possible factor is inflation. If the price of UK goods rises more rapidly than those of its main competitors, the price competitiveness of UK goods will decline. As a result, people in the UK and overseas are likely to switch from UK to overseas goods.

Answers to essay questions

1 a   Import restrictions are ways of limiting the quantity of imports which come into a country. They take a number of forms. The best known are tariffs which are sometimes also referred to as customs duties. These are taxes on imports. They may be either *ad valorem* (percentage) taxes or specific (a fixed sum) taxes. They raise the price of imports and thereby make them less price competitive against domestic goods. They also raise revenue. The diagram below shows the effect of the imposition of a tariff.

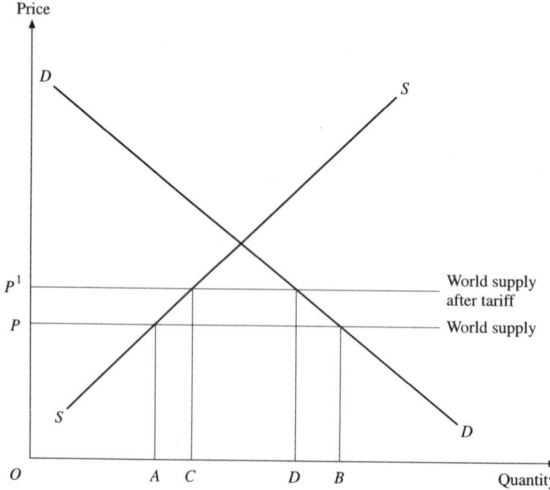

Fig. 11.5

The tariff reduces imports from AB to CD and raises domestic production from OA to OC. However, it also reduces overall domestic consumption from OB to OD and raises price.

Another well-known method is the imposition of a quota. This is a limit on the value or the quantity of a good that is allowed to enter the country, e.g. 20 000 computers from China. Quotas may be more effective than tariffs in cases where demand for imports is price inelastic.

A method which was used in the UK up to 1979 and is still used in some African, Asian and East European countries, is exchange control. This is a limit placed by the government on the amount of the country's currency which can be exchanged for foreign currencies. It can be used to control the total value of imports and to discriminate against the import of, say, luxury goods.

A radical measure is the imposition of an embargo or ban. This can be placed on the import of a particular product or on imports from a particular country.

A government can also limit the amount of imports by operating an import deposit scheme and a purchasing policy strategy. An import deposit scheme requires importers to deposit a sum (usually a percentage of the value of the product) before they can bring products into the country. A purchasing policy involves the government giving preference to domestic producers when placing orders for, say, military equipment.

Imports can also be discouraged by artificially complicated and time-consuming customs formalities and health and safety standards. These increase the difficulty and cost which overseas firms experience in exporting to the country.

In recent years there has been a growth in voluntary exports restraints (VERs). These are agreements between two countries whereby they agree to restrict the amount one or both of them export to each other.

b   In the last two decades there has been a growth in the level of protectionism that countries are giving to their domestic producers and the range of trade restrictions they use. There has been concern among European countries and the USA about the increasing competitiveness of the Asian Tigers and also about trade disputes between the EU and the USA. A number of arguments are advanced in favour of protectionism. These can be divided into arguments supporting the protection of particular domestic industries and arguments supporting the protection of all domestic industries.

One argument for selective protectionism is to help sunrise (infant) industries. These are newly established firms which some economists claim need protection until they have grown large enough to take full advantage of economies of scale and thereby compete on equal terms with overseas firms. If the sunrise industries do grow and increase their efficiency, they can add to output, employment and exports. However, there is a risk that they may become dependent on protectionism.

At the other end of the spectrum, sunset (declining) industries may be protected in order to allow them to decline gradually rather than go out of business quickly. This may enable the industries to lose labour through natural wastage rather than redundancies.

It may also be argued that strategic industries should be protected. These are industries whose continued existence is considered to be important for the country. For example, it may be considered important to ensure that domestic production of food and military equipment continues in order to avoid the disruption to supplies that would be caused by, say, trade disputes and wars.

The prevention of dumping is another argument for protecting particular industries. Dumping occurs when overseas producers sell products in a country at a low price, sometimes below cost, in order to get rid of surplus stocks and/or to drive out domestic producers.

In addition to the arguments advanced to protect particular industries, a number of arguments are advanced in favour of a general system of protection.

Import restrictions may be used to improve a country's balance of payments position. They will reduce or control imports but they may also provoke retaliation. If other countries do react by raising their tariffs, for example, a trade war may occur and sales of the country's exports will suffer. Of course, tariffs may be imposed in reaction to other countries raising their levels of protectionism.

Tariffs may be used to improve the terms of trade. Placing a tax on imports may force overseas producers to lower their prices in order to remain competitive.

Protectionism may be employed to ensure that a country maintains a diversified industrial structure and to avoid the risk involved in over-specialisation. It may also be used to help a country to restructure its economy. If a country wishes to switch from making goods which are no longer in high demand to making those which are, it may wish to help sunset industries to grow and sunset industries to decline.

However, a number of arguments can be advanced against protectionism. It reduces competition and may thereby raise the price of goods and reduce consumer surplus. It may also reduce choice and remove the pressure on domestic firms to be efficient and to produce goods of a high quality.

The key, underlying argument against protectionism is that it prevents full advantage being taken of comparative advantage. This may mean that world output is below its potential level and so economic welfare is not as high as it could be. However, it can be questioned as to what extent the theory of comparative advantage explains the reality of international trade. For example, in practice there is not perfect mobility of factors of production within a country. Nor is there perfect competition, and some argue that protectionism may offset some of the imperfections which exist.

2 a A fixed exchange rate is one which is maintained by the government at a given parity or within margins. For example the value of the pound sterling may be set at £1 = 3DM or £1 = 2.8–3.2DM.

If the exchange rate threatens to move away from its fixed rate or outside its margins, the government will intervene to maintain its value. For example, if the supply of its currency on the foreign exchange market is increasing, the government can intervene and buy up its own currency, using some of its official reserves of foreign currencies. This is illustrated in the diagram below.

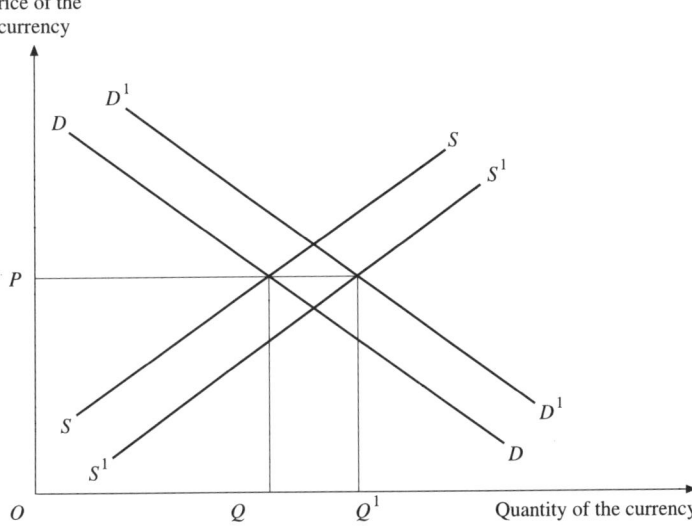

Fig. 11.6

It may also seek to avoid a downward movement in its exchange rate by increasing its rate of interest. This will be likely to reduce the outflow of currency and encourage an inflow of funds from abroad. A longer-term policy is to engage in deflation, e.g. by increasing income tax. This will reduce demand for imports and hence the supply of pounds on the foreign exchange market and may increase exports and the demand for pounds. If these measures are unsuccessful, the government will have to change its exchange rate to a lower parity, i.e. to devalue.

A freely floating exchange rate is determined by the forces of demand and supply and can vary from day to day. For example, an increase in demand for the currency will raise its price. Managed floating is an exchange rate system whereby the parity is allowed to alter in line with changes in demand and supply but the government intervenes to avoid large fluctuations in the value of the currency. Again, the two main methods used are the buying and selling of the currency and changes in interest rates.

b   The value of a currency can fall to a lower parity as the result of market forces or as the result of government intervention.

The value of the pound sterling, for example, will fall if the demand for pounds decreases and/or the supply of pounds increases. The demand for a currency is a derived demand. Pounds are demanded by those wishing to purchase UK goods, those wishing to invest in the UK and those hoping to take advantage of a future rise in the value of the pound. The supply of pounds on the foreign exchange market comes from people and firms selling pounds in order to obtain foreign currency in order to buy foreign goods, invest abroad or in anticipation of exchange rate changes.

A number of market factors can cause the value of the pound to fall. If the UK experiences inflation, the price of UK goods will rise relative to overseas goods. This will make UK goods less attractive both at home and abroad. Demand for UK exports will fall, causing the demand for pounds to fall. The UK's demand for imports will rise, causing an increase in the supply of pounds. The net effect is shown in the diagram below.

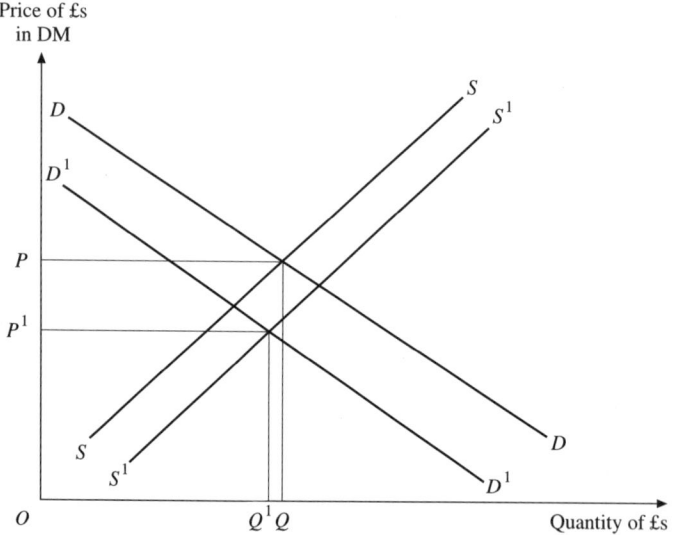

Fig. 11.7

A decline in the quality of UK goods relative to overseas goods and an improvement in the marketing of overseas goods relative to UK goods will have a similar effect.

Another cause of a fall in the value of sterling is a change in real income either at home or abroad. An increase in real incomes in the UK is likely to result in an increased demand for imports. The UK has a relatively high marginal propensity to import (the proportion of extra income which is spent on imports). Higher UK real incomes may also result in goods being diverted from the export to the buoyant home market. In contrast, it is a fall in real incomes abroad which may cause a fall in the value of the pound. This is because it will reduce the ability of foreigners to buy UK goods and may compel overseas firms to compete more actively in their home markets and overseas.

Changes in interest rates can also affect the value of a currency. A fall in UK interest rates relative to other countries' interest rates will probably discourage overseas investment in the UK (which will reduce demand for pounds) and encourage domestic residents to invest abroad (which will increase the supply of pounds). There will be a net capital outflow and a fall in the value of the pound.

Speculation is another factor. If speculators believe that the value of the pound will fall, they will sell pounds now. This will itself contribute to the fall in value they are anticipating. Overseas governments holding pounds in their reserves will also be likely to sell them if they expect the value of the pound to fall in the future.

Under a fixed exchange rate system the government can announce a decrease in the amount of foreign currency that can be bought with a given amount of the domestic currency, i.e. it can devalue the currency. Under a managed float system the government can seek to lower the value of its currency by selling it in return for foreign currencies, lowering the rate of interest or increasing people's ability to buy domestic and overseas goods by introducing reflationary fiscal and/or monetary policies.

c   A fall in the exchange rate reduces the price of exports and raises the price of imports and thereby makes the country's goods more price competitive. This may initially lead to a deterioration in the balance of payments on current account position before volumes have time to adjust to the price changes. However, if the combined elasticities of demand for exports and imports is greater than one, other countries do not follow the devaluation so that the effective exchange rate does fall, domestic costs of production do not rise and the country is able to supply more exports, the current account position should improve in the longer term. This time lag before the country sees the benefits of devaluation is known as the J effect and is illustrated in the diagram below.

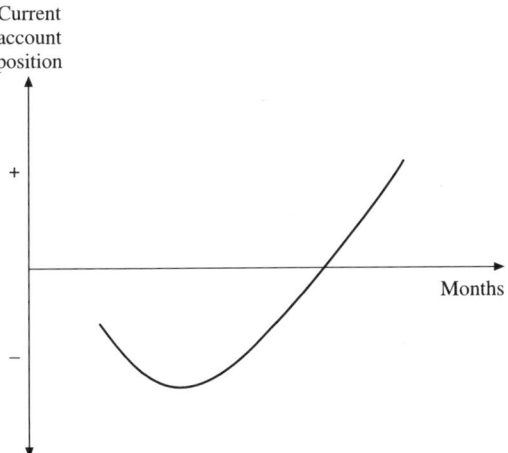

Fig. 11.8

As well as having an effect on a country's external position, devaluation will also have effects on the internal economy. If more domestic goods are sold at home and abroad, domestic production will rise, leading to an increase in growth and probably in employment.

The eventual rise in output will be greater than the initial increase. Exports are an injection into the circular flow and will result in a multiple increase in income. Those who benefit from the initial increase in sales of domestic goods will spend some of their increased income which will generate increases in incomes for others.

However, there is a risk that devaluation can give rise to inflation. Devaluation raises import prices. Countries import both finished products and raw materials. The higher prices of the finished imported goods will enter straight into the measure of retail prices. The higher price of imported raw materials will increase costs of production of those firms which use these. The impact higher import prices have on the domestic price level will depend on the amount of imported goods bought and the extent to which domestically produced goods are seen as substitutes. However, by making imported products more expensive in the domestic market, devaluation may remove the pressure on domestic producers to keep prices low. Workers may also press for wage rises to compensate for the higher imported prices and, if successful, costs of production may rise. To offset these inflationary pressures, a government may introduce deflationary fiscal or monetary policies or introduce a prices and incomes policy.

Answers to short questions

1 Monetary policy is the attempt by a government or its central bank to control the supply of money or the cost of money, i.e. the rate of interest. Fiscal policy consists of any measure which changes public spending or taxation in terms of amount, timing or composition.

2 The incidence of taxation refers to who pays a tax. The formal incidence is borne by those who have the legal liability to pay, whereas the effective incidence is borne by those who actually pay. For example, the formal incidence of excise duty on cigarettes falls on sellers of cigarettes. However, a high proportion of the burden will be shifted on to consumers who will pay higher prices for cigarettes. Indeed, the inelastic demand for cigarettes means that most of the effective incidence falls on consumers.

3 The PSBR is likely to become larger during a recession. This is because direct and indirect tax revenue will fall. Fewer people will be in employment so less income tax will be raised and falling profit margins will reduce the amount of corporation tax collected. Lower levels of spending will also reduce revenue from excise duty and VAT. Government spending on job seekers' allowance will also rise automatically in line with the increased number of people unemployed. In addition, a government may engage in discretionary fiscal management. It may raise government spending, e.g. on infrastructure, and/or cut tax rates to boost aggregate demand. As a country moves out of recession, tax revenue will rise, government spending on job seekers' allowance will fall and the PSBR will get smaller.

4 A reduction in taxation may increase employment for a number of related reasons. A cut in corporation tax will enable firms to keep more of their profits and so may encourage them to expand and take on more workers. Similarly, a fall in indirect taxes will reduce firms' costs, increase demand and, again, encourage expansion and increase employment. A cut in income tax will raise disposable income and thereby increase aggregate demand. It will also increase the incentive to work.

5 An incomes policy can be used to reduce cost push inflation without increasing unemployment. It may hold down wage increases and firms' costs by placing a limit on wage rises. An alternative measure, which a government may use to reduce inflation, is deflationary fiscal or monetary policy which may increase unemployment. An incomes policy can also be used to offset labour market imperfections. For example, the Disability Act was introduced to counter discrimination in the labour market. However, an incomes policy can create inflexibility in the labour market. A firm wishing to expand may find it difficult to attract new workers if it cannot offer a wage rise above the limit imposed. There is also the possibility that an incomes policy can cause labour unrest. For example, a flat sum limit will benefit the lowly paid, while a percentage limit will benefit the highly paid.

6 The UK government attempts to reduce inequalities in the distribution of income in two main ways. One is the use of a progressive income tax system which takes a greater percentage of the income of the rich than of the poor. The other is to provide cash benefits to the unemployed, the disabled, the sick and the retired. These benefits are sometimes referred to as transfer payments.

7 There are a number of measures which the government might adopt to raise the level of investment. These include cutting the rate of interest and/or increasing investment subsidies, which will reduce the cost of investment. Reducing corporation and income tax will raise the expected return from investment, and spending on research and development may raise the productivity of capital goods. As well as stimulating private sector investment, the government could directly increase public sector investment by, say, spending more on road construction.

8 Among the possible causes of government failure are lack of, or inaccurate, information, conflicts in policy objectives, government ministers, councillors and civil servants pursuing their own self-interest, and basing policies on incorrect economic analysis. Time lags are also a significant problem. There may be delays in identifying that a problem exists, in deciding what policy measures to use, in introducing those measures and in economic agents reacting to the measures. Meanwhile, economic conditions may have changed.

9 Fiscal policy measures include changes in government spending and taxation. A government may seek to promote growth by increasing its spending on training. A better trained workforce will increase the country's productive potential and shift the long-run aggregate supply curve to the right. It might also reduce income tax to raise disposable income. The resulting increase in aggregate demand may encourage firms to increase their output.

10 Supply side policies are policies designed to increase aggregate supply by improving the workings of markets. They include trade union reform, deregulation, privatisation, cuts in marginal rates of taxation, reduction in welfare benefits, and the promotion of training.

Answers to multiple choice questions

1 Answer **C**
An expenditure-reducing measure is one which seeks to improve the current account position by reducing domestic demand for all goods, both those produced at home and those produced abroad. The intention is to reduce expenditure on imports and, due to the lower demand at home, to divert some domestically produced goods from the home to the export market. An increase in direct taxes will reduce disposable income and lower domestic demand for goods.

A, **B** and **D** are all expenditure-switching measures which seek to encourage people at home and abroad to switch from buying overseas goods to buying the home country's goods.

2   Answer **C**
An expansionary fiscal policy seeks to increase aggregate demand and thereby reduce unemployment.
A, **B** and **D** may all increase as a result of an expansionary fiscal policy.

3   Answer **D**
A regressive tax falls more heavily on the poor. While they may pay less in tax than the rich, they pay a higher percentage of their income in tax.
A and **B** are features of a progressive tax and **C** describes an inefficient tax.

4   Answer **A**
Monetary policy covers measures which seek to change the supply or price of money. The rate of interest is the price which people have to pay to borrow money and the price which people receive for lending money and for forgoing liquidity.
B, **C** and **D** are all fiscal policy instruments.

5   Answer **D**
Job seekers' allowance is an automatic stabiliser. As economic activity increases, more people leave the unemployment register to take up jobs. So government spending on the benefit will fall automatically without any change in government policy.
A, **B** and **C** do not change automatically with changes in national income.

6   Answer **B**
Raising income tax will increase government revenue, at least in the short run. This will reduce a budget deficit. However, it will also reduce aggregate demand, which will be likely to increase unemployment and reduce economic growth. It is also likely to cause an increase in the surplus on the current account of the balance of payments as the fall in aggregate demand will reduce expenditure on imports and cause producers to switch some of their goods from the home to the export market.

7   Answer **C**
When the Bank of England buys government bonds it gives money in exchange. This increase in the money supply is likely to lead to an increase in demand.
A, **B** and **D** are all likely to reduce aggregate demand. In the case of **D**, although the same tax revenue is raised, there is likely to be a fall in aggregate demand. This is because the disposable income of the poor will fall relative to that of the rich and the poor have a higher MPC than the rich.

8   Answer **A**
Raising income tax will reduce aggregate demand. This should lower demand pull inflation. It is also likely to improve the balance of payments position as demand for imports should fall and, with lower aggregate demand in the domestic market, home firms may seek to export more of their output.
B and **C** will increase aggregate demand, which will increase a balance of payments deficit and demand pull inflation.

D will raise export prices and lower import prices. This may reduce cost push inflation but will probably increase a balance of payments deficit.

9 Answer **D**

The diagram shows that the rise in real national income to OY1 and fall in price to OP1 was caused by an increase in aggregate supply. This could have been achieved by the successful application of supply side policies, e.g. improved training, deregulation and trade union reform.

A would have increased aggregate demand in other countries.

B would have increased domestic aggregate demand.

C would have reduced the size of the working population and would have been likely to reduce aggregate supply.

10 Answer **A**

Between 1988 and 1990 there was a negative PSBR. This is a PSDR (Public Sector Debt Repayment) and it arises when government revenue is greater than government expenditure.

B Between 1988 and 1990 the government was reducing aggregate demand by withdrawing more spending power from circulation than it was injecting.

C From 1991 to 1995 there was a positive PSBR. This means that there was a need for the public sector to borrow. The largest component of the public sector financial position is the budget. If there was a PSBR, it is highly likely that there was a budget deficit.

D As the government was borrowing in this period it was adding to demand and hence pursuing a reflationary rather than a deflationary policy.

Answers to data response questions

1 a The graph shows that, over the twentieth century, the trend has been for public spending, as a percentage of GDP, to rise. There were significant rises in public spending during each of the two world wars. At the end of each war public spending fell back but in each case it did not fall back to its previous level. This may, in part, be because during a war people get used to a higher level of government spending.

Public spending rose steadily in the 1960s and early 1970s as governments employed discretionary fiscal policy in a bid to maintain a high level of employment. It was particularly high in the mid 1970s, then fell and rose again in 1982. It fell in the late 1980s during the consumer boom (when private sector spending was high) and rose in the early 1990s during the recession (when private sector spending was low).

b A government may wish to increase public spending to gain popularity before a general election. Public spending tends to rise just before a general election: pensions are often raised and expenditure on health and education increased. On the other hand, after an election public spending may fall. This pattern leads commentators to refer to political cycles of economic activity.

A government that is pursuing a Keynesian policy approach may also increase spending in order to increase employment and growth. An increase in public spending, not accompanied by a fall in private sector spending, will increase aggregate demand. Unless the economy is operating at full capacity, this should increase output and raise employment.

c   The table shows that general government expenditure rose in real terms by 27.2 per cent from 1981 to 1994. Expenditure on social security as a percentage of government spending rose over the period. Spending on health and education, again as a percentage, fluctuated but ended the period accounting for a larger percentage. It is interesting to note that, from 1992, defence accounted for a smaller percentage of total government spending. There has also been an actual reduction in government spending on defence as the threat from Eastern Europe has reduced. This has been referred to as the peace dividend. Government spending on public order and safety reached its peak as a percentage in 1991. Spending on general public services showed a similar trend.

As a share of the total, spending on housing and community amenities has declined as the provision of public sector housing has been reduced. Transport and communication also accounted for a smaller percentage. A number of transport and communication concerns were privatised in the 1980s, including the National Freight Corporation (1982), National Bus Company (1986), Cable and Wireless (1981, 1983 and 1985) and British Telecommunications (1984 and 1991). Spending on recreational and cultural items rose in 1986 and then maintained this higher percentage. Agriculture, forestry and fishing accounted for the same percentage in each year shown except 1993.

d   Social security is the largest item of government spending. It includes spending on pensions, job seekers' allowance, child benefit, disablement allowance and one-parent benefit.

The amount the government spends on social security depends on the rates of benefits paid and the number of claimants. If the government decides to raise, say, the state pension or job seekers' allowance, expenditure on social security, at least in the short run, will increase.

It will also increase if the number of recipients rises because of, say, an increase in the number of elderly people, an increase in the number of children, a rise in unemployment, an increase in divorce or a relaxation of the regulations.

e   Government expenditure on higher education provides a consumption and an investment benefit for students. People may actually enjoy studying and may develop interests in their subject and in, say, amateur dramatics and sport, which they continue after they leave university. A university education should also develop people's intellect, raise their productivity and increase their qualifications. This improvement in their skills and qualifications should make it easier for graduates to gain employment and should increase their long-term earning potential.

2 a　The first paragraph discusses time lags which often occur before a government identifies a problem, implements a policy and the policy takes effect. The first time lag is often referred to as a recognition lag. A government may fail to appreciate the early signs of inflationary pressures, e.g. reductions in stocks and shortages of skilled workers, and act only when the general price level starts to rise. It may also take time for a government to decide which policy to introduce (implementation lag) and, as the extract notes in connection with monetary policy, it can take time for a policy to take effect (behavioural lag).

b　Raising short-term interest rates may slow economic growth by reducing consumption and hence reducing the return from investment. Higher interest rates encourage saving and discourage consumption. Households have less discretionary income after paying higher mortgage interest payments. The cost of purchasing goods, e.g. cars, on credit rises. Falling consumer demand or a decline in the growth of consumer demand discourages firms from increasing their output or at least from increasing their output significantly. Demand for capital goods may also fall as the expected return from, and opportunity cost of, capital investment rises. A slowdown, or a fall, in aggregate demand will reduce the rate of economic growth.

c　The slowdown in growth in the USA was beneficial to the American economy as it was reaching full capacity. If output had continued to rise at a rapid rate, with unemployment falling, the economy could have reached full capacity. At this point it would not be possible to increase output without incurring inflation. This is because any attempt to raise output would result in producers outbidding each other for scarce resources and pushing up the costs of production in terms of higher money wages and higher raw material prices. These higher costs would be passed on to consumers in the form of higher prices.

d　The definition of recession in the extract does agree with the usual definition of a recession which is a fall in GDP over two or more successive quarters. However, not all economists specify a time period and some define a recession purely in terms of a fall in output and income. It is also sometimes defined as a period of time when output is below its long-term trend.

e　Economic slack refers to spare capacity in the economy. It occurs when there are unemployed resources or an inefficient allocation of resources. When there is spare capacity, the economy is operating inside its production possibility curve. It will be capable of producing more with existing resources. There will be a gap between actual and potential output.

f　When countries experience economic recovery, their output and incomes rise. Higher incomes increase demand for both domestic goods and imports. These countries may seek to purchase more goods from another country which is already operating at or near full capacity. The increase in aggregate demand, resulting from an increase in demand for its exports, will shift the aggregate demand curve to the right and cause the general price level to increase as illustrated in the diagram below. Real national income does not rise but nominal national income will increase because of the rise in prices.

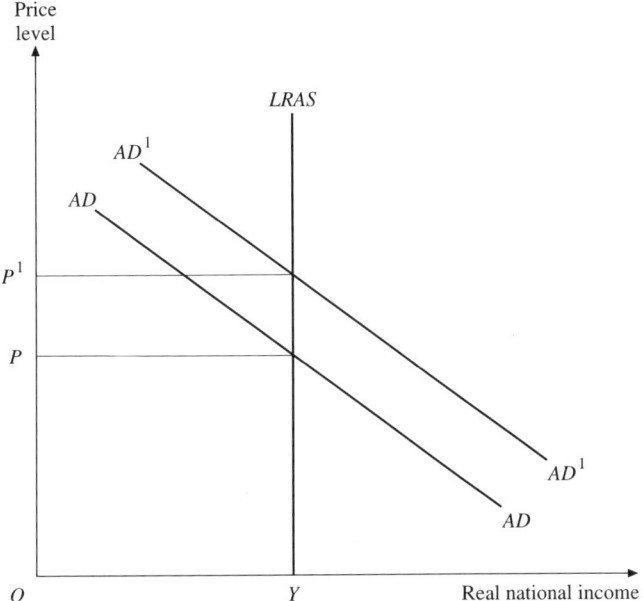

Fig. 12.4

So the higher level of demand for the same quantity of goods will result in prices being bid up and will initiate a period of inflation. There will be an inflationary gap, with planned expenditure exceeding the full employment level of income.

Answers to essay questions

1 a The policies a government uses to reduce inflation will depend on what the government believes is causing the inflation and which policies it believes are most effective.

If inflation is thought to be of a demand pull nature, the government may use deflationary monetary or fiscal policy or supply side policies. New classical economists, who argue that inflation is caused by an excessive growth of the money supply, favour deflationary monetary policy. In the 1980s the UK government concentrated on reducing the growth of the money supply and set target growth levels for the M0 and M4 measures of the money supply. In the 1990s attention switched to using interest rates as the main tool of government policy. Reducing the growth of the money supply and raising the rate of interest are likely to reduce aggregate demand and thereby lower demand pull inflation.

Keynesian economists believe that fiscal policy is more effective and suggest that deflationary fiscal policy should reduce demand pull inflation occurring at full employment. Raising income tax and/or reducing government expenditure should reduce aggregate demand and lower inflation as illustrated below.

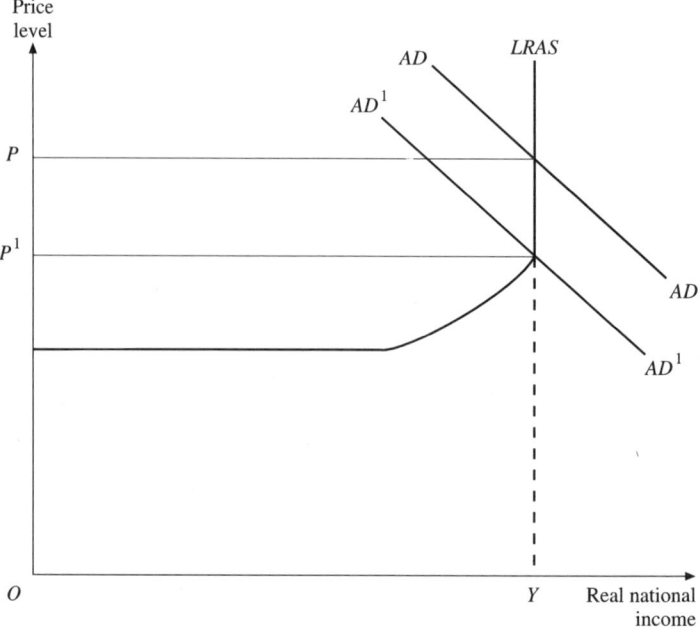

Fig. 12.5

If inflation is occurring because planned expenditure exceeds the current maximum possible output, an alternative strategy is to increase aggregate supply, i.e. shift the long-run aggregate supply curve to the right. Among the supply side measures which may increase the level of potential output are increases in spending on training, increases in investment incentives and trade union reform. Some supply side measures do actually involve increased government spending which will increase aggregate demand but the intention would be to increase aggregate supply by more than aggregate demand.

According to Keynesians, inflation may also be the result of cost push factors, i.e. decreases in aggregate supply arising from increases in costs of production, such as a rise in the price of imported raw materials and higher wage rates. Fiscal policy may again be employed to combat cost push inflation. However, this time corporation tax could be cut to reduce firms' costs. Income tax and VAT could also be reduced in order to lower workers' wages claims. The government could also raise subsidies to firms and cut the prices of goods produced by state concerns. It may have to be careful, though, to ensure that its cuts in tax rates are accompanied by cuts in government expenditure if there is a risk that cost push inflation may merely be replaced by demand pull inflation.

Exchange rate policy can also be used to reduce cost push inflation. If a stable exchange rate is maintained, domestic producers will know that competition lost, through rising domestic costs, will not be regained by a fall in the value of the currency.

A more active exchange rate policy may be pursued, whereby the government raises the value of the currency by, for example, purchasing the currency. A rise in the exchange rate will lower import prices and thereby the prices of some of the finished goods bought, reduce the cost of imported raw materials and increase the pressure on domestic firms to keep their costs and prices low.

If the cause of cost push inflation is thought to be increases in wage rates not matched by rises in productivity, a government may introduce an incomes policy which seeks to limit wage rises or even, in cases of high inflation, freeze wage rises. An incomes policy, unlike deflationary fiscal or monetary policy, is unlikely to increase unemployment. However, it does introduce inflexibility into the labour market, preventing firms wishing to expand from offering higher wages. Incomes policies do not solve inflation; they merely curb it.

b   The main objectives of government macro-economic policy are price stability, high employment, balance of payments equilibrium and growth. A government, at any particular time, may also have other objectives, e.g. reducing poverty.

The existence of inflation and the measures taken to reduce it may make it difficult for a government to achieve these objectives. For example, if domestic inflation is above that prevailing in other countries, demand for exports is likely to fall and demand for imports to rise. This would be likely to lead to a deficit on the current account of the balance of payments or to increase an existing one. Under a floating exchange rate system, the value of the currency should, in theory, float downwards to restore an equilibrium. However, even if this does occur, it would be likely to generate further inflation by raising import prices. Under a fixed exchange rate system, the government would have to take measures to correct the deficit.

Some measures to reduce inflation would tend to reduce a current account deficit. For example, deflationary fiscal and monetary policy would reduce demand for all goods, including imports, while improved training, leading to a more productive labour force, and cuts in corporation tax would make the country's exports more price competitive. Raising interest rates may attract a net inflow of investment and this increase in transactions in liabilities could offset the deficit on the current account.

Increasing the exchange rate to combat cost push inflation may increase any deficit on the current account position unless domestic firms can respond by increasing their competitiveness.

By reducing demand from domestic and overseas residents for the country's goods, the existence of inflation may reduce output and employment. It may also limit the policy measures a government may consider in order to raise employment and the rate of growth. For example, if there is inflation, a government may be reluctant to introduce measures which will increase aggregate demand and may encourage workers to press for wage rises. There may be a conflict of objectives and the government may have to decide what its priority is.

However, if inflation is occurring because planned expenditure exceeds the full employment level of output, the anti-inflationary policies may merely reduce aggregate demand to the full employment level. Some supply side measures, such as improved training, may also both reduce inflation and increase employment. In addition, the reduction or elimination of inflation should, in the long run, raise output and employment by making the country's goods more price competitive.

A government wishing to reduce poverty may find its policy options constrained by the existence of inflation. For example, it may wish to increase welfare benefits but may feel that this addition to aggregate demand may increase demand pull inflation, and so it may have to consider combining higher welfare benefits with, say, increased income tax rates.

2 a The key function of taxation is to raise revenue to pay for government expenditure. Taxation reduces the spending power of the private sector and the resources which would have been used to produce goods and services for the private sector are then released to produce goods and services for the public sector. A government can always finance its expenditure by borrowing money from the central bank. However, it avoids financing most of its expenditure this way because it would be inflationary. For example, if the full employment level of output is, say, £90 billion and private sector demand is £80 billion and the government spends £40 billion financing it all by borrowing, total planned expenditure would be £120 billion. To avoid inflation, the government would seek to impose taxes to the level that would reduce private sector demand to £50 billion.

Taxation is a fiscal policy measure. A government may alter the level of taxation to influence aggregate demand. If private sector demand is rising too rapidly, a government may increase taxation to avoid inflation and the development of a current account deficit on the balance of payments. On the other hand, if private sector demand is falling to a low level, taxation may be reduced to increase employment.

As well as being used to influence aggregate demand, taxation can also be used to influence aggregate supply. A cut in corporation tax, for instance, may encourage enterprise and innovation, and a cut in income tax may provide a greater incentive for people to enter employment and to accept promotion when in work.

Taxation, often used in combination with a system of welfare payments, is used in many countries to influence the distribution of income and wealth. For example, a more even distribution of income is created by a progressive system of income tax.

Indirect taxation is also employed to influence the goods which people buy. Most countries impose some tariffs on imported goods in order to discourage their consumption. They also place taxes (sometimes called sin taxes) on demerit goods such as cigarettes and alcohol in order to reduce demand for these goods.

b Direct taxes are taxes imposed on income and wealth. In the UK they are collected by the Inland Revenue. The burden of direct taxes cannot be shifted on to third parties. They are paid directly by the individuals and firms on whom they are imposed. Examples of direct taxes include income tax and corporation tax.

In contrast, indirect taxes (also called outlay and expenditure taxes) are imposed on expenditure on goods and services. In the UK most are collected by the Customs and Excise Department. The burden, or some of the burden, of indirect taxes can be passed by sellers of goods on to purchasers in the form of higher prices. They are paid indirectly by consumers via the sellers of the goods. Examples of indirect taxes include VAT and excise duties.

c Income tax, a direct tax, still accounts for the largest single contribution to government tax revenue in the UK. However, in the last 20 years an increasing proportion of tax revenue has been collected from indirect taxation.

Economists and politicians are divided on the merits of raising a larger proportion of tax revenue from indirect taxation. This is because there are both advantages and disadvantages to this move and because people place different weighting on these advantages and disadvantages.

Raising a higher proportion of tax revenue from indirect taxes, and hence raising a smaller proportion from direct taxes, may increase incentives to effort. It is sometimes claimed that a high level of income tax discourages some people from taking on paid employment, some from remaining in employment past retirement age, some from working overtime and some from taking highly paid but very demanding jobs. A high level of corporation tax may also discourage investment, innovation and enterprise. In contrast, indirect taxes are claimed not to discourage effort and enterprise as they are linked to expenditure rather than earning. Some also claim that they are relatively painless as people may be unaware that they are paying tax, or unaware of the amount of tax they are paying, when they buy goods.

Indirect taxes avoid the double taxation effect that income tax has on savings. Saving takes place out of income which is taxed and then the return on the saving is also taxed.

Indirect taxes are also relatively cheap to administer. In practice, much of the work is undertaken by traders. These taxes are difficult to evade by customers as they are included in the price of goods and services. They can also be changed relatively quickly and can be used selectively to influence the pattern of consumers' spending. Indirect taxes can be used to counter market imperfections. If negative externalities arising from, say, smoking can be calculated, a tax could be placed on cigarettes which matches the marginal external cost. This will internalise the cost, raise price and reduce output to allocatively efficient levels.

Indirect taxes, as well as direct taxes, influence economic activity. VAT, for example, is an automatic stabiliser and VAT revenue rises, without any change in government policy, when spending increases. The government can also choose to alter indirect taxes to regulate the economy. It may, for instance, reduce indirect taxes to combat cost push inflation.

However, there are arguments against raising a larger proportion of tax revenue from indirect taxes. One is that indirect taxes are regressive. This means that they take a larger proportion of the income of the poor than of the rich. In contrast, most direct taxes, including income tax, are progressive taxes which take a larger proportion of the income of the rich. So moving the tax base from direct to indirect taxes increases the tax burden of the poor, those least able to pay.

Depending on how they are imposed, indirect taxes may distort consumer choice. For example, in the UK some goods are exempt from VAT, some are zero rated, fuel and power bear 8 per cent VAT and most goods bear the standard rate of 17.5 per cent. There may be a case, on grounds of equity, for treating products differently, e.g. placing a higher rate of VAT on luxury goods and demerit goods, but a number of anomalies exist in the UK system. The difference in rates may, for example, encourage people to buy cakes, which are zero rated, in preference to chocolate which bears the standard rate. It also means that those adults who can fit into children's sizes for clothes do not have to pay VAT, whereas most adults do. VAT is not currently charged on newspapers and books, mainly on the grounds that these are merit goods. However, it is questionable as to what extent pornographic literature may be considered to be a merit good.

In the absence of market imperfections, the imposition of an indirect tax can reduce consumer surplus by raising price. This, by itself, will reduce economic welfare, although, to assess the net effect, the use of the tax revenue would also have to be taken into account.

Indirect taxes may also contribute to inflation. They increase firms' costs of production and are likely to be passed on to consumers in the form of higher prices.

So whether the government should or should not change the structure of taxation will depend on what its objectives are, what forms and rates of indirect taxes it is contemplating and an assessment of the relative strengths and weaknesses of the two forms of taxation.